analysing ARCHITECTURE

'*analysing* ARCHITECTURE should become an essential part of all architectural education and an informative guide to the powerful analytical tool of architectural drawing.'

Howard Ray Lawrence, Pennsylvania State University

analysing ARCHITECTURE offers a unique 'notebook' of architectural strategies to present an engaging introduction to elements and concepts in architectural design. Beautifully illustrated throughout with the author's original drawings, examples from across architectural history, from primitive places to late twentieth-century structures, are used to illustrate a number of analytical themes and to show how drawing can be used to study architecture.

Simon Unwin clearly identifies the key elements of architecture and conceptual themes apparent in buildings. He describes ideas for use in the active process of design. Breaking down the grammar of architecture into themes and 'moves', Unwin exposes its underlying patterns to reveal the organisational strategies that lie beneath the superficial appearances of buildings.

Exploring buildings as results of the interaction of people with the world around them, *analysing* ARCHITECTURE offers a definition of architecture as 'identification of place', and provides a greater understanding of architecture as a creative discipline. This book presents a powerful impetus for readers to develop their own capacities for architectural design.

Simon Unwin is Lecturer in Architecture at The Welsh School of Architecture, University of Wales, Cardiff.

analysing ARCHITECTURE

Simon Unwin

London and New York

First published 1997
by Routledge
11 New Fetter Lane, London EC4P 4EE

Simultaneously published in the USA and Canada
by Routledge
29 West 35th Street, New York, NY 10001

Printed and bound in Great Britain by
Butler and Tanner Ltd, Frome, Somerset

British Library Cataloguing in Publication Data
A catalogue record for this book is available from the British Library

Library of Congress Cataloguing in Publication Data
Unwin, Simon, 1952–
Analysing Architecture / Simon Unwin.
Includes bibliographical references and index.
1. Architectural design. I. Title.
NA2750.U58   96-34005
720'.1--dc20

ISBN 0-415-14477-9
ISBN 0-415-14478-7 (pbk)

for Gill

CONTENTS

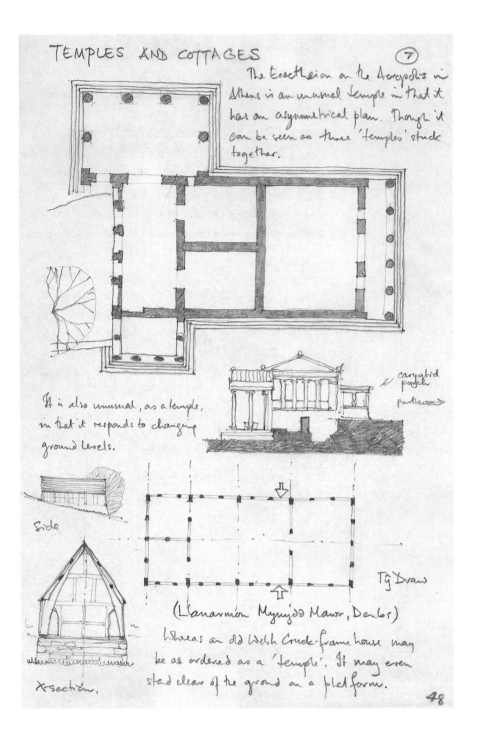

TEMPLES AND COTTAGES ⑦

The Erechtheion on the Acropolis in Athens is an unusual temple in that it has an asymmetrical plan. Though it can be seen as three 'temples' stuck together.

It is also unusual, as a temple, in that it responds to changing ground levels.

caryatid porch
parthenon →

Side

X section.

Tŷ Draw

(Llanarmon Mynydd Mawr, Denbs)

Whereas an old Welsh Cruck-frame house may be as ordered as a 'temple'. It may even stand clear of the ground on a platform.

48

INTRODUCTION

INTRODUCTION

For some years I have used a notebook to analyse architecture through drawing. I find this exercise useful as an architect, and it helps to focus my teaching. My simple premise is that one's capacity for 'doing' architecture can be developed by studying the work of others. In this way one can discover some of the powers of architecture, and, by looking at how other architects have used them, see how they might be managed in one's own design.

For teaching I have organised my notebook findings into the beginnings of a thematic framework, which can be used in analysing examples. The following chapters illustrate some of the themes that have emerged so far. They make observations on architecture as a creative discipline, its elements, the conditions that affect it, and attitudes that may be adopted in doing it.

The first chapter offers a working definition of architecture, as *identification of place*. This is put forward as the primary concern of architecture, and as a theme underpins everything that follows. Realisation that the primitive motivation of architecture is to identify (to recognise, amplify, create the identity of) places has been the key that has allowed access into the related areas explored in this book.

A large part of the book deals with conceptual strategies used in design. There are chapters which look at different ways of organising space, and at the various roles of geometry in architecture.

The poetic and philosophical potential of architecture is, I think, evident throughout. If poetry is a condensation of experience of life, then architecture is poetic, essentially. But it can be seen that some works of architecture do more: they seem to provide a transcendent poetry – a level

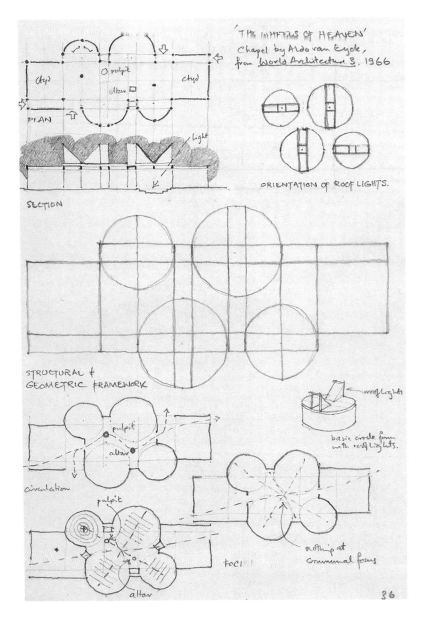

'THE INHERITORS OF HEAVEN'
Chapel by Aldo van Eyck,
from World Architecture 3, 1966

PLAN

chyd · O pulpit · chyd
· altar ·

SECTION

· light

ORIENTATION OF ROOF LIGHTS.

STRUCTURAL &
GEOMETRIC FRAMEWORK

circulation

pulpit
altar

roof lights

basic circle form
with roof lights.

pulpit

altar

foci

nothing at
communal focus

86

of meaning and significance that overlays the immediate presentation of place, and which is to be interpreted, as a complement to sensual perception and experience, for appreciation by the intellect.

The chapters deal with specific themes. These themes are like analytical 'filters' or frames of reference. Each abstracts a particular aspect of the complexity of architecture – *architecture as making frames, primitive place types, temples and cottages, stratification, geometry....*

In all the chapters there is an intimate connection between the text, which is explanatory, and the drawings, which have been the principle medium of analysis. Some of the drawings are diagrams of particular elements or ideas, but many are plans or sections of examples which illustrate the themes being discussed.

Some works have been selected as appropriate examples in more than one of the chapters, illustrating a different theme in each. Any work of architecture may of course be examined through any or all of the filters, though this will not necessarily produce interesting revelations in all

instances. Towards the end of the book there are some case studies which show how a fuller analysis of a particular work can be achieved by examining it under a number of themes.

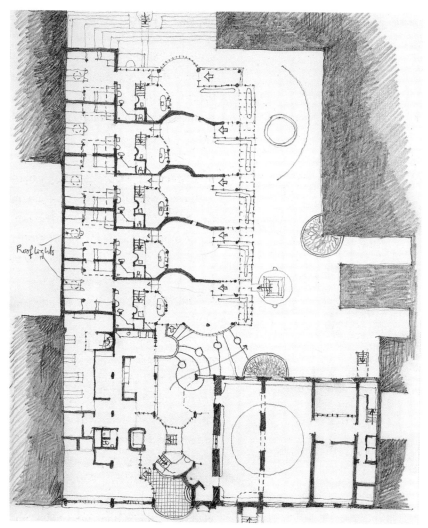

Roof lights

ACKNOWLEDGEMENTS

Many people have contributed, knowingly or unwittingly, to the preparation of this book, not least the numerous student architects who have been subjected to various forms of teaching related to its development. Some of them have said things, or done things in their designs, that have prompted thoughts which are included here.

The same is true of my colleagues in architectural education, in particular those I work with week by week in the Welsh School of Architecture. Some of the examples were suggested by Kieren Morgan, Colin Hockley, Rose Clements, John Carter, Claire Gibbons, Geoff Cheason and Jeremy Dain.

I have benefitted from many discussions with Charles MacCallum, Head of the Mackintosh School of Architecture in Glasgow, and from the encouragement of Patrick Hodgkinson, of the Bath School.

I am also grateful to the Head of Department at the Welsh School, Richard Silverman; and to various visitors to the school who have, unknowingly, stimulated ideas which are included in the following pages.

Some of my colleagues in architectural education have contributed to the evolution of this book by asserting things with which I found I could not agree. My attempts to determine why I did not agree have affected my thinking greatly; so, although I shall not name them, I must also thank my theoretical antagonists as well as my friends.

Some ideas have come from far afield, from friends and opponents I rarely or never see, but with whom I sometimes indulge in discussion across the Internet: in particular, Howard Lawrence, together with other contributors to the 'listserv' group – *DESIGN-L@psuvm.psu edu*.

Thanks are due too to Gerallt Nash and Eurwyn Wiliam at the Museum of Welsh Life for kindly providing me with a survey of the cottage Llainfadyn, on which the drawings at the beginning of the chapter *Space and Structure* are based.

I am especially grateful to Dean Hawkes, Professor of Design at the Welsh School, who was kind enough to read the material while in preparation and who made a number of useful comments.

And finally, as always, one must thank those who are close and who put up with having someone around who is writing a book. In my case these long-suffering people are Gill, Mary, David and James.

Simon Unwin, Cardiff, December 1996

ARCHITECTURE AS
IDENTIFICATION OF PLACE

ARCHITECTURE AS IDENTIFICATION OF PLACE

Before we can get on to looking at some of the conceptual strategies of architecture in detail, it is necessary to lay out some ground work with regard to the nature of architecture, and its purpose. Before we can get onto the 'how?', we need to look briefly at the 'what?' and 'why?'; i.e. 'what is architecture?', and 'why do we do it?'.

It is probably fair to say that the matters of the definition and the purpose of architecture have never been settled. These are issues about which there is a great deal of confusion and debate, which is strange considering that architecture as a human activity is literally older than the pyramids. The question 'What is one doing when one is doing architecture?' appears simple, but it is not an easy one to answer.

Various ways of framing an answer to this question seem to have contributed to the confusion; some of these relate to comparison of architecture with other forms of art. Is architecture merely sculpture – the three-dimensional composition of forms in space? Is it the application of aesthetic considerations onto the form of buildings – the art of making buildings beautiful? Is it the decoration of buildings? Is it the introduction of poetic meaning into buildings? Is it the ordering of buildings according to some intellectual system – classicism, functionalism, post-modernism...?

One might answer 'yes' to all these questions, but none seems to constitute the rudimentary explanation of architecture that we need. All of them seem to allude to a special characteristic, or a 'superstructural' concern, but they all seem to miss a central point which one suspects should be more obvious. What is needed for the purposes of this book is a much more basic, and accessible, understanding of the nature of architecture, one that allows those who engage in it to know what they are doing.

Perhaps the broadest definition of architecture is that which one often finds in dictionaries: 'architecture is the design of buildings'. One cannot contradict this definition, but it doesn't help very much either; in a way it actually diminishes one's conception of architecture, by limiting it to 'the design of buildings'. Although it is not necessary to do so, one tends to think of 'a building' as an object (like a vase, or a cigarette lighter), and architecture involves rather more than the design of objects.

One more useful way of understanding architecture can be gleaned, ironically, from the way the word is used in regard to other art forms, music in particular. In musicology the *architecture* of a symphony can be said to be the conceptual organisation of its parts into a whole, its intellectual structure. It is strange that the word is rarely used in this sense with regard to architecture itself.

In this book this is the root definition of architecture that has been adopted. Here, the architecture of a

Opposite page:
Children under a tree have,
in the most primitive way, made an
architectural decision by choosing
it as a place to sit.

building, a group of buildings, a city, a garden ... is considered to be its *conceptual organisation*, its *intellectual structure*. This is a definition of architecture which is applicable to all kinds of examples, from simple rustic buildings to formal urban settings.

Though this is a useful way of understanding architecture as an activity, it doesn't address the question of purpose – the 'why' of architecture. This appears to be another difficult 'big' question, but again there is an answer at the rudimentary level which is useful in establishing something of what one is striving to achieve when one is doing architecture.

In looking for this answer, simply suggesting that the purpose of architecture is 'to design buildings' is again an unsatisfactory dead end; partly because one suspects that architecture involves rather more than that, and partly because it merely transfers the problem of understanding from the word *architecture* onto the word *building*.

The route to an answer lies in forgetting altogether, for the moment, about the word *building*, and thinking about how architecture began in the distant primeval past. (Archaeological exactitude is not necessary in this, nor need we get embroiled in discussions about whether things were done better in those days than in today's more complex world.)

Imagine a prehistoric family making its way through a landscape unaffected by human activity. They decide to stop, and as the evening draws

on they light a fire. By doing so, whether they intend to stay there permanently or just for one night, they have established a *place*. The fireplace is for the time being the centre of their lives. As they go about the business of living they make more places, subsidiary to the fire: a place to store fuel; a place to sit; a place to sleep; perhaps they surround these places with a fence; perhaps they shelter their sleeping place with a canopy of leaves. From their choice of the site onwards they have begun the evolution of the house; they have begun to organise the world around them into places which they use for a variety of purposes. They have begun to do architecture.

The idea that *identification of place* lies at the generative core of architecture can be explored and illustrated further. In doing this one can think of architecture, not as a language, but as being in some ways like one.

The architectural actions of a prehistoric family making its dwelling place can be replicated and updated in a beach camp. The fire is the focus, and also a place to cook. A windshield protects the fire from too much breeze, and as a wall begins to give some privacy. There is a place where the fuel for the fire is kept, and the back of the car acts as a food store. There are places to sit, and if one were to stay overnight, one would need a bed. These are the basic 'places' of a house; they come before walls and a roof.

Reference for Welsh farmhouses:
Royal Commission on Ancient and Historical Monuments in Wales – *Glamorgan: Farmhouses and Cottages*, 1988.

The inside of this Welsh farmhouse can be compared with the beach camp on the previous page. The places of the beach camp have been transposed into a container which is the house itself. Although such images can feed our romantic ideas of the past, the architecture itself was, before it became anything else, a product of life.

Place is to architecture, it may be said, *as meaning is to language.* Learning to do architecture can seem to be like learning to use language. Like language architecture has its patterns and arrangements, in different combinations and compositions as circumstances suggest. Significantly, architecture relates directly to the things we do; it changes and evolves as new, or reinterpreted, ways of identifying places are invented or refined.

Perhaps most important, thinking of architecture as identification of place accommodates the idea that architecture is participated in by more than the individual. In any one example (a building for instance) there will be places proposed by the designer, and places created by adoption by the users, (these may or may not match). Unlike a painting or a sculpture, which may be said to be the intellectual property of one mind, architecture depends upon contributions from many. The idea of architecture as identification of place asserts the indispensable part played in architecture by the user as well as the designer; and for the designer who will listen, it asserts that places proposed should accord with places used, even if it takes time for this to happen.

So called 'traditional' architecture is full of places which, through familiarity and use, accord well with users' perceptions and expectations. The illustration on this page shows the interior of a Welsh farmhouse (the upper floor has been cut through to show some of the upstairs room). The places that are evident can be compared directly with those in the beach camp shown on the opposite page.

The fire remains the focus and a place to cook, though there is now also an oven – the small arched opening in the side wall of the fireplace. The 'cupboard' to the left of the picture is actually a box-bed. There is another bed upstairs, positioned to enjoy the warm air rising from the fire. Under that bed there is a place for storing and curing meat. There is a settle to the right of the fire (and a mat for the cat). In this example, unlike the beach camp, all these places are accommodated within a container – the walls and roof of the house as a whole (which itself, seen from the outside, becomes a place identifier in a different way).

Although nobody is shown in the drawing, every one of the places mentioned is perceived in terms of how it relates to use, occupation, meaning. One projects people, or oneself, into the room, under the blankets of the bed, cooking on the fire, chatting by the fireside.... Such places are not abstractions such as one finds in other arts; they are an enmeshed part of the real world. At its fundamental level architecture does not deal in abstractions, but with life as it is lived, and its fundamental power is to identify place.

Conditions of architecture

In trying to understand the powers of architecture one must also be aware of the conditions within which they are employed.

Though its limits cannot be set, and should perhaps always be under review, architecture is not a free art of the mind. Discounting for the moment those architectural projects that are designed never to be realised, as conceptual or polemic statements, the processes of architecture are operated in (or on) a real world with real characteristics: gravity, the ground and the sky, solid and space, the progress of time, and so on.

Also, architecture is operated by and for people, who have needs and desires, beliefs and aspirations; who have aesthetic sensibilities which are affected by warmth, touch, odour, sound, as well as by visual stimuli; who do things, and whose activities have practical requirements; who see meaning and significance in the world around them.

Such is no more than a reminder of the simple and basic conditions under which we all live, and within which architecture must operate. There are however other general themes that condition the operation of architecture. Just as the languages of the world have their common characteristics – a vocabulary, grammatical structures, etc. – so too does architecture have its elements, patterns, and structures (both physical and intellectual).

Though not as open to flights of imagination as other arts, architecture has fewer limits. Painting does not have to take gravity into account; music is solely aural. Architecture is however not constrained by the limits of a frame; nor is it confined to one sense.

What is more, while music, painting and sculpture exist in a way separate from life, in a transcendent special zone, architecture incorporates life. People and their activities are an indispensable component of architecture, not merely as spectators to be entertained, but as contributors and participants.

Painters, sculptors, composers of music, may complain about how their viewers or audience never see or hear their art in quite the same way as it was conceived, or that it is interpreted or displayed in ways that affect its innate character, but they do have control over the essence of their work; and that essence is, in a way, sealed hermetically within the object: the musical score, the covers of a book, or the picture frame. But even the essence of architecture is penetrated by the people whose activities it accommodates, which can change it.

[Architecture has also been compared with film-making – an art form that incorporates people, place, and action through time. But even in film the director is in control of the essence of the art object through the control of plot, sets, camera angles, script, etc., which is not the case in architecture.]

The conditions within which one can engage in architecture are therefore complex, perhaps more so than for any other art form. There are the physical conditions imposed by the natural world and how it works: space and solid, time, gravity, weather, light.... There are also the more fickle political conditions provided by the interactions of human beings individually and in society.

Architecture is inescapably a political field, in which there are no incontrovertible rights and many arguable wrongs. The world around can be conceptually organised in infinite different ways. And just as there are many religions and many political philosophies, there are many divergent ways in which architecture is used. The organisation and disposition of places is so central and important to the ways in which people live that it has through history become less and less a matter of *laissez faire*, more and more subject to political control.

People make places in which to do the things they do in their lives – places to eat, to sleep, to shop, to worship, to argue, to learn, to store, and so on and on. The way in which people organise their places is related to their beliefs and their aspirations, their world view. As world views vary, so does architecture: at the personal level; at the social and cultural level; and between different sub-cultures within a society.

Which use of architecture prevails in any situation is usually a matter of power – political, financial, or that of assertion, argument, persuasion. Launching design into conditions like these is an adventure only to be undertaken by the brave-hearted.

BASIC ELEMENTS
OF ARCHITECTURE

BASIC ELEMENTS OF ARCHITECTURE

Now that we have sorted out a working definition of architecture and its fundamental purpose – *conceptual organisation, and identification of place* – we can begin to look at the 'materials' that are available to us in doing architecture.

These are not the physical materials of building – bricks and mortar, glass, timber, etc. – but the conceptual elements of architecture. And they should be considered not as objects in themselves, but in the ways in which they contribute to the identification (or making) of places.

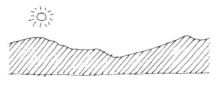

In physical terms the primary elements of architecture are the conditions within which it operates (which have already been mentioned). Principally these include: *the ground*, which is the datum to which most products of architecture relate; the *space* above that surface, which is the medium that architecture moulds into places; *gravity*; *light*; and *time* (few examples of architecture can be experienced as a whole all at one time; processes of discovery, approach, entry, exploration, memory, etc. are usually involved).

Within these conditions the architect has a palette of conceptual materials with which to work. It cannot be said that the following list is complete, but at the most basic level this palette includes:

defined area of ground

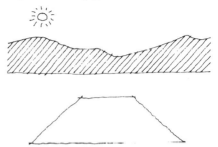

The definition of an area of ground is fundamental to the identification of many if not most types of place. It may be no more than a clearing in the forest, or it may be a pitch laid out for a football game. It may be small, or it may stretch to the horizon. It need not be rectangular in shape, nor need it be level. It need not have a precise boundary but may, at its edges, blend into the surroundings.

raised area, or platform

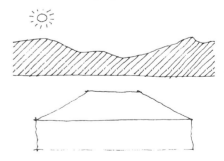

A raised platform creates a level horizontal surface lifted above the natural ground. It may be high or low. It may be large – a stage or terrace; it may be medium-sized – a table or altar; it may be small – a step or shelf.

lowered area, or pit

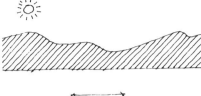

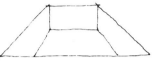

A pit is formed by excavation of the ground's surface. It creates a place which is below the natural level of the ground. It may be a grave, or a trap, or even provide space for a subterranean house. It might be a sunken garden, or perhaps a swimming pool.

marker

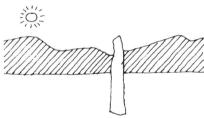

A marker identifies a particular place in the most basic way. It does so by occupying the spot and by standing out from the surroundings. It may be a tombstone, or a flag on a golf course; it might be a church steeple, or a multi-storey office block.

focus

The word *focus* is the Latin for hearth. In architecture it can mean any element upon which concentration is

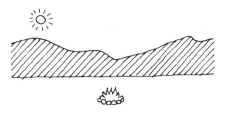

brought to bear. This might be a fire-place, but it could also be an altar, a throne, a work of art, even a distant mountain.

barrier

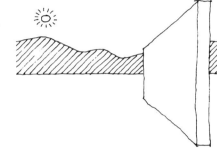

A barrier divides one place from another. It could be a wall; but it might also be a fence, or a hedge. It could even be a dyke or a moat, or just the psychological barrier of a line on the floor.

roof, or canopy

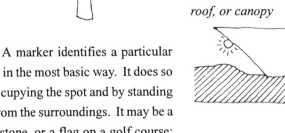

The roof divides a place from the forces of the sky, sheltering it from sun or rain. In so doing, a roof also implies a defined area of ground beneath it. A roof can be as small as a beam over a doorway, or as big as a vault over a foot-ball stadium.

Because of gravity a roof needs support. This could be provided by walls, but it could be by ...

supporting posts, or columns

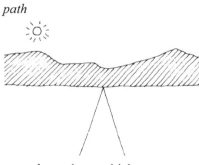

Other basic architectural elements which identify places include:

path

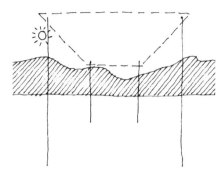

... a place along which one moves; which might be straight, or trace an irregular route across the ground surface avoiding obstacles.

A path might also be inclined: as a ramp, a stair, or even a ladder. It might be formally laid out, or merely defined by use – a line of wear across the countryside.

openings

... *doorways* through which one may pass from one place to another, but which are also places in their own right; and *windows* through which one can

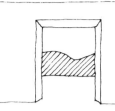

look, and which allow passage of light and air.

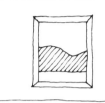

Historically, a more recent basic element is the *glass wall*, which is a barrier physically but not visually.

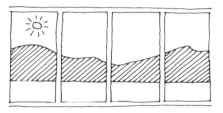

Another is the *suspension rod* or cable, which can support a platform or roof, but which also depends literally upon a structural support above.

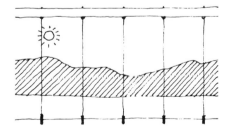

Basic elements such as these can be combined to create rudimentary architectural forms. Sometimes these combined elements have names of their own, for example:

21

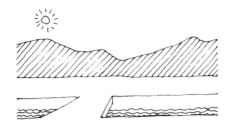

A *bridge* is a path, over a barrier; a platform; it can also be a roof.

Barriers can be combined to form an *enclosure*, which defines an area by putting a wall around it.

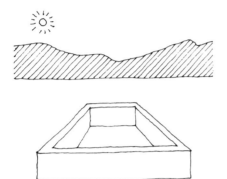

Walls and a roof create a *cell*, defining a place separated from everywhere else.

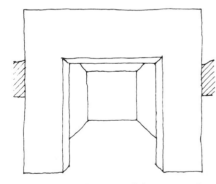

And giving a roof the supporting columns it needs, creates an *aedicule* (right).

These basic elements and rudimentary forms recur again and again in the examples in this book. They are used in architecture of all times and regions of the world.

An ancient Greek temple consists of some of these basic elements, used in a clear and direct way to identify the place of a god.

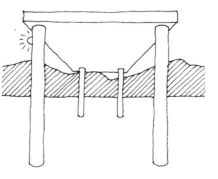

The building stands on a *platform*, and consists of *walls* which define a *cell*, which is surrounded by *columns*. The columns together with the walls of the cell support the *roof*. The cell is entered through a *doorway*, outside of which is a small platform in the form of an altar. Such a temple, often

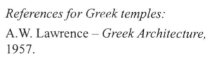

References for Greek temples:

A.W. Lawrence – *Greek Architecture,* 1957.

D.S. Robertson – *Greek and Roman Architecture,* 1971.

References for Villa Mairea:
Richard Weston – *Villa Mairea,* in the *Buildings in Detail* series, 1992.
Richard Weston – *Alvar Aalto,* 1995.

sited on a hill, as a whole acts as a *marker*, which can be seen from far away. Together, the platform, walls, columns, roof, altar, identify the place of the god, who is represented by the carved statue within.

More complex and subtle works of architecture are also composed of basic elements.

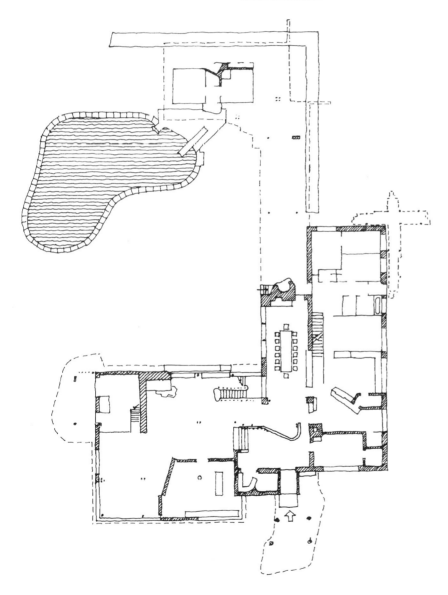

This is the ground floor plan of the Villa Mairea, a house designed by the Finnish architects Alvar Aalto and his wife Aino, and built in 1939.

Although it is not drawn in three dimensions, you can see that the places which constitute the house are defined by the basic elements of wall, floor, roof, column, defined area, pit (the swimming pool), and so on. Some places – the approach to the main entrance (indicated by an arrow) for example, and the covered area between the main house and the sauna – are identified by roofs (shown as dotted lines) supported by slender columns. Some places are identified by particular floor materials, timber, stone, grass, etc. Some places are divided by low walls (not hatched), others by full-height walls (hatched), or by glass walls.

Architecture is not just as easy as knowing the basic elements. A large portion of its subtlety lies in how they are put together. In language, knowing all the words in the dictionary wouldn't necessarily make one a great novelist. Having a good vocabulary does however give greater choice and accuracy when one wants to say something. In architecture knowing the basic elements is only the very first step, but knowing them gives one a choice of how to give identity to places in appropriate ways.

MODIFYING ELEMENTS
OF ARCHITECTURE

MODIFYING ELEMENTS OF ARCHITECTURE

The basic elements of architecture as described in the previous chapter are abstract ideas. (That is why they were illustrated in such a sparse way.) When, by being built, they are given physical form, various additional factors come into play.

In their physical realisation and our actual experience of them, basic elements and the places they identify are modified: by light, by colour, by sounds, by temperature, by air movements, by smells (and even possibly by tastes), by the qualities and textures of the materials used, by use, by scale, by the effects and experience of time....

Such modifying forces are part of the conditions of architecture; they can also be elements in the identification of place.

The possible configurations of basic and modifying elements are probably infinite. The inside of a cell might be dark, or bright; it might muffle sound, or have an echo; it might be warm, or cool; it might be dank, or fresh; it might smell of expensive perfume, or of stale sweat, of fruit, or of fresh cooking. A pavement may be rough, or as smooth and slippery as ice. An enclosure (a garden) might be sunny, or shady. A platform (a seat) might be as hard as stone or metal, or soft, padded with foam or feathers. An aedicule may be sheltered from wind, or be exposed and breezy. And so on.

As abstract ideas, basic elements are subject to complete control by the designing mind; modifying elements may be less compliant. One might decide on the precise shape and proportions of a *column*, a *cell*, or an *aedicule*, but the matter of how it sounds, or is lit, or smells, or changes with time, is a more subtle issue. Control over modifying elements is a continuing and evolving battle. For example: in primitive times, light would have been that provided by the sky, and not subject to control; now there is electric light which can be controlled precisely. In the distant past, materials for building, whether stone or timber, were rough hewn; now their textures and qualities can be finely controlled.

Though use of the basic elements may be the primary way in which a designing mind conceptually organises space into places, modifying elements contribute a great deal to the experience of those places.

Light

First amongst the modifying elements of architecture is light.

Light is a *condition* of architecture, but it can also be used as an element. Light from the sky is the pervasive medium through which sighted people experience the products of architecture; but light, both natural and artificial, can be manipulated by design to identify particular places and to give places particular character.

If one is thinking of architecture as sculpture it is by light that it is seen and its modelling appreciated. If one is thinking of architecture as identification of place, then one is aware that there can be light places and dark places, places with a soft even light and places with the strong brightness and sharp shadows of sunlight; places where the light is dappled, or constantly but subtly changing; places, such as theatres, where there is a stark contrast between light (the stage – the place of the action) and dark (the auditorium – the place of the audience).

Light can be related to the activity in a place. Different kinds of light can be appropriate for different kinds of activity. A jeweller at his workbench needs strong light over a particular area. An artist in her studio needs constant and even light by which to paint. Children in school need good general lighting for work and play. In all instances light contributes to the identification of place.

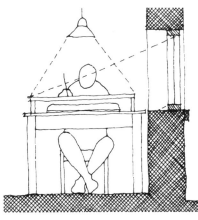

Light changes and can be altered. Light from the sky varies through the cycles of night and day, and during different times of the year; sometimes it is shaded or defused by clouds. The variations can be stimulating.

Daylight can be exploited in making places. Its qualities can be

changed by the ways in which it is allowed into a building.

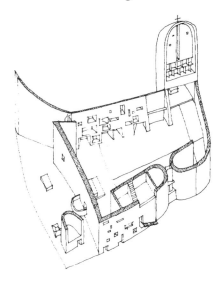

Some old houses have broad chimney stacks. Open to the sky they allow a dim 'religious' light to illuminate the hearth (when there is no fire). Le Corbusier used a similar effect in the side chapels of Notre-Dame du Haut at Ronchamp. Using light 'scoops' he identified the places of the side altars with daylight softened by its reflection off white roughcast walls.

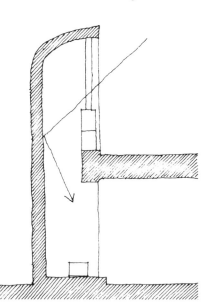
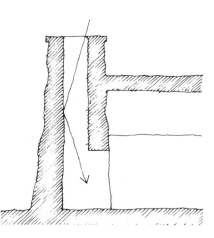

The way light is admitted into the side chapels at Ronchamp is similar in effect to that of light filtering down an old broad chimney stack.

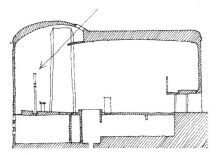

The same sort of effect is used in this crematorium at Boras, Sweden, by Harald Ericson. It was built in 1957, three years after the Ronchamp chapel. The drawing shows its long section.

In the same year, Ralph Erskine used a roof-light cum light scoop to identify the place of a small winter garden in the middle of a single-storey villa which he built at Storvik, also in Sweden.

Beams of light can also work in the opposite way, drawing attention to their source.

In identifying places through architecture, light – both the varying light from the sky, and the precisely controllable light from electric bulbs – can contribute in many ways.

The way in which light contributes to the identification of place is part of architecture. Decisions about light play their part in the conceptual organisation of space, and affect the ways in which basic elements of architecture are used.

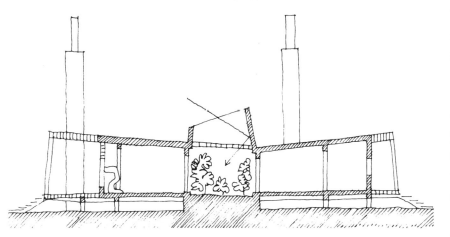

In this villa in Sweden, Ralph Erskine used a roof-light to identify the place of a small winter garden at the heart of the house.

Light from an electric bulb is more constant and controllable than daylight: it can be switched on and off, or precisely varied in intensity, colour and direction. One of the most intense uses of electric lighting is in the theatre; but any place can be considered as a 'theatre' and lit accordingly.

A spotlight can identify the place of an actor, a singer, a painting, an object ... anything on which attention is to be focused.

Light contributes to the ambience of place. One is likely to make the quality of light in a place of contemplation or worship different from that in a place for playing basketball or one for performing a surgical operation.

Without changing the physical form of a place its character can be radically altered by changing the way in which it is lit. Think of the dramatic change in the appearance of a friend's face when you hold a flashlight under his or her chin. The same changes can occur in a room when it is lit in different ways, at different intensities, and from different directions. A room's character changes radically when, in the evening, the electric lights are put on and the curtains are drawn; the fading dusk light is replaced with a

A spotlight can identify the place of anything upon which one wishes to focus attention.

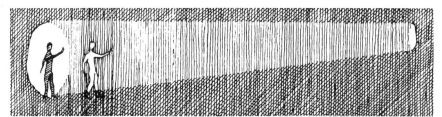

constant brightness. We are perhaps so familiar with this event that we do not recognise its drama.

The device of reversing the lighting conditions in a theatre, when the house lights go out and the stage lights come on, is an important ingredient in the magic of theatre.

Light can make the fabric of a building seem to dematerialise. A well lit, completely smooth, surface (of a wall, or a dome, for example), of which one perhaps cannot see the edges, can appear to lose its substance and become like air. The absence of light can have a similar effect. The surfaces in the distant recesses of the interior of a gothic church can seem to disappear in the gloom.

There are places where light is constant, and places where light changes. In some buildings (hypermarkets or shopping malls for example) electric bulbs supply light which is exactly the same all the time, at 9.30 on a winter evening, and at 12 noon on a summer day.

Making a clearing in a forest is an architectural act. It removes the obstruction of tree trunks, but it also changes general shade into a place with bright light from the sky. The removal of obstruction means that the place becomes a 'dancing floor'; the admission of light accentuates the place, and allows it to be a garden rather than a forest.

Erecting a roof under desert sun creates a patch of shade. The creation of a place of shade is essential to the architecture of a Bedouin tent.

A roof, which might in some climates be considered primarily as protection against rain, is also a shade. Putting a roof-light in it can be like making a clearing in a forest, creating a pool of light surrounded by shade.

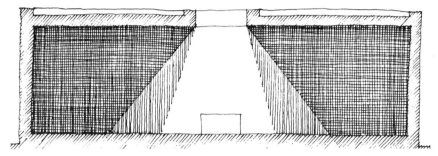

A lone lamp in a dark street identifies a place; a red light maybe identifies somewhere more specific.

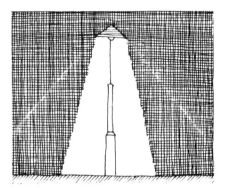

The doors of ancient Greek temples faced the morning sun. The red light from the east must have dramatically illuminated the figure of the god within. Like a cannon operating in reverse, the sun's horizontal light, striking deep into the interior of the temple helped to identify the place of the image of the god at a particularly significant time of day.

In the ceiling of the large church of the abbey of La Tourette in southern France, the architect Le Corbusier designed a relatively small rectangu-

A tent in the desert identifies a place of shade.

A roof-light in a room identifies a place of light.

Inside the tower of Brockhampton Church, designed by William Richard Lethaby in 1902, the windows cast shadows of their tracery as a pattern of sunlight on the white walls.

In this image you have to imagine the statue of the god illuminated by the golden light from the rising sun.

In the Aye Simon Reading Room (in the Guggenheim Museum of Art designed by Frank Lloyd Wright) Richard Meier, who was remodelling the room, used three existing roof-lights to identify three specific places (from left to right): the built in seat; the reading table; the receptionist's desk.

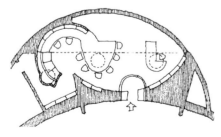

lar roof-light. As the sun moves across the sky, through the dark interior a rectangle of its beams tracks like a slowly moving searchlight.

In the side chapel of the same church Le Corbusier used deep circular roof-lights, like broad gun barrels with brightly coloured inner surfaces, to illuminate the places of the altars.

In the crypt chapel of the church intended for the Güell Colony in southern Spain, the architect Antonio Gaudi created a place of darkness in which columns and vaults melt into shadow, lit only by the stained glass windows. This chapel, rather than making a clearing, recreates the forest, with stone tree trunks and coloured dappled light seeping under a canopy of shade.

Colour

Issues of colour are of course inseparable from those of light. Light itself can be any colour; coloured glass changes the colour of light which

passes through it; the apparent colours of material objects are affected by the colour of the light that falls on them.

Colour, with light, can play a part in identifying place. A room painted a particular shade of green has a particular character, and is likely to be know as the 'Green Room'; a room lit only by a blue electric lamp has a particular character; a room lit by daylight passing through coloured glass windows has a particular character. Different colours and qualities of light may seem to suggest different moods.

Colour is not only a matter of decoration or the creation of places with particular moods. Colour plays a part in place recognition. The importance of colour in place recognition is underlined by camouflage, which conceals by destroying or obscuring colour differences.

Colour is also used in coding. In directing someone to your house, you might describe it as the house with the red (or blue, or green, or whatever colour) door (or walls, or windows, or roof). A coloured line can indicate a place where you should wait (to have your passport checked). A change in the colour of paving slabs, or carpet, might indicate a particular pathway, giving it special importance (as when a red carpet is laid down for an important person), or help people find their way.

Temperature

Temperature plays a part in the identification of place too. The chief purpose in building an igloo is to organise a small place of relative warmth amidst the snowfields of the arctic north.

A reason for the shaded patios, full of plants, in the houses of Cordoba, is that they create a relatively cool place as a respite from the heat of southern Spain.

Temperature has always been a central consideration of architecture when thought of as identification of place.

Temperature may or may not be associated with light. In the temperate zones of the northern hemisphere a south facing wall can make a place which is both bright and warm from the light and heat of the sun. An air-conditioning outlet, however, which emits no light, can identify an attractively warm place on an icy day. A bright room can of course be cold; a dark one warm.

The interiors of some buildings (recent art galleries for example) have constant, unvarying temperature in all parts, carefully controlled by air-conditioning and computer systems.

In other buildings, a rambling old house for example, there may be places with different temperatures: a warm place by a fire, a cool hallway, a warm attic, a cool cellar, a warm living room, a cool passageway, a warm courtyard, a cool pergola or verandah, a warm conservatory, a cool larder, a hot kitchen oven, a cold ice-house...; moving from place to place one passes through zones of different temperatures, related to different purposes and providing different experiences.

Ventilation

Temperature is involved with ventilation and humidity. Together they can identify places which may be warm, dry, and still; cold, damp, and draughty; warm, humid, and still; cold, dry, and draughty; and so on.

A fresh breezy place can be refreshing after a warm, humid one; a warm, still place is welcome after a cold windy one.

In the ancient palaces of the Mediterranean island of Crete, which has a hot, dry climate, royal apartments had open terraces and tiny courtyards shaded from sun, and positioned to catch or produce air movement to cool the interior spaces.

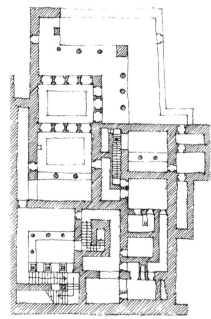

In the front elevation of the Altes Museum in Berlin, designed by Karl Friedrich Schinkel in the nineteenth century, there is a loggia, once open to the outdoor air, containing a pair of stairs from ground to first floor, and looking over the square (the

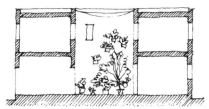

The small courtyards (patios) of houses in southern Spain are shaded by their high walls and, when the sun is at its highest, by awnings. They are packed with many plants, and maybe a small fountain. Evaporation from these creates cool air which flows through the rooms and into the narrow streets.

The residential quarters in the palaces of ancient Crete were well shaded. They were also provided with many openings and small light wells which, by providing ventilation, helped keep the rooms cool in the severe Cretan summer heat. (This is part of the palace of Knossos.)

An air-conditioning outlet can identify a warm place to stand on a cold day.

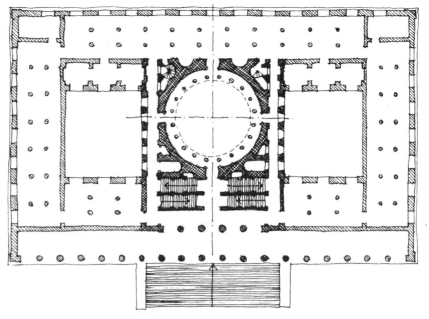

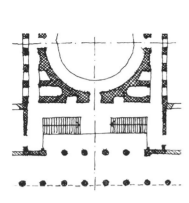

Above right is the ground floor plan of the Altes Museum in Berlin; above left is part of the second floor plan, showing the loggia. Below is a sketch of the loggia looking out towards the Lustgarten, (there is a much better version of this drawing in Schinkel's own Collection of Architectural Designs, *originally published in 1866 but republished in facsimile in 1989).*

Lustgarten) in front of the museum. Before it was enclosed with a glass curtain wall (in the early 1990s) this loggia, which is encountered during one's progression through the museum as well as at the beginning and end of a visit, provided a reminder of the fresh air and the openness of the outside, as a contrast to the enclosed interiors of the galleries.

Sound

Sound can be as powerful as light in identifying place. Places can be distinguished by the sounds they make, or by the ways in which they affect sounds made in them.

Some religions use sound to identify their places of worship: by bells, or gongs, or wind chimes, or a priest calling from a minaret.

A place might be distinguishable by the sound of the wind in the leaves of its trees, or by the sound of a stream or fountain of water. One's experience of a hotel room might be spoilt by the constant hum of its air-conditioning. A particular place in a city might be associated with the music of a particular busker. A place – an examination room or a library or a monastery refectory – might be distinguished by its silence; a restaurant by its taped background music.

Places can be identified by sound, but they can also be identified by the

ways in which they affect sounds made within them.

A sound in a cathedral which is large and with hard surfaces, will echo. A sound in a small room with a carpet, soft upholstered furniture and curtained windows, will be muffled. A hall for the performance of music, or one for drama, or a courtroom in which witnesses, lawyers and judges must be heard, has to be made with careful consideration of the quality of sound it will allow.

In the large church which is part of the monastery of La Tourette (the same church which has the rectangular roof-light), Le Corbusier has created a space which seems to hum of its own volition: its hard parallel concrete surfaces reflect, and even seem to magnify, every small noise – someone's shoe scraping on the floor, someone clearing their throat. When the monks sang in this space....

Sometimes odd acoustic effects can be produced inadvertently. In the early 1960s the American architect Philip Johnson designed a small art gallery as an extension to a house. Its plan is based on nine circles arranged in a square; the central circle is a small open court; the other eight circles form the

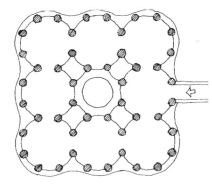

galleries and entrance lobby. Each of the galleries has a shallow domed roof. At the centre of each gallery one's voice seems amplified, as the circular surfaces of the walls, and the spherical surface of the domed ceiling, reflect it directly back.

A related effect occurs in an amphitheatre. If one stamps at the central focus, the sound reflects back from each step in turn, producing a very rapid 'machine-gun' sound.

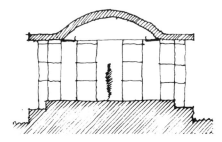

If you stand at the centre of one of the galleries in this building by Philip Johnson, your voice is reflected back to you by the curved surfaces of the walls and the ceiling, making it sound louder than elsewhere.

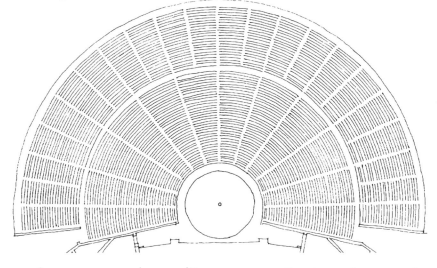

Some composers have written music specially to exploit the acoustic effects of particular buildings. The sixteenth-century composer Andrea Gabrieli wrote music especially for the cathedral of St Mark's in Venice. For his *Magnificat* he would position three choirs and an orchestra in different parts of the church, producing a quadrophonic effect.

There have also been occasions when the fabric of a building has been used as a musical instrument: this happened apparently at the opening of an arts building at Gothenberg University, Sweden, in the early 1990s, when the

Standing at the centre of an amphitheatre, a sound is reflected back from each tier in turn, extending it into a string of echoes which sound like a rapid machine-gun.

balcony rails were used as percussion instruments.

Smell

A place can be identified by its smell; a smell can make a place.

A schoolboy's stink bomb identifies a place to avoid. A public lavatory tends to smell one way, a ladies' hairdresser's another, a perfume shop another, a fishmonger's another.

The character of an old library is partly due to the smell of polished wood and musty leather book-bindings; that of an artist's studio to the smell of oil paint. Food halls in department stores cultivate odours of roasted coffee, delicate cheeses, and fresh-baked bread. Chinese temples are pervaded by the perfume of burning incense. The bedroom of an adolescent boy might be distinguished by the smell of old socks or deodorant. The lounge in a gentleman's club might smell of polish and old leather armchairs. Different parts of a garden might be distinguishable by the perfume of roses, honeysuckle, jasmine, lavender....

Texture

Texture is a characteristic which one can see – in this it relates to light and the sense of sight; but it is also a characteristic which one can feel – in this it relates to the sense of touch. In both ways, texture contributes to the identification of place.

Texture can be achieved by surface application, of paint or of polish or of fabric; but texture is also intimately related to the innate qualities of materials and the ways they can be treated and used.

We identify places by changing their texture. We do this inadvertently when, for example, by repeatedly walking the same route across a field or a yard, we (or some sheep) wear away a smooth path. We do it consciously when we define a pathway with grit, or cobbles, or paviours, or tarmacadam. These changes are apparent to our eyes, but they are also appreciated by our sense of touch, through our feet, and provide a harder wearing surface than the earth.

On some roads the white lines which mark the verges are textured with rough ridges. If a car deviates from its lane it is communicated to the driver by the vibration and the noise of the tyres on the ridges; the place of the roadway is identified not only by sight, but by vibration (and sound) also.

Changes of texture are useful in the dark, and for people with partial sight. In some places road crossings are indicated by a change in the pavement texture.

In old houses, when the making of hard pavements was a laborious activity, the places of hardest wear, around the doorways, were often identified and protected by large slabs of stone, or aprons of cobbles.

Floors and pavements figure so prominently in discussion of the ways in which textures can identify place because it is through our feet that we make our main tactile contact with the products of architecture. Carpets change the texture of floors, making them warmer and more comfortable, particularly to bare feet. In some places consideration of bare feet is more problematic; around a swimming pool there is conflict between the need for comfort for feet and the need for a non-slippery texture.

Texture is important in other places where we come into contact with architecture.

If the top surface of a low wall is also intended as a casual seat, then one might change its texture from hard stone, brick or concrete, to soft fabric or timber, thereby identifying it as a place to sit. The change is apparent to the eye, but also to another part of the body.

Texture is also important where our hands or upper bodies touch buildings: door handles, counters, sleeping places, and so on. Beds are essentially matters of changes of texture – making a place upon which it is comfortable to lie and sleep.

Scale

This drawing shows a man standing on a rather small stage.

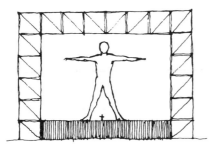

If however one is told that this man is only a piece of stage dressing, and that the real man on the stage is actually the dot between its legs, one's perception of the size of the stage is dramatically changed.

Scale is about relative sizes. A scale on a map or drawing indicates the sizes of things shown on it relative to their sizes in reality. On a drawing which is at 1:100 a doorway which in reality might be one metre wide would be shown as one centimetre wide.

In architecture scale has another meaning, still to do with relative sizes. It refers to the size of something relative to oneself.

The experience of a place is radically affected by its scale. A football pitch, and a small patch of grass in a back garden, though both defined areas of grass, present very different experiences because of their different scales.

(Scale is also discussed in the chapter on *Geometry in Architecture*, under 'Measuring'.)

Time

If light is the first modifying element of the products of architecture, then time is perhaps the last. Light provides instant stimulation; but time takes ... time.

Time plays a part in architecture in various ways. Although architecture produces lasting products, none of them is immune to the effects of time: materials change – develop a patina, or deteriorate; original uses become more ingrained in a building, or are displaced by others; people make places better, or alter them for new uses.

Sometimes the effects of time are positive, sometimes negative. They are

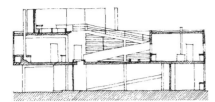

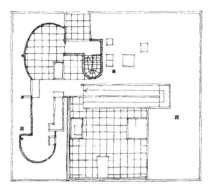

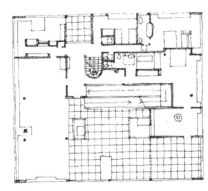

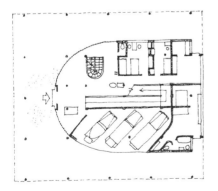

usually considered to be 'natural' in that they are not subject to control by human decision; but that does not mean that they cannot be anticipated and used positively. It is possible to choose materials, or to design generally, with maturity rather than early use in mind.

Time is a modifying element of architecture in another sense; one which is more under the control of the designer, though not totally so.

Although it takes time to achieve a profound understanding of a great painting, one is able to take in an initial impression literally in the blink of an eye. With a piece of music it takes the duration to be able to get even this initial impression; the achievement of a profound understanding probably takes many listenings.

With a product of architecture it takes time to get an impression too. Though we see a great deal of architecture illustrated by photograph in books and journals, this is not of course the way in which it is intended to be experienced.

When we experience a building in its physical existence there are many stages to the process. There is the discovery, the view of the outward appearance, the approach, the entrance, the exploration of the interior spaces (the last of which probably takes the greatest amount of the time).

Some architects consciously try to manipulate the temporal experience of the products of their architecture.

All processional architecture encapsulates time. In ancient Athens there were processions which led from the agora, up the acropolis, to the Parthenon. The route took time. Great cathedrals seem to encapsulate the time it takes to pass from the entrance, along the nave, to the altar; as in a wedding. The production line in a car plant takes cars through a process of assembly, which takes time.

In the Villa Savoye (1929) Le Corbusier used time as a modifying element of architecture. The three floor plans are shown on the left. Approaching it, entering it, and exploring within it, he created a route – an 'architectural promenade'.

The approach works whether one is on foot, or in a car. The 'front' entrance into the house is on the left of the ground floor plan (bottom); but one approaches from the rear. In a car one passes under the building following the sweep of the glass wall around the hallway.

One enters the house, and there is a ramp which takes one, slowly, up to the first floor, which is the main living floor. You can see the ramp on the section (top).

At that level there is the salon, and a roof terrace.

From the roof terrace the ramp continues to an upper roof terrace, where there is a solarium, and a 'window' just above the entrance, completing the route.

ELEMENTS DOING
MORE THAN ONE THING

A window can 'do' many things architecturally at the same time. It lets light into a room, or out. It provides a view out, or in. It might set up an axial relationship. The formation of an opening creates a cill, which can be a shelf for books or plants. The window can be a place for display.... All this without even considering its role in the pattern of an elevation.

The front wall of the Alcazar, in Toledo, also displays the credentials of its sixteenth-century owner, Charles V of Spain, identifying the place as his palace.

ELEMENTS DOING MORE THAN ONE THING

In architecture elements often work to identify place in more than one way at a time.

A gable wall of a house, for example, which plays its part in enclos-

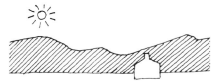

ing the interior of the dwelling, can also be a marker identifying a place where someone lives.

The top surface of a wall can be a pathway, for a cat, or as in a pier or a castle wall.

And the side surface of a wall can be a place for display, as in a cinema, or an art gallery; or in the way that any building presents a 'face' to the world.

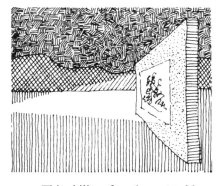

This ability of an element to identify different places in a variety of ways is an essential feature, and one of the most intriguing aspects, of architectural design. It involves the mental processes of both recognition and creation in an interactive way – creation of one place leads to recognition of others – and comes into operation at all scales.

Occurrences are innumerable. This will be seen to be a theme which recurs over and over again in the examples used in this book.

Part of the reason for the importance of this theme in architectural design is that architecture does not (or should not) operate in its own hermetic world. Its work is (almost) always relating to other things which already exist in the conditions around.

Any wall built in a landscape creates at least two places – one sunny, one shady.

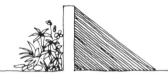

If it forms an enclosure then it divides an 'inside' from the 'outside'; giving something to and taking something from both.

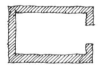

The theme also reaches into the work itself. A single 'party' or dividing wall makes two rooms.

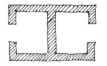

A flat roof is also a platform.

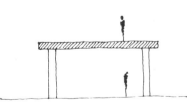

A series of roofs which are also floors creates a multi-storey building.

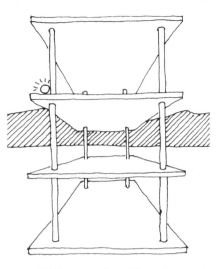

Walls are often (though not always) structural – they hold up a roof; but their primary architectural role is to define the boundaries of place. Other structural elements can have this role too. A line of columns can also define a pathway.

In this apparently simple plan (examples of which can be found in the

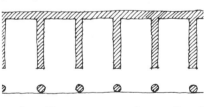

ancient Roman agora, the medieval cloister, town squares, and the shop

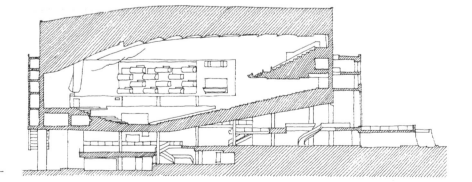

In this small apartment by the Swedish architect Sven Markelius, a number of elements do more than one thing at once. For example: the one structural column (near the balcony door) helps to suggest different places within the generally open plan; the bathroom and kitchen are grouped together and form a division between the entrance lobby and the rest of the apartment.

In the Royal Festival Hall, London, the stepped floor of the auditorium also provides a distinctive raked ceiling for the foyer spaces. The building was designed by Robert Matthew, Leslie Martin, and others, and was completed in 1951.

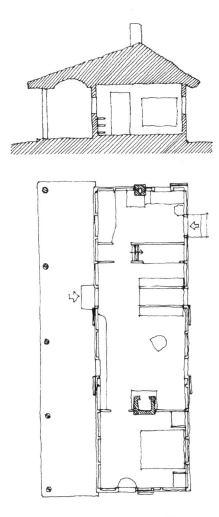

In this small summerhouse, (shown here in section and plan), the four columns not only hold up the roof, but also help to define the boundary of the verandah – a place for sitting and looking over the nearby lake which is at Muuratsalo in Finland. It is called the Villa Flora, and was designed by Alvar and Aino Aalto in 1926.

houses of Malaysia) a few basic architectural elements are composed to identify a number of different places: the cells themselves; the street or square outside; and the covered pathway, which also makes a transition space between the outside and the insides. (The concept of 'transition spaces' is discussed in more detail later, under *Transition, Hierarchy, Heart*.)

One of the indispensable skills of an architect is to be conscious of the consequences of composing elements; being aware that they are likely to do more than one thing. These consequences can be positive: cut a window into a wall, and you create a window cill which is a shelf for books or for a vase of flowers; build two rows of houses and you also create the street between them.

But the consequences can also be negative: build two houses too close together but not joined and you might create an unpleasant unusable space be-

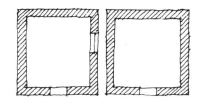

tween; build a wall for display, and you may also create a 'non-place' behind.

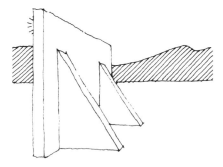

This is one of the most important aspects of architectural design. It is a matter in which an architect can achieve great subtlety; but it is also one that can cause problems.

This is the plan of an English house built in the early part of the twentieth century.

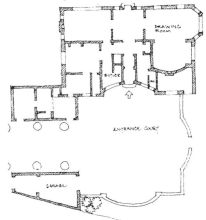

The forecourt is a square with cusps taken out of three of the sides. The cusp which bites into the house might help to identify the place of the entrance, but it also causes problems with the internal planning of the house. In the awkward spaces alongside the doorway the architect has placed the butler's pantry (to the left) and the cloakroom and lavatory (to the right). A similar problem occurs in the drawing room where the same device is used to identify the place of the fire; but here it also makes an odd shaped garden room (in the bottom right corner of the house).

Elements can often be found to be doing two things at once (it is actually difficult to find elements in architecture which are only doing one thing at once!), but one sometimes finds elements which are doing many things.

(This might be one of the measures of architecture.)

In this section through a hillside house – The Wolfe House – designed by Rudolf Schindler in 1928, you can see that the simple thin horizontal concrete slabs, tied back into the hill, act not only as floors and ceilings, but also as outdoor terraces and sunshades.

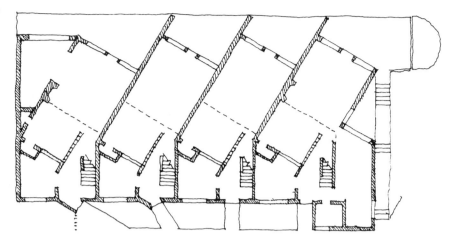

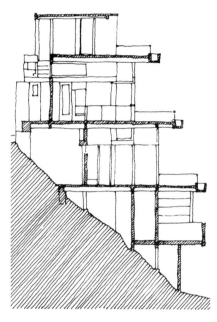

Their precipitous edges are protected by balustrades which are also planting boxes.

In the Falk Apartments of 1943 (shown in plan, top right), by the same architect, it is not so much the element but the way it is positioned that does more than one thing at once.

The party walls between the apartments have been angled so that the living rooms face a lake. But this device has other effects too. It allows the terraces outside each apartment to be larger; it also gives these terraces more privacy. Deeper into the plan the angled walls open up a place for each

staircase, which would otherwise be more cramped. The non-orthogonal geometry also helps the end apartments to be larger and different in plan from the intermediate ones. Schindler has been careful not to let the deviation from right-angles create awkward shaped rooms; it is as if almost all the problems which might have been caused by the shift from rectangular geometry have been reduced down to one tiny triangular cupboard in the left-hand end apartment.

As with the Wolfe House, these apartments were designed for a hillside, though one which is less steep. Their section is stepped, so that a roof can also be a terrace. In the section of an individual apartment you can see that the bedroom is almost like an enclosed gallery in the living room. This de-

In the plan of the Falk Apartments, it is the angle of the party walls that does more than one thing.

Reference for the architecture of Rudolf Schindler:

Lionel March and Judith Scheine – *R.M. Schindler*, 1993.

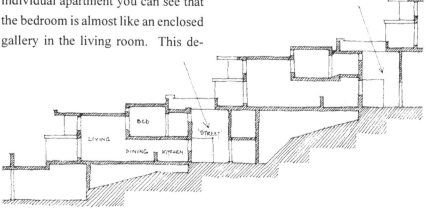

Reference for Swiss villages:
Werner Blaser – *The Rock is My Home*, WEMA, Zurich, 1976.

This plan is of a village in the Ticino region of Switzerland. It shows cellular houses (hatched), walls, and some platforms adjacent to houses. It is difficult to find an element which is not doing more than one thing at once: mainly, defining private, semi-private, and public spaces – pathways and small 'nodal' squares.

vice too does more than one thing. One can see from the bedroom down into the living room, and thus the bedroom is less enclosed than is traditionally the case. But also the position of the bedroom in the section creates two different ceiling heights which relate to the places they cover: a high ceiling over the living room making it more spacious; and a low ceiling over the entrance and kitchen. The line where the low ceiling changes to the high also suggests the division between the living room and the dining area. The dining place is identified by the lower ceiling.

One of the drawbacks with stepped sections is that inside spaces close to the hill can be dark. Notice that in the Falk Apartments Schindler counters this problem by making 'streets' between the layers of apartments. These pathways do at least three things at once: they give access into the apartments; they provide light into the back spaces – the kitchens, hallways, and bathrooms; and they allow cross-ventilation through the apartments.

There are many too many instances of elements doing more than one thing at once in the products of architecture to be able to cover them adequately here. This is a characteristic of architecture at all scales and types, and from all periods of history. When an ancient Greek hung his shield on the roof-post of his megaron, he was using an architectural element to do two things at once; if that post was also a corner of his bed-place, then it was doing three.

The process of introducing one element to do a particular purpose, and then seeing what else it does (and so on), is an essential part of the 'organic' tradition in architecture. This is how settlements have grown into villages, and villages into towns, through history.

USING THINGS
THAT ARE THERE

USING THINGS THAT ARE THERE

In this small crevice in a huge rock face (in the Carnarvon Gorge in Queensland, Australia), an aborigine family laid the dead body of a small child, wrapped in bark. They marked

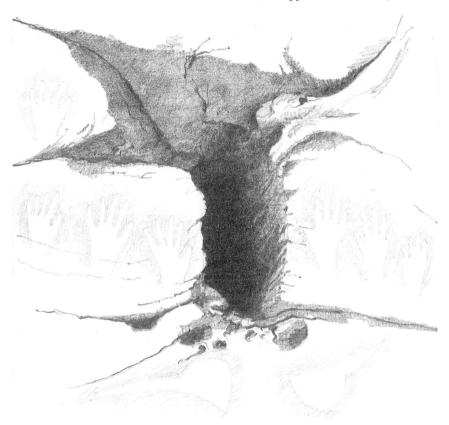

the place with silhouettes of their hands, made with pigment. This grave is as much a piece of architecture as is the Great Pyramid of Giza (and more poignant).

Although architecture is always an activity of a mind, it does not follow that architecture always entails building something physically. As identification of place, architecture may be no more than a matter of recognising that a particular location is distinguishable as 'a place' – the shade of a tree, the shelter of a cave, the summit of a hill, the mystery of a dark forest....

In daily life, one is constantly recognising places. This is how one knows where one is, where one has been, and where one is going. With many of these thousands of places one does not interact; they are left unchanged except for the recognition itself, which may be fleeting and hardly acknowledged.

Some places however stick in the mind. They are remembered because of some particular distinction: a fine view, shelter from the wind, the warmth of the sun; or because they are associated with a particular event: falling off a bicycle, fighting with a friend, making love, witnessing a miracle, winning a battle....

The next significant step in a relationship with place is that one might choose to use it for something – the shade of that tree for a brief rest on a long and arduous walk, the cave as a hiding place, the hill top to survey the surrounding countryside, the darkest part of the mysterious forest for some spiritual ritual....

Maybe the recognition of a place is shared with other people, the memory and use associated with it becomes communal.

In these ways places acquire significance of many kinds – practical, social, historical, mythical, religious....

The world has many, many such places: the cave in Mount Dikti on the

Opposite page:
A cave that is used as a dwelling is architecture, just as much as is a built house, by reason of having been chosen as a place.

island of Crete, believed to have been the birthplace of the Greek god Zeus; the route of the Muslim pilgrimage – the *hajj* – in and around Mecca; the mount from which Christ delivered his sermon; the stretch of boulevard in Dallas, Texas, where President Kennedy was shot; the places in the Australian outback which are identified and remembered in the 'songlines' of aborigine culture....

Recognition, memory, choice, sharing with others, the acquisition of significance; all these contribute to the processes of architecture.

Of course architecture also involves building – the physical alteration of a part of the world to enhance or reinforce its establishment as a place. Recognition, memory, choice, sharing ... operate at the rudimentary levels of identification of place. Architecture makes more difference when it proposes and puts into effect physical changes to the fabric of the world.

Architecture always depends on things that are already there; it involves recognising their potential or the problems they present; it involves, maybe,

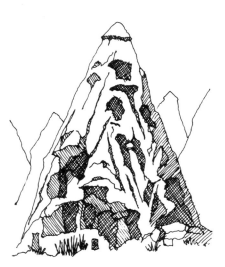

Castle builders through history have built their fortifications on sites which, though often powerfully dramatic, were chosen primarily for their defensibility. Even if identically rebuilt somewhere else, such buildings would not be architecturally the same on another site.

remembering their associations and significances; it involves choice of site, and sharing with others.

Fundamentally all terrestrial architecture depends upon the ground for its base, something that we perhaps tend to take for granted.

In a flat and completely featureless landscape the establishment of a place would have to be an arbitrary decision; (once established however the place would provide a catalyst for other places). The irregular shape of the ground, together with the courses of the

Simeon the Stylite lived in a cave dwelling within one of the volcanic cones of the valley of Göreme in Anatolia. The caves were extended and refined by carving into the rock.

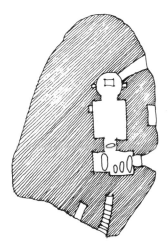

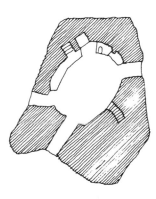

References for architecture using natural forms:

Bernard Rudofsky – *Architecture Without Architects,* 1964.

Bernard Rudofsky – *The Prodigious Builders*, 1977.

African baobab trees have thick trunks and soft wood. With space carved out inside, they can be made into dwellings.

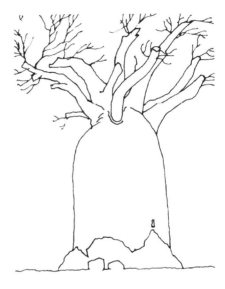

The Dome of the Rock in Jerusalem is built over a rock which is sacred to Jews, Christians and Muslims.

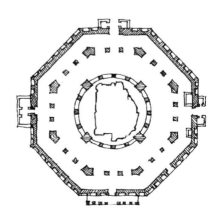

water that flows through it, the wind that blows across it, and the things that grow on it, all under the sun, often suggests places which are seeds of architecture. Dealing with them, taking advantage of them, mitigating their effects, exploiting their character ... can be important factors in architecture.

In the untouched landscape, doing architecture can involve using hills, trees, rivers, caves, cliffs, breezes from the sea: things said to be 'provided by nature'.

Examples in which natural features or elements contribute to architecture are innumerable and can be aesthetically and intellectually engaging in the way they seem to symbolise a symbiotic relationship between people (and other creatures) and the conditions in which they live.

People have lived in caves since time immemorial; they have altered them, flattened their floors, extended them by excavation, enclosed their entrances, built outwards from them ... to make them more commodious. It is said that proto-people descended to the ground from living in trees; people still make houses in trees. Since ancient times too people have used the walls of caves and of cliff-faces as places for the display of images – wall paintings and carvings. Through history people have found ways to cool and dry their dwellings with natural breezes, and warm them with the sun. Domineering or frightened people have chosen hills and craggy rocks as places for fortresses or defensible villages. The constant need for water and food has led people to build near rivers and adjacent to fertile land. And so on.

Each of the major buildings on the acropolis in Athens identifies a place that was already there: the Parthenon identifies the highest point, dominating the city around; the Erectheion an ancient sacred site; the Propylon the easiest access onto the summit; and each of the theatres an accommodating bowl of land where spectators probably watched performances even before they were provided with formal performance places and stepped seating.

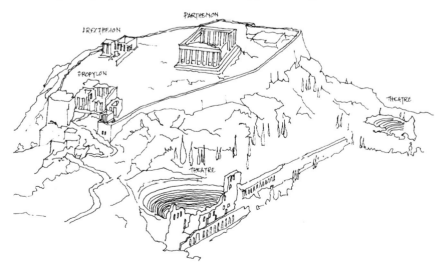

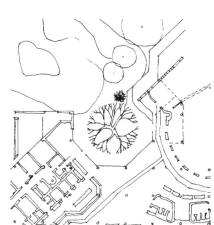

Reference for Stoneywell Cottage:
W.R. Lethaby and others – *Ernest Gimson, His Life and Work*, 1924.

Reference for the Student Centre by Ralph Erskine:
Peter Collymore – *The Architecture of Ralph Erskine*, 1985.

At the base of Ayer's Rock in central Australia there are some natural alcoves, apparently carved out by wind erosion. Each provides a place of shade, stones to sit on, and also a surface on which to draw. Some of them appear to have been used as schoolrooms.

Erskine used a particularly fine tree, already on the site, to determine the position of an outside space taken like a bite out of the plan of the building. The tree, with the natural contours of the ground, contributes to the identity of the place, and to the views from inside the building.

Reference for Mexican house:
'Maison à Santiago Tepetlapa', *in L'Architecture d'Aujourd'hui, June 1991*, p.86.

This cottage in Leicestershire (UK) was designed in the 1890s by Ernest Gimson. It was built hard against a natural rocky outcrop, which contributes part of the enclosure of the house, and also affects the levels of its floors. The land, as found and chosen, is an integral part of the work of architecture.

In designing the Students' Union building at Stockholm University in Sweden, built in the late 1970s, Ralph

The drawing to the right is a section through part of a small dwelling in Mexico, designed by Ada Dewes and Sergio Puente. It was built in the mid-1980s. The designers used basic elements of architecture to make a number

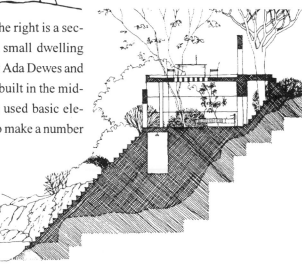

Reference for the 'timeless way of building':
Christopher Alexander – *The Timeless Way of Building*, 1979.

Reference for BBC Radio Centre: 'Foster Associates, BBC Radio Centre', *in Architectural Design 8*, 1986, pp.20-27.

The atrium of the proposed BBC Radio Centre at Langham Place in London was to have been oriented towards All Souls Church, using it as a visual focus for the space.

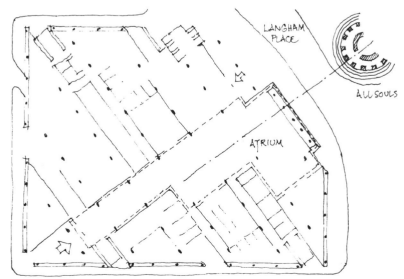

of places; these are used in concert with modifying elements and things already on the site to make the complete experience of the house.

The house is built amongst trees on the steep side of the valley of a fast-flowing river. The first element of the house is a horizontal platform built out from the slope. This is approached from above by steps; and there is a stepped pathway down from it to the river below. This platform is further defined by a single screen wall on the upslope side through the middle of which it is entered. It also has a roof over it supported by the screen wall and by two columns. The other three sides of the platform, which is a bedroom, are enclosed only by mosquito netting, which keeps out biting insects but allows in the songs of the birds in the trees. Steps in the platform lead to a shower room below. The roof of the bedroom is also the floor of the living room above. This 'room' has only one wall, a vertical extension of the screen wall below, through which it too is

entered; the other 'walls' and its 'roof' are provided by the canopy of trees around.

Using the natural things that are already there is an ingredient in what has been termed, by Christopher Alexander, the 'timeless way of building'. As such it is as relevant today as ever, though in regions of the world which have been inhabited for many centuries one is less likely to have the opportunity to use natural features and elements, and more to have to relate to previous products of architecture.

On a crowded beach, if there is a small space left amongst other people's towels, wind breaks, barbecues, deck-chairs, sunshades, etc., you make your own settlement, accommodating yourself to the space available, the direction of the sun and wind, the route to the sea, as best you can.

It's a similar situation when one does architecture amongst existing products of architecture – in a village, a town, a city; one interacts with what is already there.

In cities the task is often to make places in spaces between existing buildings, and relate to the places around that are already there.

When Foster Associates designed a new Radio Centre for the BBC (left, which has not been built) they took care to fit the building into its site, and relate to things around.

The building was to have stood at Langham Place in London, the junction between Regent Street and Portland Place, and on the urban route between Regent's Park and Piccadilly

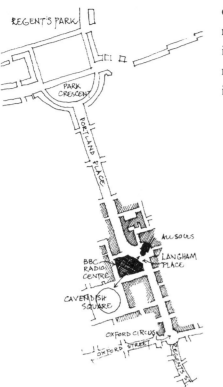

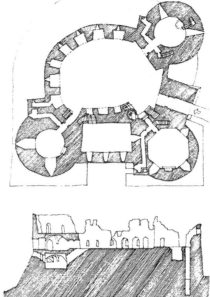

of Bute, he was presented with the ruins of a Norman castle as the starting point. His design grew from little more than a ground plan, already there in stone.

Circus designed by John Nash in the early nineteenth century. Not only is the building's plan shaped to fit the site like a jigsaw piece, thus providing walls to define the adjacent roads, but it also provides a pathway, passing through the building, from Cavendish Square into Langham Place. The building has a six-storey atrium at its heart; this is oriented towards Nash's All Souls Church across the road, which its large glass wall frames like a picture, using it to add identity to the place of the atrium within the building.

Sometimes architecture involves using the fabric of an existing building, or its ruins.

When the Victorian architect William Burges was given the commission to design a hunting lodge, a few miles north of Cardiff, for the Marquis

Using these remains as a base, physically and creatively, Burges designed his own interpretation of a

Reference for Castell Coch:
John Mordaunt Crook – *William Burges and the High Victorian Dream*, 1981.

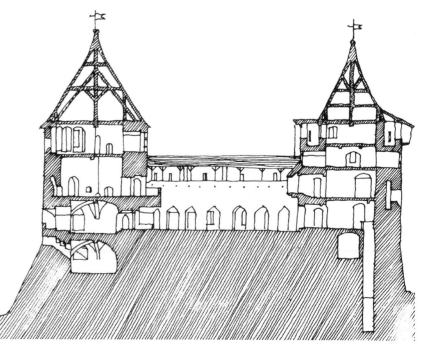

medieval castle. The result is a collusion of the past with Burges's present. *Castell Coch* (The Red Castle) is not an accurate reconstruction of the original castle. In the 1870s when it was built, it was a new building (except that is for the foundations), but one in which Burges took prompts from what was already there. His imagination benefited from working on a base, and on a site (the castle overlooks the Taff Valley running north from Cardiff), inherited from seven centuries earlier. His intention was to make a romantic recreation of a medieval place, as an entertainment for his client and an ornament in the landscape.

In the late 1950s and early 1960s the Italian architect Carlo Scarpa was presented with a commission which similarly involved using an old building and making it into a new work of architecture. His base (there was more remaining of it than Burges had at *Castell Coch*), was a fourteenth-century castle in the northern Italian city of Verona – the *Castelvecchio* (Old Castle).

Scarpa's attitude to the past and how its built remains might be used architecturally was different from that of Burges. It was not his intention to realise a romantic image of the past, but rather to use remains of the past as a stimulus to present aesthetic interest.

In dealing with, and remodelling the Castelvecchio, Scarpa created an architectural experience which is one of the present, but which also exploits accidents and collisions, juxtapositions and relationships, spaces and their character, that derive from arrangements which existed in the building before he came to it. To these arrangements he has added some more, from his own responsive imagination, as one more layer – belonging to the mid-twentieth century – on a building which already had many, from various periods of history.

Perhaps the most impressive place in Scarpa's *Castelvecchio* is the 'Cangrande space', named after the equestrian statue which it frames. This is a place that had not existed in the

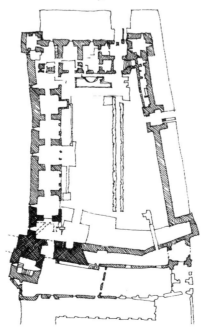

Reference for Castelvecchio:
Richard Murphy – *Carlo Scarpa and the Castelvecchio*, 1990.

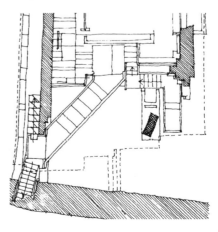

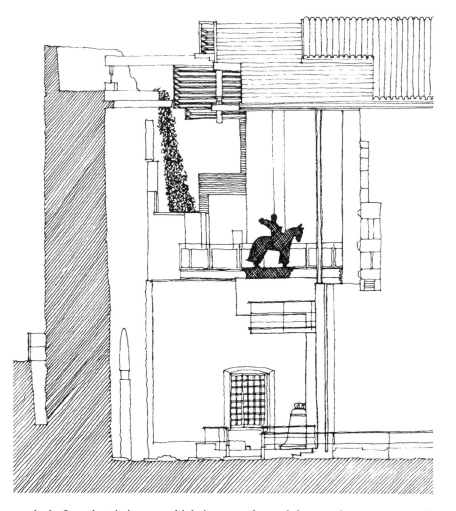

The 'Cangrande' space at the Castelvecchio in Verona, as remodelled by Carlo Scarpa. Scarpa interpreted the history of this particular corner of the castle, to identify an impressive place within which to display an equestrian statue.

castle before, but it is one which is deeply conditioned both by the existing fabric of the old stone walls, and by an appreciation by Scarpa of the historical changes which had occurred in that particular part of the building.

When the Danish industrialist Knud Jensen commissioned Jørgen Bo and Vilhelm Wohlert to design the Louisiana Art Museum north of Copenhagen, there were various things that he wanted the architects to use in their design – things that were already there on the site:

First, the old house had to be preserved as the entrance. No matter how elaborate the museum might become in later years .... Second, I wanted one room ... to open out into that view, about two hundred metres to the north of the manor, overlooking our lush inland lake. Third, about another hundred metres farther on, in the rose garden – on the bluff overlooking the strait and, in the distance, Sweden – I wanted to have the cafeteria and its terrace.

The first phase of the art museum that was built in response to Jensen's brief, which occupies the left two-thirds of this plan, uses all the innate

Reference for Louisiana Art Museum:
Michael Brawne – *Jørgen Bo, Vilhelm Wohlert, Louisiana Museum, Humlebaek*, 1993.

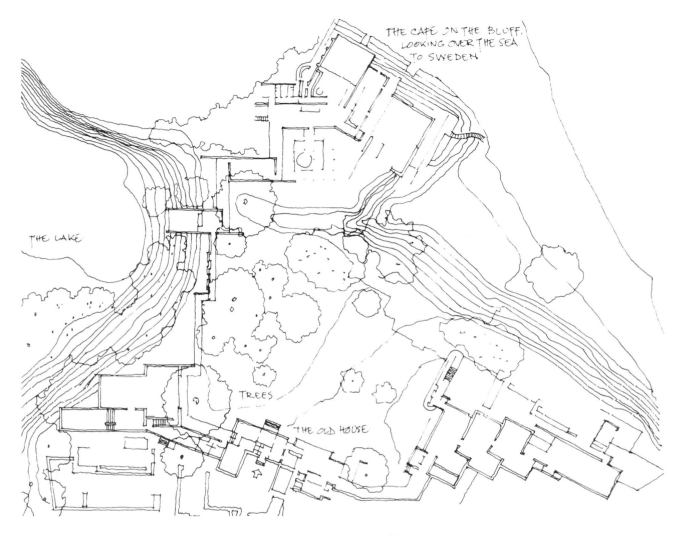

THE CAFE ON THE BLUFF, LOOKING OVER THE SEA TO SWEDEN

THE LAKE

TREES

THE OLD HOUSE

The ground plan of the Louisiana Art Museum in Denmark, designed by Jørgen Bo and Vilhelm Wohlert. A old house is used as the entrance; the galleries and the cafeteria respond to other places on the site.

features of the site which he identified. The old house, at the middle-bottom of the plan, is the main entrance. The route through the museum then moves through some galleries and then north along a stepped series of walkways to a particular gallery which has a large glass wall looking out over the lake. The route continues through more galleries to the bluff, where there is a cafeteria looking out across the sea to Sweden. The architects also used other features already on the site, especially some of the mature trees, and the contours of the ground.

This building, the architecture of which takes its visitors on a tour of its site, and of places that were already there, could not be the same anywhere else.

PRIMITIVE
PLACE TYPES

PRIMITIVE PLACE TYPES

As time has passed the places people use have become more diverse, more sophisticated, and more complex in their interrelationships. Some types of place are ancient: the hearth as the place of the fire; the altar as a place of sacrifice or a focus for worship; the tomb as a place for the dead. Other place types are more recent: the airport, the motorway service station, the cash-dispenser.

The most ancient types of place are those which are to do with the fundamental aspects of life: keeping warm and dry; moving from location to location; acquiring and keeping food and water, fuel and wealth; cooking; sitting and eating; socialising; defecating; sleeping and procreating; defending against enemies; worshipping and performing ritual; buying or exchanging goods and services; story-telling and acting; teaching and learning; asserting military, political, and commercial power; discussing and debating; fighting and competing; giving birth; suffering 'rites of passage'; dying.

It is the concept of place that links architecture to life. The places which people use are in intimate relation to their lives. Living necessarily involves the conceptual organisation and physical arrangement of the world into places: places to work, places to rest, places to be seen, places to spectate; places which are 'mine', places which are 'yours'; places which are pleasant, places which are nasty; places which are warm, places which are cold; places which are awe-inspiring, places which are boring; places that protect, places for exhibition; and so on.

Like language, architecture is not stagnant. Both language and architecture (as identification of place) exist through use, and are subject to historical changes and cultural variation. Social institutions evolve; beliefs differ about the relative importance of particular facets of life, and hence so does the need for places to accommodate them. Aspirations become more, or less, sophisticated; some places become redundant; needs for new types of place become apparent; fashions come and go; linkages (physical and electronic) between places become more sophisticated.

In language a particular meaning can be conveyed in different ways, using different words in different constructions. The words and their patterns have to be in accord with the intended meaning, otherwise it is lost in nonsense or a different, unintended, meaning emerges. The various ways of saying something may just be different; but variations in vocabulary and construction can also add subtlety, emphasis, stylistic nuance, or aesthetic quality. It is the same in architecture; places with similar purposes can be identified architecturally in different ways.

Places are identified by the elements of architecture. A place for performance might be identified in any of a number of ways: by a platform, by a spotlight, by a circle of stones, by a number of marker poles setting out an area of ground; a place of imprisonment might be a small dark cell, or an island, or a deep pit, or the corner of a classroom.

The identity of a place also depends on the ability of someone to recognise it as such. A person has to be able to recognise a place as a place; otherwise, for that person, that place does not exist.

A place might have many interpretations. A person might see a wall as a barrier, another see it as a seat, another see it as a path along which to walk; one might see it as all three at the same time.

Places can overlap with others. A bedroom has a place to sleep (the bed), but it also has places for getting out of bed, for sitting and reading, for dressing and undressing, for looking in a mirror, for standing looking out of the window, maybe for doing press-ups; these places are not distinct, but intermingle within the room, and perhaps change their identities from time to time. At a larger scale, a town square can be a market place, a car park, a place for performance, a place for eating, a place for meeting, for talking, for wandering ... all at once.

Primitive place types

Amongst this complexity, some place types have acquired their own names – hearth, theatre, tomb, altar, fortress, throne – that reach far back into history. Their ancient names are testament to their age-old roles in the lives and architecture of people through history.

Although such place types are ancient, and have a consistent conceptual identity (a hearth is a place for a fire, a theatre for performance, a tomb for the dead, an altar for worship, a fortress for defence, a throne a seat of power), their architecture (their conceptual organisation by the use of basic and modifying elements) can vary greatly. A purpose does not necessarily determine the architecture of its place; many purposes, even the most ancient, have been accommodated architecturally in very different ways.

The relationship between architecture and the names of place types with ancient purposes can be confusing. The word *tomb* might evoke a particular example in one's mind, but the architecture of tombs through history has been very varied.

The names of place types in architecture can seem clear, but be vague. If one says that a place is 'like a theatre' one might be exact in so far as it may incorporate a place for performance with a place for spectating, but architecturally it might be an amphitheatre, a courtyard, a street, or have a proscenium arch.

There is often a rough and ready relationship between architecture and the words through which it is discussed. Words that are specific in one context may be imprecise and analogical in another. Words such as *hearth, theatre, tomb, altar, fortress, throne* are not necessarily specific in the architectural forms to which they refer.

Reference for hearth:

Gottfried Semper *identified* hearth *as one of the four fundamental elements of architecture, along with the* earthwork*, the* roof*, and the* screen wall*, in...*

Gottfried Semper – *The Four Elements of Architecture*, 1851.

(With regard to these 'Four Elements', in this book the hearth *is categorised as a 'primitive place type', the* earthwork *and the* screen wall *both as the 'basic element' of* barrier*, and the* roof *as the 'basic element' of* roof*.)*

Hearth – the place of the fire

The hearth has had a traditional significance in many cultures, as the heart of the home, or the focus of a community – a source of warmth, for cooking, a point of reference around which life revolves.

Its essential component is the fire itself; but the ways in which the place of the fire is identified can vary greatly. Even a simple outdoor fireplace can be formed of different configurations of basic architectural elements.

In the most rudimentary way a fire identifies its own place, creating a sphere of light and heat, a column of smoke and sparks, and a rough circle of scorched earth. But often its place is marked in other ways too.

A fire can be framed in various ways: the circle of scorched earth may be contained with a circle of stones;

the fire might be set against a large stone which protects it from excessive draught and stores some of its heat;

or it may be flanked by two parallel walls of stone that channel draughts and provide a platform for cooking.

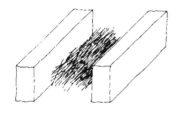

The place of a fire might be identified in more elaborate ways too: maybe provided with a tripod from which a cooking pot is hung, but which also forms an aedicule emphasizing the hearth;

or perhaps set in a more sophisticated construction, like a seat or table that lifts it off the ground for convenience;

or perhaps provided with its own small building.

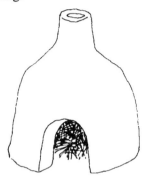

A fire not only has its own place, but also creates a place where people can occupy its sphere of light and warmth. The extent of this sphere can vary. It might be defined by a tight circle of people around a campfire on a cold night; or it might be the extensive circle of visibility of a hill-top beacon seen across miles of countryside.

Through history the architectural role of the hearth as an identifier of place of human occupation has been to do with how its sphere of light and warmth has been defined, contained, or controlled.

In the countryside – the landscape of the primitive family or the present-day camper – a fire makes its own place by its light and warmth. But when one wants to make a fire, a place for it has to be chosen. In doing this

various factors may be taken into account; factors which are related to the purpose of the fire.

If there is a dell, protected from the wind and provided with rocks for seats, and if the purpose of the fire is to provide a cooking-place and a focus for a summer evening of eating and talking, then it is likely to be chosen as a place for the hearth. In doing this the dell becomes a container of the sphere of light and warmth from the fire. It also becomes a room within which friends may cook, eat and talk.

The fire is in the middle of a sort of natural room; its light and warmth seem bounded by the rocks around and the canopies of the trees above.

In many cultures, particularly in cool and cold regions of the world, domestic architecture has been primarily concerned with enclosing the place of the fire and containing its sphere of light and warmth.

An igloo contains the sphere (or hemisphere when the fire is on the flat surface of the earth) literally – with a dome.

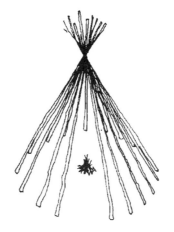

Materials more difficult to shape than ice are not so easy to form into a dome ... so a teepee limits the hemisphere with a cone.

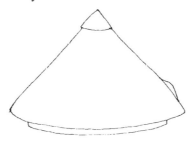

The primitive round house does similarly.

In an ancient Mycenaean megaron (here shown in plan) the place of the fire was identified by a circle on the ground, by the four columns which held up the roof, and also by the rectangular form of the room itself, which was the place of the king.

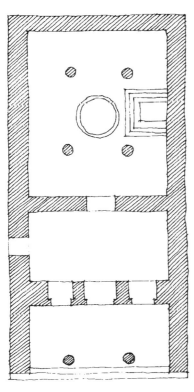

And an orthogonal room converts the hemisphere into a rectangular volume of space.

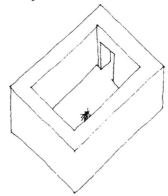

The architecture of the fireplace within a dwelling cell is stimulated by the organisation of the space around it into subsidiary places. As a source of warmth and light the fire is a focus for life; but it can also be an obstacle.

In the remains of some early dwellings archaeologists have found hearths located arbitrarily on the floor, with little clear organisational relationship between their position and the space enclosed around them.

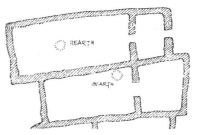

Other ancient remains suggest tidier, more formal arrangements. In the megaron of the palace of Mycenae (*c.*1500 BC; far left) there is a clear relationship between the hearth and the throne, the entrance, and the structure of the room. Sitting here, Agamemnon, the king of ancient Mycenae, was enthroned within his own 'fireplace'.

The consequences of changing the location of the fireplace from a central position to a peripheral one is shown in these two Norwegian traditional timber houses. Their plans are similar, except for the position of the hearth.

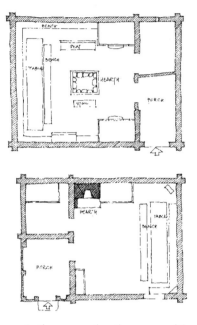

In the upper plan the space of the living room is dominated by the central hearth. Subsidiary places – for sitting and eating, for storage – are arranged around this central focus. Moving around the room is a matter of moving around the fire.

In the lower plan the fireplace is situated in the corner of the room, and built as a small cell of stone, non-combustible to protect the timber of the outer walls. The consequence of this change is that, although the fire no longer occupies its central symbolically important position, movement within the room is less constrained. The floor becomes more open for human occupation – a 'dancing floor'.

The decentralised fireplace need not be positioned in the corner of its room. In this small Welsh cottage the hearth takes up almost all of one wall.

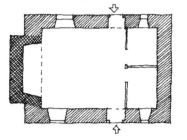

A consequence of putting a fireplace on the periphery of a room is that the fabric of the hearth (and of the chimney stack it acquires) contributes to the enclosure and structure of the room; it assumes another architectural role, as wall. In this Welsh example it is the fireplace that divides the cell of the house into two rooms.

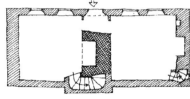

In fact the fireplace stack in this example does more than that. Each of its four sides contributes a wall to four places: the two rooms already mentioned, plus an entrance lobby; and a stair to the upper floor, which the stack similarly divides into two.

In another Welsh example (right) the space defining role of the hearth and its massive chimney stack is taken further, with each of its four sides playing a part in the composition of each of four sections of the house – three wings of accommodation plus an entrance porch. Here the fireplace is once more central to the house, but in a way

Reference for Welsh rural houses: Peter Smith - *Houses of the Welsh Countryside*, 1975.

In this summer cottage, designed and built in 1940, Walter Gropius and Marcel Breuer used the chimney stack to separate the living area from the dining.

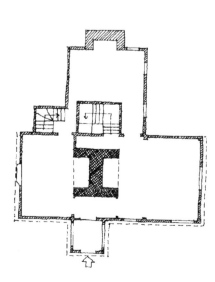

architecturally different to that of the open hearth in the centre of a room. The central stack generates four spaces like spokes radiating from a hub.

The same architectural idea is taken a step further in the next example, and formalised into a square plan by enclosing the four corner spaces as

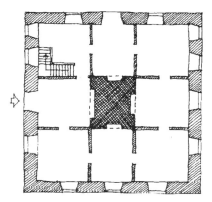

rooms. These rooms don't have fireplaces; and the circumambulatory route from room to room reintroduces the sort of circulation problems of the hearth in the centre of the floor, though of a different order.

In this house (below), another building by Rudolf Schindler, designed (but never built) when he was an ap-

prentice fellow of Frank Lloyd Wright, the fireplace plays a number of the roles already mentioned. It provides the focus of the house, and is its main structural anchorage. It divides the living room from the work room. It also contributes a wall to the entrance lobby. Its fourth side is however more curious. The fire itself is not set beneath the chimney stack, but on a low platform between the stack and the outer wall. It seems the idea was that one fire could warm both rooms.

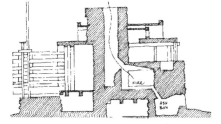

In large rooms a fire can only warm a fraction of the space; its sphere of warmth does not extend to the walls. In these circumstances the fire, like an outdoor fire, identifies its own small place within a larger one.

Sometimes this is recognised architecturally too. This is a plan of

In the Ward Willits House, designed by Frank Lloyd Wright in 1901, the central chimney stack plays a pivotal role in the organisation of the accommodation into four wings.

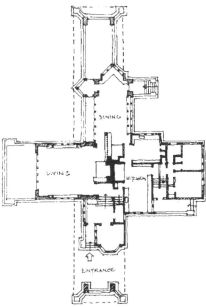

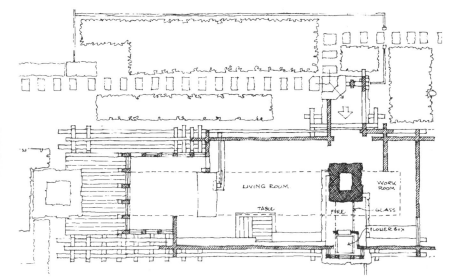

two of a number of 'co-operative dwellings' which Barry Parker and Raymond Unwin designed (in about 1902) for 'a Yorkshire town' (right). If they had ever been built they would have formed part of a quadrangle of similar houses, also provided with common rooms for social activities. In the right hand plan you can see that the place around the fire is identified architecturally as an 'ingle-nook'. Notice too how Parker and Unwin architecturally identified other 'sub-places' within the living room: a place to sit by the window; a place at the table to eat; a place to play the piano; a place to study at a desk.

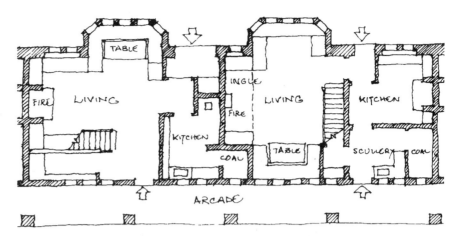

In houses with central heating the hearth is less important as a source of warmth; but it can retain its role as the focus of a particular place, for sitting and reading, or knitting, or talking, or going to sleep. Rather than the hemisphere of warmth having to fill the interior of the cell, it can be used merely to heat, and more importantly provide a vital focus for, a small portion of the space within the cell, leaving the rest of the space to be heated by the background central heating system.

In Le Corbusier's design for a Citrohan House (1920, right) the fireplace is the focus of a small part of the living room, under the 'boudoir' balcony and rather like a simplified inglenook. The rest of the house was to be heated by radiators fed from a boiler positioned under the outside steps to the roof, which therefore did not contribute to the conceptual organisation of the living spaces of the house.

With central heating the hearth in a dwelling is practically redundant, or at least not required to heat the whole space. In these circumstances its role in spatial organisation can change. It can become more like a fire in an internal landscape.

In this design for a house by Hugo Häring (1946, right) the fireplace is almost completely detached from the rest of the fabric of the house. From

In this house designed by Hugo Häring, which is determinedly not orthogonal, the hearth is separated from the walls in a irregular pattern.

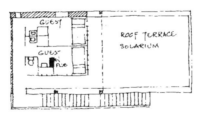

second floor

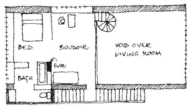

first floor

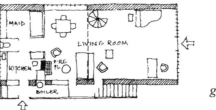

ground floor

its central position other places, defined by the activities they accommodate, radiate with an irregularity more associated with the natural landscape.

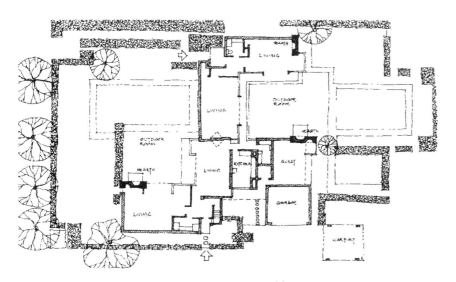

This plan is of a pair of houses designed by Rudolf Schindler, in 1922, for himself and his wife, and another couple. Set in the reasonably comfortable climate of southern California, the gardens are treated as outdoor rooms bounded by hedges rather than constructed walls. These outdoor rooms, as well as small parts of the inside spaces, were provided with their own fireplaces. There is not one central chimney stack, but three, positioned between the rooms with roofs over them and those without.

Below is a plan of Fallingwater, by Frank Lloyd Wright (1935). This house is built above a waterfall. Its floor platforms and flat roofs echo the horizontal strata of the surrounding rocks. The symbolic power of the hearth was important in many of Wright's designs for houses. Though it does not provide all the heating, it is the social focus and heart of the house. Set against, and on, the rock of the waterfall itself, it is as if the hearth has escaped from the containment of the cell and returned to its place in the natural landscape.

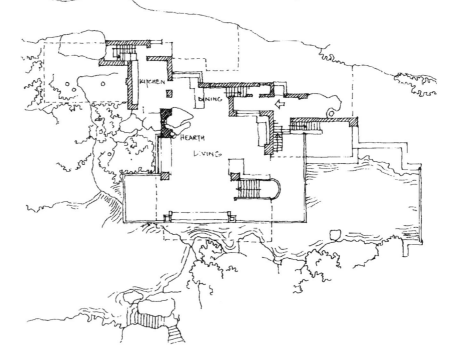

Bed – a place for sleep, sex, sickness

A bed is not just a piece of furniture; conceptually it is a place. It might be argued that the most fundamental purpose of a house is as a secure place for sleep. The bedroom is the innermost, most private, most protected part of a house. It is a place where one must feel safe enough to sleep, or to be ill, and private enough for sex.

The earliest houses were, and the most primitive houses are, little more than bedrooms, with most other activities associated with dwelling taking place outside.

The development of the house through history includes the invention of the separate bed chamber, and its progressive segregation from other internal living places in the interests of increasing privacy and security.

The bedroom has become a room on the conceptual, and often also the physical, periphery of a house – upstairs or set aside from the living rooms, private to its owner, and often considered less important than the reception rooms.

A bed can be a separate piece of furniture, with its own self-contained form, or it can be fixed into the architecture of its house.

Like a hearth, a bed may be no more than the patch of ground which a sleeping creature occupies.

Or it might be identified as a defined area by a material which makes it more comfortable – leaves, soft grass, a ground sheet, a foam mattress, a towel, a rug....

A bed may be a platform, lifting the sleeping surface off the ground...

... and fitted with one, two, three or four walls.

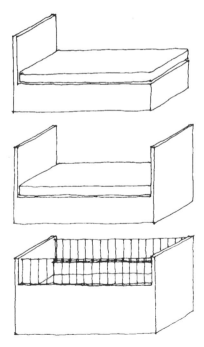

A bed might be fitted with a roof, supported on its own columns, making it into a bed-aedicule.

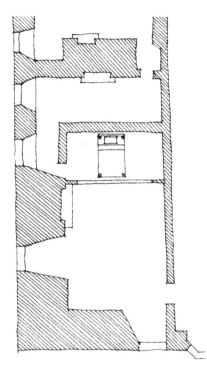

In Powis Castle in Wales there is a state bedroom which is spatially organised like a proscenium arch theatre: the bed is the stage, and is set in an alcove framed by a proscenium arch, outside of which is an area for those seeking an audience.

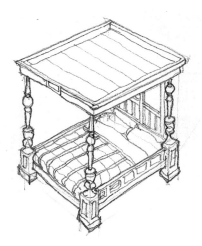

A bed may be an aedicule, provided with its own roof supported on columns, or walls.

It may even be completely enclosed within in its own 'cupboard'.

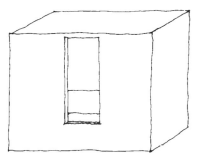

It might even be a complete room in itself – a bed-cell.

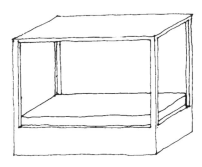

Not only do beds have architecture in themselves, they contribute to the composition of places in larger works of architecture.

A hiking tent, like a primitive bivouac made of branches and leaves, is a bed-roof – a small building.

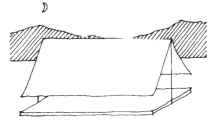

In more complex buildings the bed does not occupy the whole internal space, but it does play its part in the organisation of spaces into places.

According to accounts in the writings of Homer, some three thousand years ago, ancient Greek kings slept in beds in their megarons, and their visitors slept in the porches, as

someone nowadays might, on a hot night, sleep on a verandah.

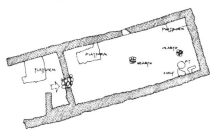

Some small old houses had sleeping floors built between the side walls at the end of an open hall, lifting the bed up into the warmer air that collects in the upper levels of any heated space, and freeing more space on the ground floor. This is a long section through a tiny Welsh cottage.

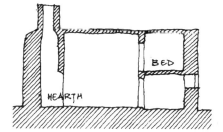

Some had box-beds – sleeping-cells like cupboards built alongside the hearth. This is the plan of a house the inside of which is illustrated earlier in this book (in the chapter on *Architecture as Identification of Place*). It also

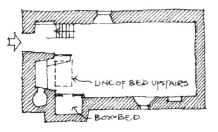

has a bed upstairs, formed of a box in the ceiling below which was used to store and smoke joints of meat. Both beds are near the hearth for warmth.

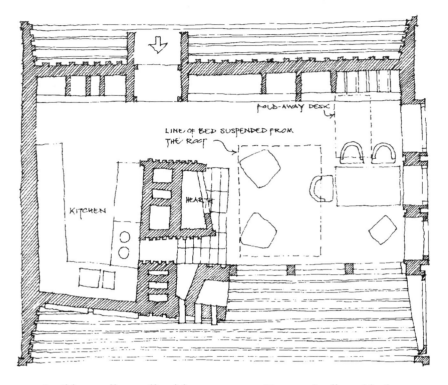

Reference for Ralph Erskine:
Peter Collymore – *The Architecture of Ralph Erskine*, 1985.

Reference for Charles Moore:
Charles Moore and others – *The Place of Houses*, 1974.

In this tiny house which Ralph Erskine built for himself when he went to live in Sweden, space is saved by having furniture which can be stowed away; the bed lifts into the ceiling space.

In this small woodland house which Ralph Erskine built for himself when he went to live in Sweden during the Second World War, the bed could be lifted into the ceiling during the day, to save space.

In some of the houses that Charles Moore has designed, the bed is a platform on top of an aedicule, with the space defined beneath used as a sitting place, with its own hearth.

Even an 'ordinary' bed – a movable piece of furniture – contributes to the architecture of its room. The Victorian architect Robert Kerr, in his book *The English Gentleman's House* (1865), used four-and-a-half pages discussing the relative positions of windows, doors, hearth, and bed in a sleeping-room, and comparing typical English arrangements, where the bed stood as a free-standing piece of furniture positioned to avoid draughts, with French bedrooms where the bed was sheltered in its own alcove.

According to Robert Kerr, the English Victorian architect, the English gentleman's bedroom should be arranged so that the bed avoided draughts; one should be able to draw a straight line from the door to the hearth without it cutting across the bed. In French examples, he said, beds were protected from draughts by being provided with their own alcoves planned into the bedrooms.

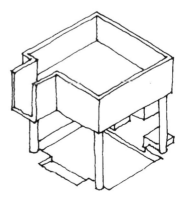

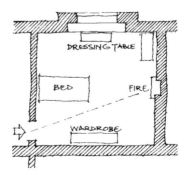

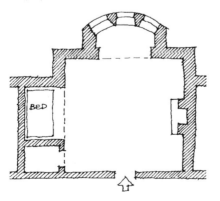

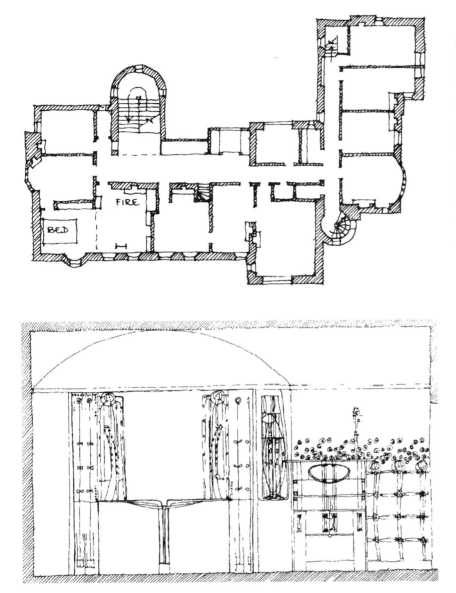

Hill House was built in 1903 at Helensburgh, Scotland, designed by the architect Charles Rennie Mackintosh. The main bedroom is at the bottom left of this plan, which shows the first floor of the house. Though apparently very simple, Mackintosh subtly divided the room into various places for particular purposes. There is a hearth with a seat. The washstand is just inside the door. There is a dressing place by the pair of windows, between which stands a tall mirror. The bed lies in its own generous alcove, which has a vaulted ceiling; originally Mackintosh intended to define the bed-alcove even more with two decorated side-screens making an entrance, but these were not built. The lower drawing shows these screens, the bed, the washstand, and the decorative scheme for the bedroom walls.

In the Farnsworth House (below) by Mies van der Rohe, the places of the two beds are not as definitely identified by the architecture. Though their positions are hinted at by the organisation of space in the house, they take their own places rather than have them given to them by the architecture.

In the main bedroom in Hill House, the architect Charles Rennie Mackintosh placed the bed in its own alcove, with an arched ceiling.

Reference for Mackintosh:
Robert Macleod – *Charles Rennie Mackintosh, Architect and Artist*, 1968.

Reference for Mies van der Rohe:
Philip Johnson – *Mies van der Rohe*, 1978.

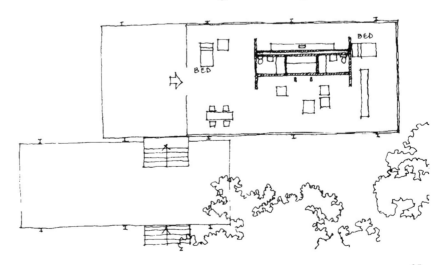

Altar – a table for sacrifice or worship

The architecture of an altar may be more consistent than that of a hearth or of a bed – it is almost always a table (a platform) for ritual or symbolic sacrifice, or which plays the role of focus for worship.

In ancient Egypt altars were tables on which nourishment for the dead pharaoh was placed. Altars were hidden away in the deepest recesses of the mortuary temples that were attached to the bases of the pyramids. Though they were concealed from public view, and attended only by the priests, they were usually positioned on the east–west axis of the pyramid, and the long axis of the temple.

This is a small early example from the pyramid of Meidum:

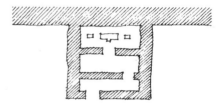

The same principles of arrangement apply in the much larger and more complex example at the pyramid of Chephren (which is one of the well-known group at Giza, far right). The mortuary temple lies at the base of the pyramid (at the top of the drawing); the altar is in a small chamber close to the pyramid; the spirit of the pharaoh would reach the food through the image of a doorway, which appeared to lead from inside the pyramid.

At Stonehenge the place of the altar is identified by a circle, and a horseshoe, of standing stones. The

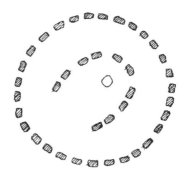

altar is positioned not quite at the geometric centre of the circle, offset in response to the approach to the circle and the open end of the horseshoe.

In ancient Greece altars were positioned outside the temples. The image of the god was housed within. This is the temple of Athena Polias at Priene. The altar and the god inside the temple are linked by the long axis which they share. As in Egyptian pyramids, this was often the east–west axis.

In the pyramid temple of Chephren, the altar is hidden away in the deepest recesses. The god king would come to collect the food through an imitation doorway which 'connected' the chamber with the inside of the pyramid.

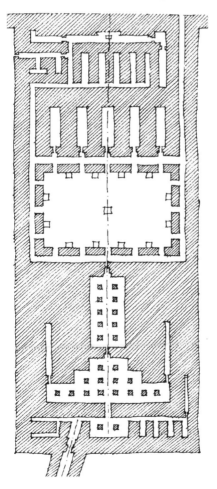

The spire of a traditional church acts as a marker, identifying the place of the altar in a way that can be seen for miles around.

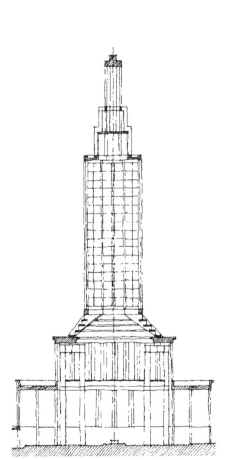

This church designed by Auguste Perret is one big spire. The altar is positioned centrally, directly under the spire.

In medieval churches and cathedrals the altar is inside. This is the

church of S. Maria del Mar in Barcelona. Still, the altar relates to an east–west axis that provides the backbone for the whole building. The principal purpose of all Christian churches is to identify the place of the altar. In this example the way that the building focuses on the altar is clear.

During the Renaissance, some architects and theologians wondered whether the altar should be positioned at the centre of the church, rather than at one end.

In the church of St Peter in Rome the high altar is placed at the centre of the main part of the building. An ex-

tension to the nave stops the building being a fully centralised church.

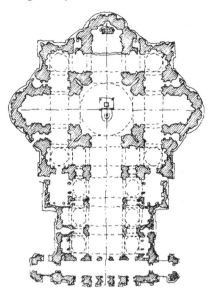

Some twentieth-century churches have centralised plans too. This is the plan of one in Le Havre, France, designed by Auguste Perret, and built in 1959. This church is a large spire (far

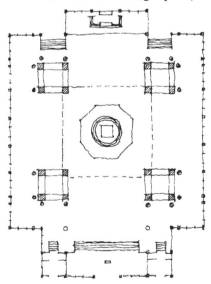

left), which, like spires on traditional medieval churches, also identifies the place of the altar. In Perret's church the altar is placed on three axes: the two horizontal axes, and the vertical.

This church too has a centralised plan, with the altar at the focus of a square, and with its presence emphasised from the outside by a spire supported on the eight timber columns

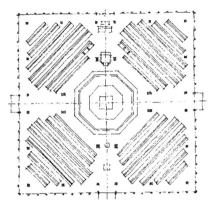

around the octagonal platform. It is a chapel dedicated to St James the Fisherman, and was designed by Albert Christ-Janer and Mary Mix Foley. It was built in Wellfleet, Massachusetts, in 1956.

Another way in which the place of the altar can be identified by a church building is by the effect of the perspective of a long space. This effect works because the altar is on the long axis of the building. This axis is so powerful, symbolically as well as architecturally, that entrances into churches often avoid aligning with it.

By the twentieth century the symmetrical arrangement had become so orthodox that architects were keen

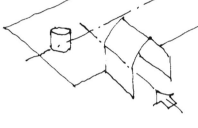

The place of the altar in a traditional church is identified by the axes of the building.

The axis of a church creates perspective which focuses on the altar.

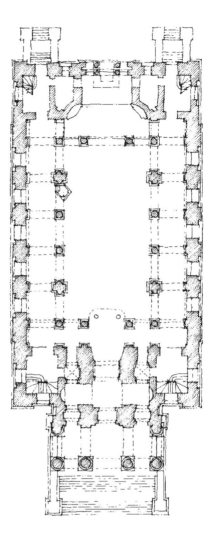

Christ Church, Spitalfields, has a symmetrical plan, and its altar lies on the long axis (in this case sharing that axis with the entrance). This London church was designed by Nicholas Hawksmoor in the mid-1720s.

to explore other ways of positioning an altar in a church.

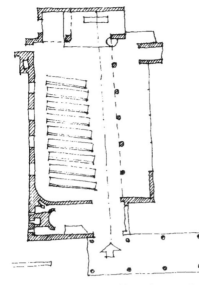

The Cemetery Chapel at Turku in Finland (above), designed by Erik Bryggman, and built in 1941, has an asymmetrical plan, but the altar remains the focus of the building. Attention is drawn to it by the axis of the entrance and the pathway leading to it (as in more traditional church plans), but in making an asymmetrical layout the architect recognised the relationship between the inside of the church and the outside. The context of the church is not symmetrical; Bryggman's

layout allows the sun in to illuminate the altar alcove, and the congregation to look out through the glass south wall.

Some things in architecture, without being altars, can be like them. This is a part of sketch 'ideal' plan for the Abbey of St Gall in France. It dates from the 9th century AD, and shows the intended infirmary.

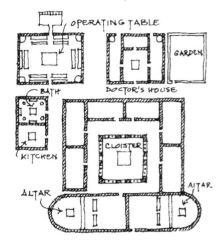

The operating table (at the top left) has the same sort of architectural relationship with its room, as the altars in their chapels (bottom).

Many ordinary everyday things can be like altars. When someone, in

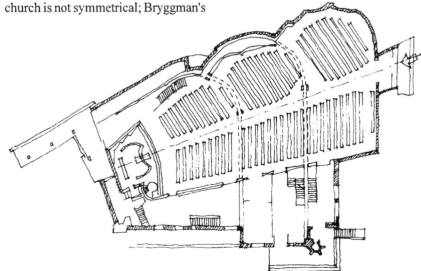

Alvar Aalto's design for the Vuoksenniska Church at Imatra in Finland is asymmetrical in its plan. But still the building, by various means, focuses on the altar.

their room, devotes a table to memorabilia of a favourite football club, it can be like an altar.

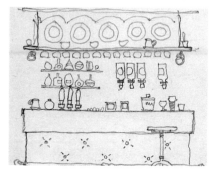

A museum curator may place precious objects on their own altars.

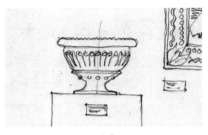

A grandmother might make a piano into an 'altar' to her family.

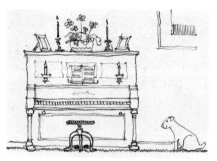

A bar might be considered by some to be an altar to drinking.

A kitchen stove might be like an altar to cooking.

A mantelpiece can be an altar to the fire.

A dressing table may be an altar to one's self.

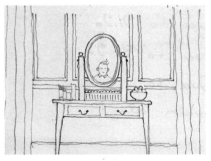

A dining table can be an altar to a family eating together.

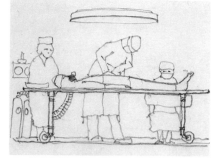

An operating table might be interpreted as an altar, as might a mortuary table.

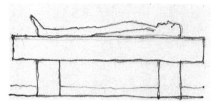

Performance place

A performance requires space; whether religious ritual, dance, music, drama, football ... it is not as focused a place as a hearth or an altar. A performance place also requires protection from encroachment by those not involved in it, who may be spectators.

When a clown performs in a field it becomes a stage. He defines its area

When a clown performs on a patch of ground it becomes a stage.

by his movement and by positioning his props. He protects it from encroachment by force of his presence and pretend personality. The ring of spectators that he attracts also contribute to the identification of place, to the architecture of this impromptu theatre.

In primitive times a place for the performance of ritual may have been no more than a clearing in a forest, or a trampled piece of grassland. But by

the powers of architecture performance places can be made more formal and more permanent.

In Minoan and Mycenaean times (about 3500 years ago) the 'dancing floor' – *orkestra* – was a specific place.

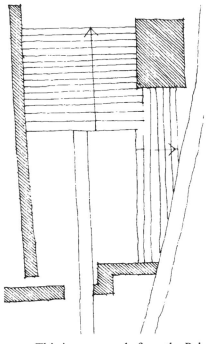

This is an example from the Palace of Knossos on the Mediterranean island of Crete. It is thought to have been built by Daedalos, architect to King Minos, as a place for his daughter to dance; but it might have been a place for displaying bulls before they went into the courtyard of the palace to be fought by young Minoans. This small dancing floor is a flat, almost rectangular, paved area, with low sitting steps on two sides. The rake of the steps takes advantage of the natural slope of the ground.

By a thousand or so years later, architects had formalised the outdoor theatre into the grand amphitheatre, which was much larger and more

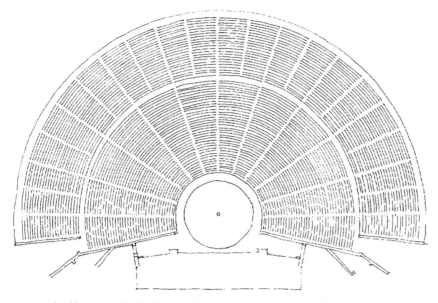

geometrically organised, but which also made use of the lie of the land.

Behind the *orkestra* in a Greek amphitheatre there was a building – the *skene* – which in Greek drama was a background to the action. Through Roman and into modern times this building came to be used as a performance place in its own right – a stage. It was also, like the altar, brought inside.

The stage became framed by a proscenium arch. In the Greek amphitheatre the magic of the place of performance had been defined by the circle of the *orkestra*; in this type of theatre the separation of the special world of the actors and the ordinary world of the audience was defined by the platform of the stage, and by this rectangular opening – a window into a make-believe world.

With the development of cinema and television the window into other worlds became more far-reaching, and encroachment impossible.

Some architects have tried to design performance places in which the separation between performers and spectators is reduced.

In the Philharmonie, a concert hall in Berlin designed by Hans Scharoun, the performers are surrounded by their audience.

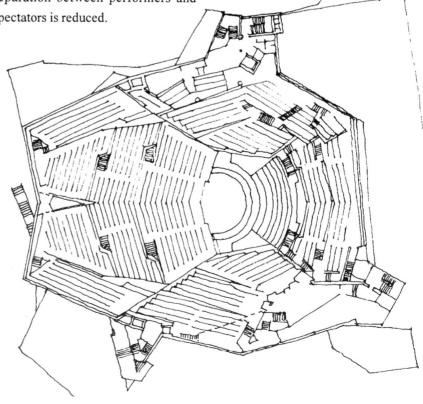

Reference for The American Center in Paris, by Frank Gehry:
Lotus International 84, February 1995, pp.74-85.

This section shows how theatres are often designed to be insulated against outside noises by their ancillary accommodation.

The plan at the bottom of the previous page shows the auditorium of the Philharmonie in Berlin (1956). As in his designs for houses, Hans Scharoun, the architect of the Philharmonie, was determined to be non-orthogonal. In this plan, he has placed the performers on their stage, not in opposition to the audience, but surrounded by them. Listeners sit in tiers as if on the slopes of a small valley. The sanctity of the performance place is preserved, by the platform, but the separation between audience and players is reduced.

Whether or not there is the illusion of separation between audience and performers it is often thought necessary to protect performance places from the encroachment of things that have nothing to do with them – traffic noise, the sounds of the weather, sunlight, and so on. This section through a theatre designed by Frank Gehry shows how performance places are often designed to be isolated in the core of their building, insulated from outside distractions by ancillary accommodation wrapped around them.

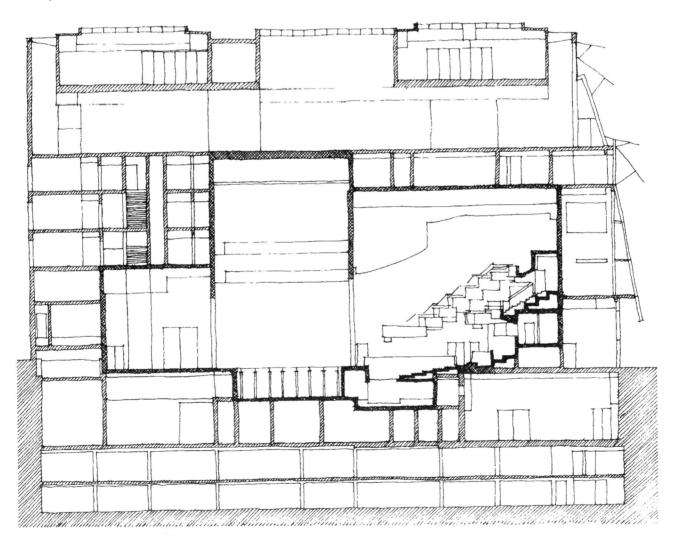

ARCHITECTURE AS
MAKING FRAMES

ARCHITECTURE AS MAKING FRAMES

Architecture is more to do with making frames than painting pictures; more a matter of providing an accompaniment to life than the dance itself.

Certainly it is within the capacity of architecture to frame 'pictures' – as the rectangle of a window frames a view, or a doorway the figure of a person.

It is also possible to compose the products of architecture, in town- or landscape, as if they themselves were objects in a picture, perhaps to be seen from a particular point of view.

accommodates movement and change – and those more abstract and subtle dimensions – patterns of life, of work, of ritual. The products of architecture can frame images of gods; they can frame the remains of dead people; they can even frame the family pet. But perhaps their noblest purpose is to frame the lives of people.

Thinking about architecture as frame-making is part of conceiving it as identification of place. Frames define boundaries. Places in which things happen or are kept are made by the

Opposite page:

In this carving the image of a person (called Rhodia) is framed by the representation of a building. It is a pictorial composition, and a memorial, but it also illustrates a recognition that buildings are 'frames' within which people live, and that buildings can be identified by the people that inhabit them. (The carving is a grave stele from Egypt, and is about 1200 years old.)

But architecture is not primarily about contriving 'picturesque' compositions; nor is the power to frame limited to distant hills or someone standing in a doorway.

The dimensions of architecture include more than the two of a picture-frame. It is obvious that they include the third spatial dimension, but there is also the dimension of time – which

means of architecture. Products of architecture are frames: the rooms within which we work, the pitches on which games are played, the streets along which we drive, the table where a family eats, the gardens in which we sit, the floors on which we dance ... are all 'frames'; and together they constitute a complex and extensive *framework* within which we live (which though vast can be like the musical accompaniment which sets the metre of a song).

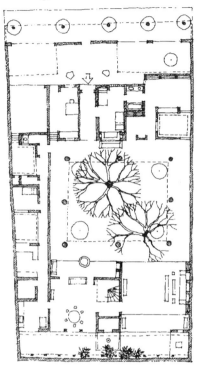

This plan illustrates how a work of architecture frames life. It is a house in Colombo, Sri Lanka, designed by the architect Geoffrey Bawa, and built in 1962. The house as a whole is framed by the outer boundary wall, but it contains many other frames too: the living and bedrooms frame social activities and sleeping; the dining table frames dinner parties; the courtyards frame the trees, plants, fountains, and large stones they contain; even the bath is a frame, and the garage frames the car.

Apparently, the word 'frame' comes from the old English word *framian,* which means 'to be helpful'. A frame is 'helpful' in that it provides support. The physical frame of something – a loom, a body, a building – is its structure, without which it would

be formless. A frame also 'helps' by defining space: creating demarcations and an ordered relationship between 'insides' and 'outsides'.

A frame is a principle of organisation. Whether it is a picture frame, or a sheep pen, or a room, it is rarely (if ever) sufficient by itself (except perhaps in the poetic device of the 'vacant frame'); it has a relationship with what it frames (actually or potentially) and with what is 'outside', setting something in its place, mediating between it and the rest of the world. That something may be a picture, or an object, but it might also be a person (the hermit in his cave, or 'Mrs Clark' in her house, St Jerome in his study, or one's self in a room), an activity (tennis on a court, or car manufacture in a factory), an animal (a pig in its sty, or a bird in its cage), a god (Athena in the Parthenon, or Vishnu in his temple).

This drawing is based on the painting of *St Jerome in His Study* by the fifteenth-century Italian painter Antonello da Messina. As a picture it has a frame; but within the picture St

Photographs often portray buildings not as frames but as objects. This is a consequence of the process of photography, which is one of placing a two-dimensional frame around something. This process deprives us of our experience of buildings as frames, turning them into objects which are themselves framed.

This image portrays the building as an object, and is unable to let us experience it as a frame.

We are used to looking at the world through frames: the frames of pictures, the frames of television screens, the frames and sub-frames of computer screens. It might be argued that since these frame remote places that they constitute an abstract, supra-real architecture: that the World Wide Web, for example, is a form of architecture which reinterprets or overlays the physical world.

Jerome is framed, physically and symbolically, by the architecture of the building in which he sits.

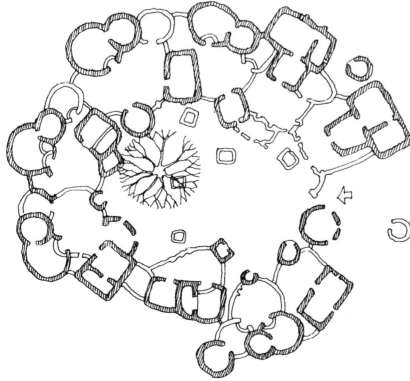

A frame can be a structure and a boundary; but its helpfulness also comes from being a frame *of reference*, according to which one develops an understanding of where one is. The squares on a chessboard, or the floors of an apartment block, or the streets of a city, make frames that condition how

Not only is the plan of this African village a diagram of the communal life it accommodates, but the village itself is a conceptual frame which responds to the order in the lives of its inhabitants.

pieces, people, or vehicles move, and by reference to which their locations can be described.

In an abstract sense, a frame can be a theory. (The intention of this book, for example, is to be 'helpful' by offering a framework of concepts for understanding architecture.) Architecture involves considering how things should be framed, theoretically as well as physically: designing a museum involves thinking about how objects should be exhibited and the routes people might take through its galleries, but it also involves taking a theoretical stance on the notion of a museum and its role in culture; designing an opera house involves thinking about how the spectacle of an opera, and the dressed-up people who come to see it, might be displayed, which depends on a theory of the culture of opera; even the design of a kennel poses the problem of how a dog should be framed.

In more complex cases, the design of a house involves theorising on how the lives it will accommodate might be lived and producing an appropriate frame; the design of a church involves understanding the liturgy – the theory of how it is to be used for worship and ritual.

Architecture, in all these cases, involves the responsibility of proposing a physical, and a theoretical, framework within which art can be viewed, opera watched, dances danced, gods worshipped, meals eaten, produce sold, or whatever.

A picture frame, or a museum exhibition case, or an ancient Greek temple, holds something which is static, something for which time has been halted. Through architecture, however, people also make frames for movement and for change: a football field is a frame on which an artificial battle is fought; a street frames its traffic; the track of a fairground ride describes the passage of its carriages; a church frames a ceremonial route, from lychgate to altar.

Frames (physical and theoretical) are used to give the world, or part of it, some sort of order. These pages (which are themselves frames) have been organised into two-dimensional rectangles, (the graphic 'architecture' of the page); some computer programmes are based on the use of frames for different tasks. The range of types of frames in architecture is greater; and they are not always simple or rectangular.

* *

A conceptual requirement of a frame is that it must have something to frame, whether or not that something is temporarily or even permanently absent. (A chair is not always occupied. A *cenotaph* is, literally, an empty tomb; though permanently empty it is a frame for the 'idea' of the dead.) It is not necessary that a frame always contains something, but its relationship with content is essential.

One usually assumes that a picture frame is of lesser importance than the work of art which it contains. One similarly assumes that the glass case which protects, for example, the bust of Nefertiti in the Egyptian Museum in Berlin is less important than the bust

itself. But the question whether the products of architecture are of lesser, or greater, importance than the things they frame is more difficult.

The answer of moderation is that the two are in a symbiotic relationship; it may be that a frame is secondary to its contents; but the contents also benefit from their frame – in the protection it gives, in the accommodation it provides, in the amplification which it gives to their existence. A room provides a service as a frame; as does a chair, a bookcase, a pulpit, an aircraft

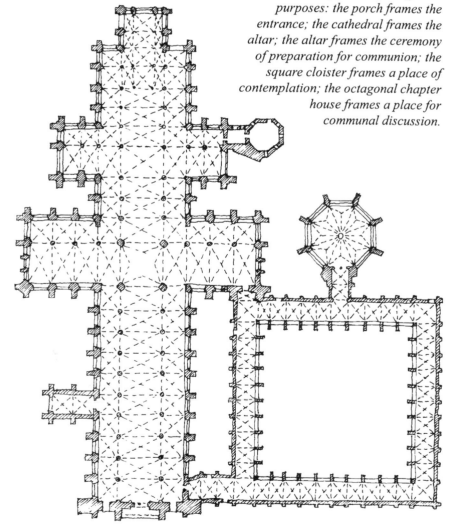

Salisbury Cathedral is composed of a number of frames for different purposes: the porch frames the entrance; the cathedral frames the altar; the altar frames the ceremony of preparation for communion; the square cloister frames a place of contemplation; the octagonal chapter house frames a place for communal discussion.

The aedicule of the Albert Memorial in London frames a statue of Prince Albert, but in death it also frames his memory.

A table, in its space, frames the life of a meal.

hangar, even a bus shelter. Each protects, accommodates, and reinforces the existence of its contents (or its inhabitants). The relationship between contents and frame is pivotal.

Architecture is most often a matter of framing the ordinary and the everyday, but famous instances make the point and are memorable: the simple blue garage in Laugharne on the South Wales coast is the frame within which Dylan Thomas wrote his poetry; the new palace in Bucharest, Romania, was intended to frame and amplify the political power of the dictator Nicolae Ceausescu; the Dome of the Rock in Jerusalem frames a sacred place; the concentration camp at Auschwitz framed the deaths of a million people.

Thinking in this way, one realises that human beings surround themselves with frames, by which they organise the world architecturally. Sitting writing this I am surrounded by many frames: the frame of streets of the planned village in which I live; the frame of our piece of ground, our house, my study. In the study there are: shelves which frame books (themselves frames of ideas and facts); a table which frames a surface for work; a drawing board; windows; a door; a fireplace; lights; pictures; cupboards; and computers, which frame lots of things from all over the world.

Architectural frames, and the ways in which they can be used, are innumerable. There are simple frames (an aedicular porch), and complex (the network of routes in a modern air terminal). There are small frames (a keyhole), and large (a city square). There are two-dimensional (a snooker or pool table), three-dimensional (a multi-storey structure), and four-dimensional (a labyrinth), and many dimensional (the Internet).

Frames need not be constructed of tangible material – a spotlight can frame an actor on a stage – and can apply to senses other than the visual: a beautiful woman might be framed by an aura of scent; the warm air from an air vent might frame a group of people trying to keep warm on a cold day; a mosque is in a way framed by the sound of the *muezzin* calling Muslims to prayer.

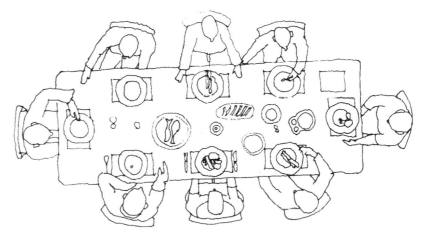

Russian Dolls

Frames often overlap one another in architecture, or fit one within another. Frames can be like Russian Dolls, each of which has an inside into which fits a slightly smaller doll, to the limits of practicability.

In architecture frames are rarely simply concentric like Russian Dolls; frames overlap, combine in complex ways, intrude one on another, and operate at vastly variable scales.

Imagine a walled town. The 'first' frame is the wall itself; there are

Some works of architecture can be like this. The plan of Beaumaris Castle on the island of Anglesey off the coast of North Wales shows five concentric layers: the moat; the outer defensive wall; the outer ward; the inner defensive wall; and the inner ward.

the gateways through the walls; then there is the network of streets, geometric or organic; each of the houses or church or civic buildings is a frame itself, but together they might define a market place or town square; in the square there might be a fountain set in

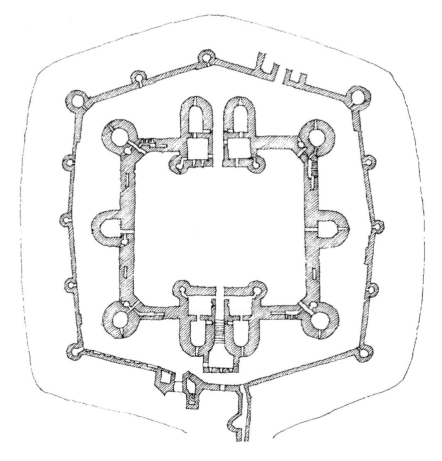

Beaumaris Castle on the island of Anglesey off the coast of North Wales, consists of a concentric series of defensive barriers.

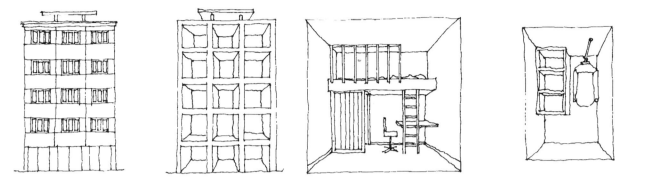

A condominium frames a number of apartments, that frame rooms, each of which contains a number of smaller frames.

its own frame of water; inside each of the houses there are a number of rooms, each of which contain frames of different kinds – tables, chairs, fireplaces, cupboards, chests, beds, a bath, a sink, even a carpet can frame a place; a table might be set for a meal, each person having their own place framed by a chair and some cutlery; the table is maybe framed in a pool of light; a desk might frame work in progress; a television frames views of the outside world; and so on.

Buildings can be frames structurally, but architecture makes frames conceptually too. This is a diagram of a small house which the American architect Charles Moore designed for himself and which was built in California in 1961. It is not a large house, but it contains two aedicules, like small temples. Each of these frames its own place: the larger, a living area; the smaller, the bath and shower. Both aedicules are lit by rooflights, so both places are also framed by light. The house as a whole is framed by the envelope shown dotted on the diagram. Other places within the house are framed by a combination of the aedicules and the outer envelope, together with pieces of furniture. Taken

Reference for Moore House:

Charles Moore, Gerald Allen, and Donlyn Lyndon – *The Place of Houses*, 1974.

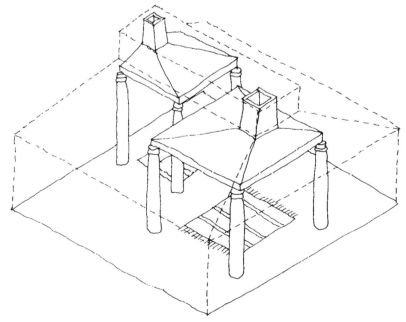

altogether the house is a complex matrix of overlapping frames.

This is another building in which aedicules of different scales are used to frame places. In this case the places are not to do with dwelling, but with death and bereavement. The Chapel of the Resurrection, designed by Sigurd Lewerentz, was built in the extensive grounds of the Woodland Crematorium in Stockholm in 1925.

In the plan one can see a number of aedicules and other types of architectural frames. The entrance, from the north, is framed by a large porch of twelve columns supporting a pediment; this porch is not actually attached to the main part of the building. Then there is the body of the chapel itself: on the outside this is very plain, rather like an austere tomb; on the inside surfaces of the walls there are shallow relief columns, so that this cell is also a temple-like aedicule.

Within the chapel, and very carefully positioned, is a smaller, more elaborate aedicule, which identifies the place of the altar and frames the cross

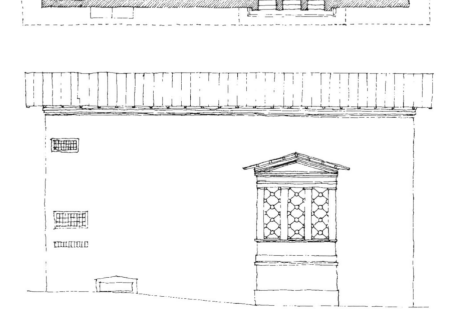

The Chapel of the Resurrection, designed by Sigurd Lewerentz is composed of many architectural frames.

Reference for Chapel of the Resurrection:
Janne Ahlin – *Sigurd Lewerentz, architect 1885-1975*, 1987.

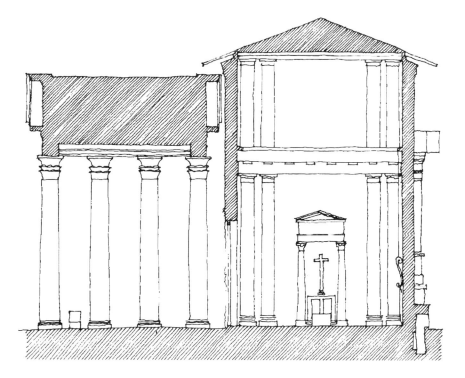

(both of which themselves are symbolic frames); and in front of this aedicule there is the catafalque, which provides a frame for the coffin during funeral ceremonies. The coffin, of course, frames the dead person. All together, the coffin and the mourners, with the altar and cross in their own aedicule, are framed by the chapel itself.

The Chapel of the Resurrection is composed of many architectural frames. The window in the south facing wall is in the form of an aedicule. Its primary architectural role is not to frame a view of the outside but, as the sole source of daylight in the chapel, to allow the sun into the cell, to frame both the altar and the coffin on the catafalque.

The First Church of Christ, Scientist, in Berkeley, California, is an aggregation of many aedicules. It was designed by Bernard Maybeck, and built in 1910.

Reference for First Church of Christ, Scientist:

Edward Bosley – *First Church of Christ, Scientist, Berkeley*, 1994.

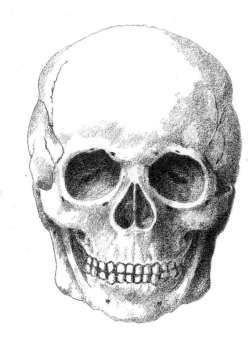

TEMPLES
AND
COTTAGES

TEMPLES AND COTTAGES

In dealing with the world, people sometimes accept what the world provides or does, and at others, they try to change it to achieve a view of how it should be – how the world might be more comfortable, more beautiful, or in better order than it is.

Our interaction with the world can be thought of as a mixture of these two responses: to accept or to change. Hamlet was not the only one to be afflicted with this quandary; it is particularly alive in architecture, where the designing mind has to engage directly with the world.

It is not possible to change everything by the powers of architecture; but neither is it feasible to leave everything as it is; merely by lighting their campfire our prehistoric family changed the world. Architecture therefore involves both acceptance and change. The designing mind is faced with the double question, 'What should one try to change; and what should one accept as it is?'.

In this question, architecture is philosophy; it is to do with how the world works, and what the response should be. There is no single correct answer, but a mixture of wondering and assertion.

The following two quotations, both by writers concerned with architecture, illustrate different philosophical positions on how the designing mind should relate to the world. The first is taken from *The Ten Books on Architecture* written by the Roman architect Vitruvius in the first century BC; (he is paraphrasing an earlier, Greek writer, Theophrastus):

The man of learning ... can fearlessly look down upon the troublesome accidents of fortune. But he who thinks himself entrenched in defences not of learning but of luck, moves in slippery paths, struggling through life unsteadily and insecurely.

The second quotation is from *The Poetry of Architecture*, by the nineteenth-century British critic, John Ruskin. He is imagining the quintessential mountain cottage:

Everything about it should be natural, and should appear as if the influences and forces which were in operation around it had been too strong to be resisted, and had rendered all efforts of art to check their power, or conceal the evidence of their action, entirely unavailing... it can never lie too humbly in the pastures of the valley, nor shrink too submissively into the hollows of the hills; it should seem to be asking the storm for mercy, and the mountain for protection: and should appear to owe to its weakness, rather than to its strength, that it is neither overwhelmed by the one, nor crushed by the other.

The attitudes which these two writers express are poles apart. Vitruvius puts forward the idea that architecture is about changing the world for the benefit of people, and that such change is to be achieved by the application of human intellect and the assertion of human will. Ruskin, on the other hand, unsteadies this simple idea by suggesting that it is not the role of human beings to contend against nature for their own benefit, but to recognise that they are part of (not separate from) nature, and to accept its authority, in the faith that nature 'knows best' and will provide. (Ruskin first published the above passage under the *nom de plume* '*KATA PHUSIN*' which is Greek for 'according to nature'.)

It would not be fair to suggest that these two quotations represent the full bodies of thought that Ruskin and Vitruvius offered in their writings. Nor do the attitudes presented belong only to these two writers; they have been echoed by many others through history. These two passages do however identify the horns of an abiding dilemma for architects.

In a previous section of this book it was suggested that to understand the powers of architecture one should be aware of the conditions within which they may be employed. The conditions which the world presents can be categorised in various ways; here is one way which seems appropriate for discussing architecture.

Generally speaking, in doing architecture, one has to deal with all or some of the following, which are extrinsic to the conscious designing mind:

• the *ground*, with its earth, rock, trees; its stability, or instability; its changes in level; its dampness; its flat- or unevenness;

• *gravity*: its constant verticality;

• the *weather*: sun, breeze, rain, wind, snow, lightning;

• the *materials* available for building: stone, clay, wood, steel, glass, plastic, concrete, aluminium;

• the *size* of people, and of other creatures: their reach, their movement, their eyes, how they sit;

• the *bodily needs and functions* of people, and maybe other creatures, for warmth, security, air, food;

• the *behaviour* of people, individually, or in groups; social patterns, and political structures;

• *other products of architecture* (other buildings, places) that already exist;

• *pragmatic requirements*: the space needed for various activities;

• the *past*: history, tradition;

• the *future*: visions of 'Utopia', or of 'Apocalypse';

• the *processes of time*: change, wear, patination, deterioration, erosion, ruin.

To each or all of these the designing mind may adopt different attitudes, maybe in differing circumstances, for example: to make shelter against a cold wind, or to enjoy the benefits of a cooling breeze; to try to control patterns of behaviour, or to allow (or accept, or cultivate, or concede to) their contribution to the identity of places; to submit materials to carving and polishing, or to accept their innate finish, or the finish they are given by the processes of their acquisition (such as that of stone broken by quarrying); to fight (or disregard) the effects of time, or to anticipate (or exploit) the patination of materials by sun, wind and wear; to provide for bodily needs and functions, or to dismiss them as beneath architectural consideration; to accept human size as a basis of architectural scale, or to create a hermetic rule for proportion, one which does not refer to anything outside itself; to follow the precedents of history (even to submit to the 'authority' of history), or to seek the new – making the future different from the past.

Any product of architecture (e.g. a building, a garden, a city, a playground, a sacred grove...) is informed by, and hence expresses, such attitudes. If an architect wishes to fight against the force of gravity, then it will show in the form of the building produced (for examples, a Gothic cathedral vault, or one of the cantilevers of Frank Lloyd Wright's design for the house called 'Fallingwater'). If an architect seeks to control the behaviour of people, then it will show in the form of the building (for example in a 'panopticon' Victorian prison, in which all cells could be watched from a single central viewpoint). If an architect wants to cool the interior of a house with breezes, then this too will affect the form of the building.

Products of architecture combine acceptance of some aspects with change of others. There is, however, no general rule to dictate which aspects are accepted, and which should be changed or controlled. This fundamental uncertainty lies at the heart of many of the great debates about architecture,

in history and in the present: should architects follow tradition, or should they strive for novelty and originality; should materials be used in the state in which they are found, or be subject to processes of manufacture that change their innate character; should architects dictate the layout of the places where people live, or should cities grow organically, without a master plan? People find different answers to these and many other similarly difficult questions.

Designing minds combine *change* and *acceptance* in varying degrees. In some products of architecture the attitude of change and control seems to dominate; in others it is the attitude of acceptance and responsiveness which appears to prevail. The archetypal 'temple' and the archetypal 'cottage' illustrate these differences.

The archetypal 'temple'

The archetypal 'temple' is not a real temple, but an idea. The illustration on the next page shows a building which looks like an ancient Greek temple, but as we shall see later there are other buildings which can be classified as 'temples', in the philosophical sense.

The 'temple' can be characterised in terms of the ways its architect dealt with various aspects of the world. It is not necessary to look at the temple in terms of all the aspects of the world listed above; seeing the treatment of some of them will illustrate the point.

The 'temple' stands on a platform which replaces the uneven *ground* with a controlled surface as a foundation for

building. This flat platform (or in some historical examples subtly curved – as that of the Parthenon on the acropolis in Athens) is a starting level (a datum) for the geometric discipline of the 'temple' itself, and detaches it from the found world. Even if the platform had no 'temple', it would define a special place, distinct because of its flatness and its separation by height above the landscape around.

The 'temple' provides shelter against the *weather*, to protect its content (the image of a god). Its form concedes little to the forces of climate; it stands prominently in an exposed location.

Its *materials* are carved into abstract or geometric shapes, and carefully finished – smooth, painted, and with precise mouldings. The stone is probably not that which is readily available at the site, but has been brought some distance, with the expenditure of substantial effort and money, because of its quality.

The scale of the 'temple' doesn't relate to the usual *size* of human beings, but to the indeterminately larger stature of the god to whom it is dedicated. The module on which the size of the 'temple' is based exists only in the dimensions of the building; the 'temple' has its own ideal system of proportions within its own fabric; this characteristic contributes to its detachment from the found world.

As a house of a god the 'temple' does not provide for the *bodily needs or functions* of mortals.

The 'temple' is complete in itself, and does not respond to *other architecture*. It is more likely that other architecture will relate to it, as a focus and point of reference. The 'temple' represents a stable centre. Though not responding to other buildings around it, the 'temple' probably does relate,

Though ancient temples are now in ruins, they were not built with this fate in mind, but to stand against the *processes of time*, rather than submit to them. (For the later Romantic mind the reduction to ruin of these icons of human self-confidence – or maybe hubris – is filled with poetic significance.)

by axis, to something distant and above the ordinary: a sacred place on the peak of a distant mountain, a star, or the rising sun.

As a shrine the 'temple' has a simple function, which is not complicated by messy *pragmatic requirements*. Its form is ideal, dictated by geometry and axial symmetry rather than by the spaces needed for a mixture of activities.

The form of the classic Greek temples was the product of refinements made over a number of centuries, but as an idea the 'temple' is timeless – belonging equally to *the past* and *the future*.

The archetypal 'cottage'

Like the 'temple', the archetypal 'cottage' is not a real building but an idea. Whereas the 'temple' manifests humanist detachment from the found world, the 'cottage' fits in with its surroundings. The drawing above shows what appears to be a British cottage (of somewhat vague origin), but there are many other buildings (and gardens) which illustrate the 'cottage' idea.

Unlike the 'temple', the archetypal 'cottage' sits on the *ground*. The unevenness of site is incorporated into its form. Not detached from the landscape, its walls may extend into the surroundings as field walls.

Like the 'temple' the 'cottage' provides shelter against the *weather*, but for people and animals rather than the image of a god. Its architect has responded to climate: it has a steeply pitched roof to shed the rain, and is located to find what protection there is from trees, and from the lie of the land. Its relationship with the sun is not one of setting up a significant axis, but maybe a matter (in a cool climate) of taking advantage of its warmth, or (in a hot climate) of providing shade from its heat.

The 'cottage' is built of *materials* that are ready to hand. Though necessarily subject to some shaping and finishing, they are used in a rough state.

The scale of the 'cottage' relates directly to the actual *size* of people, and perhaps also livestock. This is particularly evident at doorways, where height corresponds to human stature, and width, if the door is giving access to a cowshed, maybe to the span of cattle's horns.

The 'cottage' provides for *bodily needs and functions*. Its main purpose is to house people who spend their time working to keep themselves alive. There is a hearth for warmth; there are places to sit, to prepare food, to eat, to sleep.

The 'cottage' and the places around it accommodate many different *pragmatic requirements*. In response to these the layout is not formal, but complex and irregular.

The 'cottage' is mutable, and accepts the *processes of time* – wear and age. It is probably never complete; additions are added as more space is needed, or removed when redundant. Its fabric acquires a patina which deepens with age; lichens grow on its stones; and plants grow in their own way, establishing themselves in the crevices of the walls.

Attitude

Though the above descriptions are analyses of the images of apparently real and plausible buildings – a 'temple' and a 'cottage' – the issue for the designing mind is the underlying one of attitude. The mind that is engaged in architecture must have an attitude, or a permutation of attitudes, to the conditions which impinge. Attitudes may be held unthinkingly, or asserted consciously, but they always affect the character of the work produced. There is not one attitude which informs all architecture; in this, variety in works of architecture is the result of variety in the philosophical approaches of architects.

Broadly, the attitudes which designing minds adopt exist on a dimension which stretches from submission, through symbiosis, to domination; one may submit to the conditions that prevail, seek to work in harmony with them, or seek to dominate them. But they also include many, more subtle, nuances of attitude: ignorance, disregard, acceptance, resignation, response, change, mitigation, amelioration, exaggeration, exploitation, contention, subjugation, control; all of which can combine in a variety of ways in dealing with the many different aspects of the world perceived as conditioning the production of works of architecture.

With regard to climate for example: on a particular site you, as an architect, might be ignorant of some wind that blows with potential destructive force in the same month each year; you might know about the wind and yet disregard it; you might seek to mitigate, or even exploit its effects for the environmental benefit of the users; or you might perhaps suggest a windbreak to deflect or control it. Some of the options may be negligent, reckless, or downright stupid; others may be subtle, poetic, and intelligent; some might exist in a grey zone between the two; but the options in attitude are always there, to be adopted with regard to different aspects of the conditions, according to your judgement.

Attitudes, consciously or unselfconsciously adopted, are manifest in the character of the work of architecture which is produced. If an attitude of domination is adopted, it will be there in the work; if submission, it too will be there.

Attitudes may be personally asserted by architects, or inherited by them from their culture, in which case their works manifest not just their personal attitudes but those of their culture or sub-culture.

The representation of attitude in works of architecture is also open to manipulation: by those who wish to use architecture as a means of poetic expression; or by those who wish to use it as a medium of propaganda, or symbol of national, personal, commercial

status. When architects of the Third Reich in Germany during the 1930s wanted to use architecture to symbolise the power the Reich asserted, they used a style of architecture (based on Classical architecture and its 'temples') which evokes an attitude of control. When the Nazis wanted to suggest that their politics were of those 'of the people' they insisted on a folk style (based on 'cottages') which seemed to suggest acceptance and celebration of national traditions with roots deep in history. Neither the Classical style of architecture, nor the traditional, was, in these instances, born of an attitude of acceptance; both were imbued with a spirit of control.

Manipulation of the appearance of works of architecture to suggest that they are born of particular attitudes is not always associated with dark or political propaganda. It is also a facet of the poetic potential of architecture. The other face of propaganda, in this regard, is romance; whether it is the romance of the heroism of ancient Rome, or of idyllic rural life, or of high technology, or of ecological harmony, works of architecture can be made to appear to have been born of the appropriate attitudes.

It may seem cynical to say so, but sometimes the attitude superficially suggested by the appearance of a work of architecture may not be the same as the one which actually underlay its conception and realisation.

One attitude which is not compatible with being an architect is abdication. As an architect one may accept, respond to, or change (the lie of the land for example), but if one abdicates from decision, or tries to suggest that the driving attitude lies elsewhere (in nature, nation, history, climate), then, in the fine grain of things, one is no longer an architect. It is not nature, society, or history, nor climate, gravity, or human scale, that determines the way a work of architecture comes about, but an architect's attitude to them and to other aspects of conditions which appear to prevail.

'Cottage' and 'temple' as ideas

'Cottage' and 'temple' are architectural ideas that are not restricted to cottages and temples.

Confusingly, it is quite easy to find cottages (i.e. small dwellings) that are to some degree 'temples' (architecturally, that is), and temples (i.e. religious buildings, loosely speaking) that architecturally are 'cottages'. The architectural ideas are not restricted to their nominal roles as 'grand shrine for a god' and 'humble home of

man'. Architectural ideas are not necessarily specific to purpose.

In its irregular composition of forms this church on Corfu (bottom of page), though functionally a temple, is architecturally a 'cottage'...

... while this cottage (right), with its geometric order and axial symmetry, standing on a small plinth is architecturally a 'temple'.

The 'cottage' and 'temple' ideas can equally well be applied to garden design. In the traditional English cottage, and 'cottage', garden (right) plants in irregular groups are apparently allowed to grow in their innate ways, with no formal organisation...

... whereas in the ornamental garden of a French chateau, for example, the plants are arranged in geometric patterns and clipped into unnatural shapes.

The English cottage garden implies acceptance of the providence of nature, appreciation of the innate characters of the different species of plant, and enjoyment of an aesthetic effect which appears independent of human decision and control. By contrast, the geometric garden of the French chateau celebrates human control over nature; the plants do not grow into their natural shapes, but are clipped into regular forms.

Many products of architecture are neither pure 'cottage' nor pure 'temple', but a mixture of both. Parts of a rambling house may be little 'temples': such as the porch, the fireplace, the four-poster bed, the doorcase, the bay-window, and the dormer window, in this cutaway drawing.

associated with the architectural idea of 'temple'.

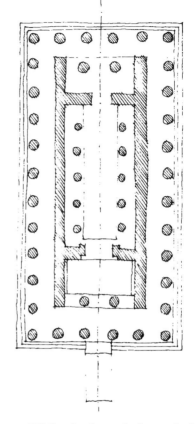

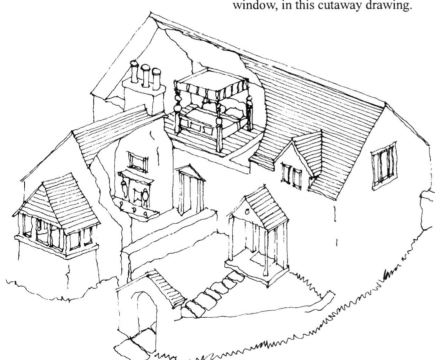

The architectural ideas of 'temple' and 'cottage' are evident in the plans of works of architecture, as well as in their outward appearances.

This is the plan of the ancient Greek temple of Aphaia at Aegina. It illustrates abstract characteristics of axial symmetry and regular geometry

While the irregularity and absence of strictly orthogonal geometry in the plan of this Welsh farmhouse (Llanddewi Castle Farm, Glamorgan)

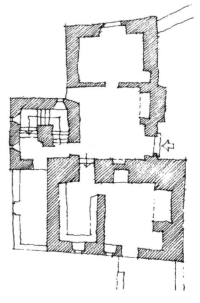

is typical of the 'cottage' idea: its plan is not complete within itself; some of its walls enclose patches of outside space, and others stretch out into the landscape; the rooms are not laid out formally, but more as an accretion of places for different purposes.

Where the 'temple' plan imposes, the 'cottage' plan responds.

The Erectheion, a temple on the acropolis in Athens, has an irregular asymmetrical plan...

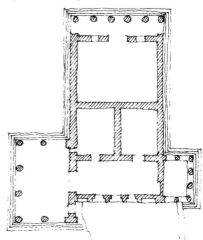

... and relates to the lie of the land by responding to varying ground levels.

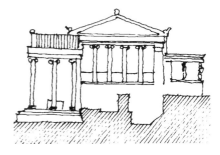

The Erectheion is composed of parts of three 'temples' put together, but in its relation to the ground, it also has some 'cottage' characteristics.

This Welsh farmhouse, by contrast, exhibits some of the architectural characteristics of a 'temple'.

It has a regular plan...

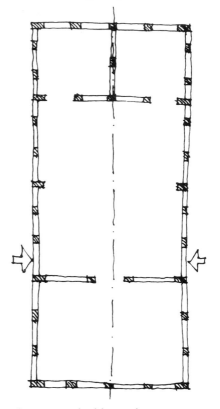

... is symmetrical in section...

... and stands clear of the uneven ground on a level platform.

So far in this discussion of the 'temple' and the 'cottage' as architectural ideas we have looked only at examples from the distant past. These

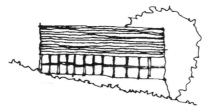

In some of its characteristics, this Welsh cottage is, architecturally, a 'temple'. It is symmetrical in plan and section, and stands on a platform, separated from the natural lie of the ground.

ideas are ancient in the production of architecture, but they have been used in the twentieth century too.

directly responds to the accommodation of different purposes, appears to be architecturally a 'cottage'.

The Einstein Tower (1919) by Erich Mendelsohn is, even with its curved forms, a 'temple'.

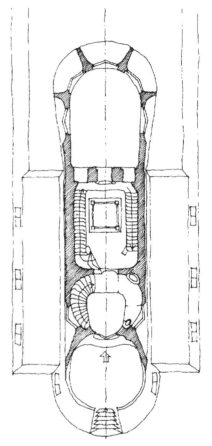

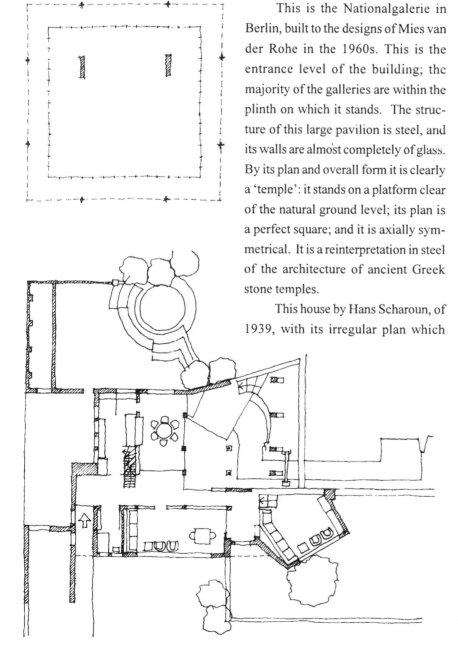

This is the Nationalgalerie in Berlin, built to the designs of Mies van der Rohe in the 1960s. This is the entrance level of the building; the majority of the galleries are within the plinth on which it stands. The structure of this large pavilion is steel, and its walls are almost completely of glass. By its plan and overall form it is clearly a 'temple': it stands on a platform clear of the natural ground level; its plan is a perfect square; and it is axially symmetrical. It is a reinterpretation in steel of the architecture of ancient Greek stone temples.

This house by Hans Scharoun, of 1939, with its irregular plan which

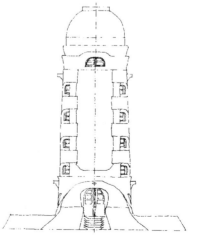

Whereas the civic centre at Säynätsalo, Finland (right), designed by Alvar Aalto (1952), with its careful but irregular planning, response to changing ground levels, and incorporation of external places, tends more towards the architectural 'cottage'.

Philip Johnson and John Burgee's AT&T Building in New York, built in 1982 (below), is a tall 'temple'.

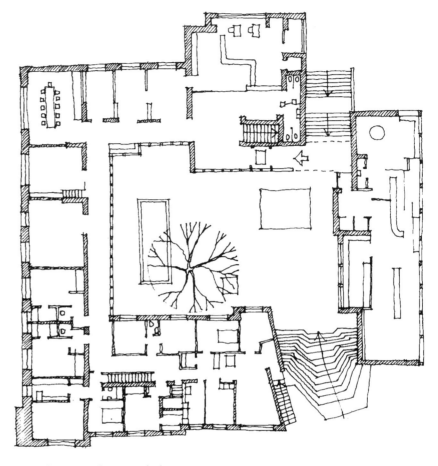

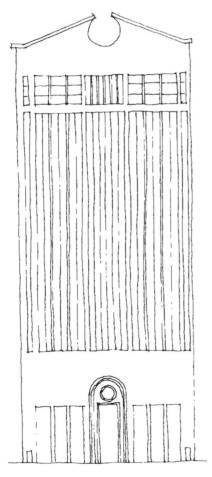

And the Inmos Research Centre near Newport, Gwent, designed by Richard Rogers is a wide 'temple'.

There are also twentieth-century buildings that combine 'temple' with 'cottage' characteristics.

From the outside, Le Corbusier's Villa Savoye (1929) appears to be a 'temple' (though it is a house). Its main living spaces are lifted clear of the natural ground, not on a solid platform, but on a series of columns. Its outer form is generally symmetrical but with small deviations; and it is ordered according to geometric proportions. But its plans,

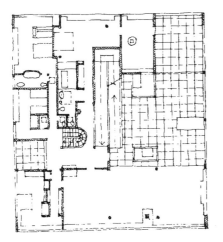

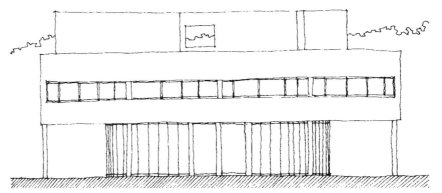

Reference for 'exclusive' and 'selective' modes of environmental design:

Dean Hawkes – *The Environmental Tradition*, 1996.

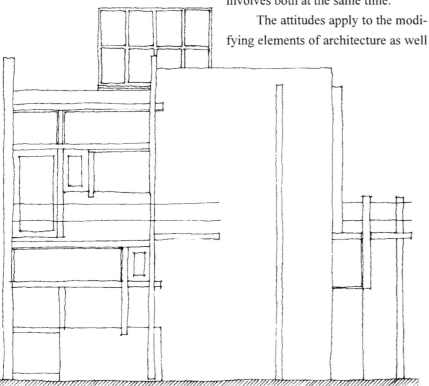

though based on a regular structural grid, are an irregular composition of spaces arranged without reference to axial symmetry.

The dichotomy of attitudes and related architectural ideas associated with 'temple' and 'cottage' run through all dimensions of architecture. An architect can impose an abstract order onto the world, or respond to what the world provides. Often architecture involves both at the same time.

The attitudes apply to the modifying elements of architecture as well as to the formal. In environmental design (which deals with warmth, light, sound, ventilation) a distinction has been drawn between 'selective' and 'exclusive' design: in selective mode a building is conceived to respond to and exploit the environment around; in exclusive mode the internal environment of a building is artificial, hermetically separated from the outside climate. In the terms discussed here, the selective mode accords with the 'cottage' idea, and the exclusive with the 'temple'.

'Temple' and 'cottage' exist conceptually on a philosophical dimension which is pertinent to all stages of design. Their application is not subject to rules, but to judgement and opinion, and can be influenced by prevailing trends of the time.

Some works of architecture are not easy to analyse in these terms. One is Gerrit Rietveld's Schroeder House (left), built in Utrecht in 1923. Its form is irregular; it has no axial symmetry; and it does not sit on a platform. Yet it has an abstract, idealised, unresponsive character which seems to separate it from the world as found, and which suggests it is a 'temple'.

GEOMETRY IN
ARCHITECTURE

GEOMETRY IN ARCHITECTURE

There are many different ways in which geometry plays a part in architecture.

The previous chapter, *Temples and Cottages*, discussed some of the different attitudes that a designing mind can adopt towards the conditions within which architecture is done. In particular it identified the attitudes of *control* and *acceptance* as they can be exemplified in an archetypal 'temple' and an archetypal 'cottage'.

The architectural uses of geometry can be discussed in these terms too. There are ways to use geometry that emerge out of the conditions of being, and there are others that may be imposed or overlaid upon the world. The latter, termed 'ideal' geometries, are the subject of the last section of this chapter; the chapter begins with some of the geometries 'of being'.

The word *geometry*, as a subject in school for example, suggests circles, squares, triangles, pyramids, cones, spheres, diameters, radii, and so on. These play an important part in architecture; as abstract ideas they belong in the category of ideal geometries – their perfection can be imposed on the physical fabric of the world as a means for identifying place.

But geometries emerge from our dealings with the world too; geometry can derive from an attitude of acceptance as much as it can be associated with an attitude of control. Geometries of being are inherent to the identification of places.

Circles of presence

People and objects introduce geometry into the world just by being.

Every body has around it what might be called a 'circle of presence', which contributes to its own identification of place. When a body is in relationship with others, their circles of presence affect each other. When a body is put into an enclosure or cell its circle of presence is also contained and perhaps moulded.

An object standing on a flat landscape occupies its own space, but it also exerts concentric circles of presence, to which we can relate.

If one discounts electronic and radio presence, the broadest of these circles of presence is the visual, described by the distance at which the object is visible. This circle may stretch as far as the horizon, or it might be contained by a forest, or a wall.

In terms of sound this large circle of presence would be the distance at which a sound emanating from a body is audible; smell, smellable; radio waves, receivable.

The smallest circle of presence, physically, is described by the distance within which one is able to touch, and perhaps embrace, the body.

The most difficult circle of presence to determine rationally is the intermediate, the one within which one feels that one is 'in the presence' of the body. It might be said that it is this circle of presence that delimits the place of the body.

Architecture uses all three: the extensive circle of visibility; the intimate circle of touchability; and the intermediate circle of place. Much architecture, from prehistoric times to the present, has been concerned with asserting, defining, amplifying, moulding, or controlling circles of presence.

A tree defines one of its circles of presence by the extent of its canopy of branches.

A candle, or a lighthouse, describes its circle of presence by the light that it emits.

A fire, as suggested in the chapter on *Primitive Place Types*, identifies a place by its sphere of light and warmth.

A standing stone exerts its presence in the landscape, as an assertion of the presence of those who put it there.

It is perhaps in the handling of circles of place that architecture can be at its richest and most subtle.

A tree defines one of its circles of presence by the extent of its canopy of branches.

Circles of presence are rarely perfect circles; they are almost always affected by local conditions and topography. The world is generally so full of bodies that their many circles of

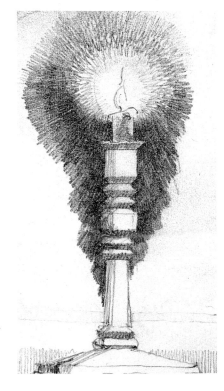

A candle or a lighthouse describe their circle of presence by the brightness of the light they emit.

The statue of Athena Promachos asserted the circle of presence of the goddess over the ancient city of Athens.

A standing stone asserts its circle of presence in the landscape, and establishes the place of those who put it there.

presence overlap, interfere, or maybe reinforce one another in complex ways which are sometimes too difficult to analyse fully.

Circles of place have been manipulated by architecture since ancient times, for various purposes.

Most of the buildings on the acropolis in Athens were built during the classical age of ancient Greek culture, around the fifth century BC. The top of this rocky hill in the plain of Attica had been a place sacred to the goddess since time immemorial. Such elevated places were sacred partly because they had a clear identity; they were elevated and sanctuaries in times of trouble; they also possessed extensive circles of presence – they could be seen (and from them one could see) for long distances across the landscape. The hill of the acropolis retains this circle of presence over modern Athens.

By their architecture the ancient Greeks manipulated the circles of presence of the sacred place of Athena. The extent of the circle of place around the sacred site was defined partly by the

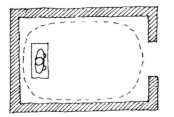

The circle of presence of a significant object can be contained and distorted by the enclosure or cell within which it stands.

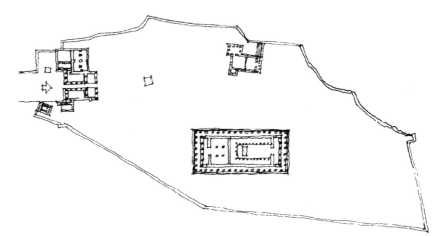

reasonably level area of land on top of the hill, but this was extended and established more firmly by the huge retaining walls which still define the sacred precinct – the *temenos* – around the temples. The shape of this temenos in plan is not circular, but represents an interaction between the circle of presence of the sacred site and the topography of the hill.

There were two important statues of Athena on the Athenian acropolis. The giant *Athena Promachos* stood in the open air near to the entrance into the temenos, projecting its own circles of presence over the city, even to ships on the sea some miles away. The other statue was enclosed within the main temple, the Parthenon, which had (and maintains) its own circle of visibility across the city, and which amplified the hidden presence of the image whilst controlling its circle of place and protecting its intimate circle of touchability, both of which were probably only ever penetrated by priests.

In these ways the acropolis illustrates some of the ways in which circles of presence play their parts in architecture: the retaining walls of the temenos define the 'circle' of the sacred site; the Parthenon amplifies the presence of the statue it contains, and its cella controls and protects the statue's circles of place and touchability.

Lines of sight

We human beings seem fascinated by the fact that we see in straight lines. This fascination is evident in the way one might vacantly line up the toe of one's shoe with a spot on the carpet, or more purposefully when one sights a distant object with the end of a finger to point it out. The fascination with lines of sight is evident in architecture too.

An alignment of three or more things, one of which is one's eye, seems to possess some peculiar significance. The precise alignment of the sun, the moon and the earth, at a solar or lunar eclipse, has always been considered a significant event. The builders of Stonehenge appear to have erected the Hele Stone to align the centre of the henge with the sun rising over the horizon on the Summer Solstice. Standing on a pier, we notice when a ship crosses the line projected by the pier out into the sea. Driving through the countryside we remark when a distant feature is exactly aligned with the road along which we are moving.

Alignment imparts significance, to both the distant object and the

We are intrigued when the landscape appears to contain alignments.

The Hele stone aligned the centre of Stonehenge with the sun rising on the Summer Solstice.

It appears that sometimes buildings were aligned with sacred mountains.

viewer. The 'sight' – the finger tip or the Hele Stone – is a medium, a fulcrum between the two, a catalyst which projects a line between the viewer and the object. Alignment implies a line of contact – an axis – between oneself and the distant object, exciting in the viewer a thrill of recognition of the linkage (which is even stronger when 'eyes meet across a crowded room').

Thinking of architecture as identification of place, a line of sight establishes contact between places. In the ancient world it was one of the ways in which architects tied places into the world around them, establishing them as fragments of matrices which centred on particular sacred sites. It is a power which is important in the design of places for performance, where engagement between actors and spectators depends on sight. It can also be important in designing art museums, where lines of sight can influence the positioning of exhibits.

Lines of passage

In the physical sciences, one of the laws of motion is that a body remains in a state of rest, or moves in a straight line with uniform speed, unless compelled by a force to change that state. This is often a presumption in architecture too.

Lines of passage are usually considered to be straight, unless diverted by some 'force'. A sensible person usually moves in a straight line between a starting point and a goal, unless there is some obstacle which

When he was remodelling the Castelvecchio in Vicenza, Carlo Scarpa would draw lines of sight onto his plans. Emanating from particularly important points in the building – the entrance, or a doorway – these would influence his deliberations on the positions of exhibits, or pieces of landscaping.

Reference for Carlo Scarpa at the Castelvecchio:

Richard Murphy – *Carlo Scarpa and the Castelvecchio*, 1990.

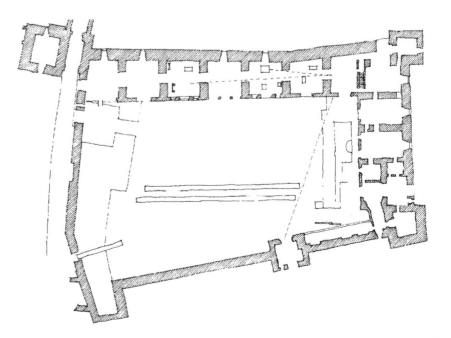

makes this unwise or impossible. In organising the world into places, architecture also establishes lines of passage between those places, using them as ingredients of serial experiences.

The line of a pathway in the landscape is often a result of people's and animals' tendency to move in straight lines being diverted by changes in the surface of the ground.

Reference for ancient Egyptian pyramids:
I.E.S. Edwards – *The Pyramids of Egypt*, 1971.

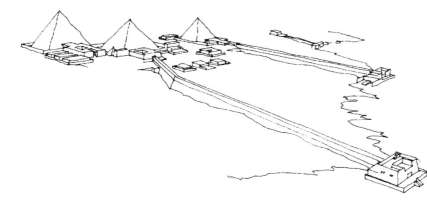

The ancient pyramids of Egypt were connected to valley buildings on the river Nile by long causeways. Sometimes these were straight; sometimes they had to take account of local land conditions, or perhaps changes in plans during construction, and deviated from the direct line.

Lines of passage are often related to lines of sight; but they are not necessarily congruent.

A line of passage can set up or reinforce a line of sight, as when a road aligns with a distant feature in the landscape; but they might not coincide. Sometimes architecture can make a play of aligning a line of passage with a line of sight (as in the nave of a church); but sometimes the line of passage deviates from the line of sight, so that a pathway does not take the most direct route between starting point and goal.

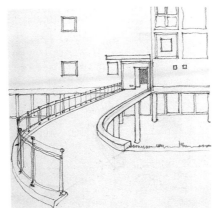

In this drawing the goal (the entrance) is clear, but the approach is diverted from the line of sight.

Approaching the entrances to the Carpenter Center, lines of passage are not congruent with lines of sight.

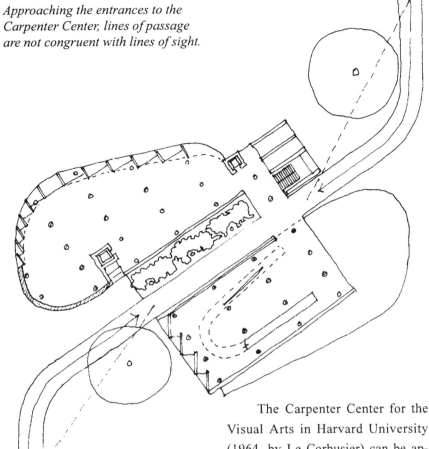

The Carpenter Center for the Visual Arts in Harvard University (1964, by Le Corbusier) can be approached from two diagonally opposite corners of the site. The ramps that rise to the entrances are curved. At the start of either ramp the line of passage to the entrance does not follow the line of sight.

Sometimes a line of passage does not have an obvious goal which can be

seen. Interplay between lines of sight and lines of passage can create a sense of mystery in the experience of a work of architecture.

Sometimes a work of architecture presents a choice of lines of passage, each of which has to be assessed by sight.

Measuring

The word *geometry* derives from two Greek words, for earth (*ge*) and measure (*metron*). Measuring the world is essential to life; people measure their environment all the time, and in lots of different ways. Measuring with a ruler or tape measure is only one of those ways, and an artificial one. The more immediate ways in which people measure the world is with their own bodies.

People measure distance by walking. They may do it consciously by counting their paces; but they also do it subconsciously, merely by walking from one place to another. In connection with walking, people estimate distance or the height of a step with their eyes, and assess the amount of effort needed to cover the distance or climb the step.

People estimate the width of doorways and passageways, estimating whether there is space to pass others.

People estimate the height of openings to assess whether or not they must stoop to pass through.

People are conscious of the size of a room, and can estimate what it will accommodate. They do this primarily by means of sight, but the acoustic of a

105

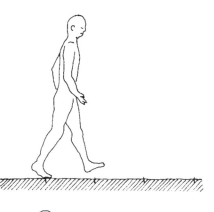

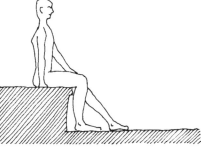

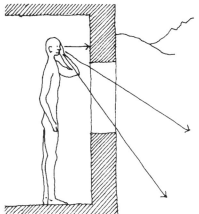

People measure the world with their movement, their bodies, and their senses. A stair measures a difference between levels in equal steps.

space can also indicate its size. People also subconsciously calculate how the size of a room, and the distances between pieces of furniture in it, can influence social interrelationships within it.

People might estimate the height of a wall to assess whether it may serve as a seat; or of a table to assess its use as a work bench.

People literally measure out the lengths of their own bodies on the beds in which they sleep.

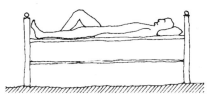

A person stands by a window conscious of the heights of the cill and of the head, and of whether the horizon can be seen.

People set the scale of a work of architecture in comparison with their own stature as human beings, and with the ways in which their bodies may move.

These are all transactions between people and works of architecture. People set the measure of the buildings they use; but buildings also set the measure of the lives they accommodate. People take measure from the works of architecture they inhabit, and use their measurements to make different types of assessment.

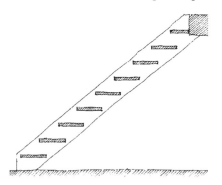

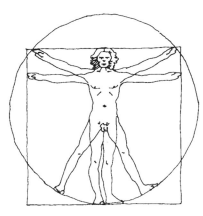

In the late fifteenth century Leonardo da Vinci constructed this drawing illustrating the relative proportions of an ideal human frame as set down by the Roman writer on architecture, Vitruvius. It suggests that in its ideal form the human frame conforms to geometric proportions; it also suggests that the measurements of the human frame are tied in with those of nature, and the universe.

allowed for the different postures that the human frame adopts: sitting, leaning, working at a table....

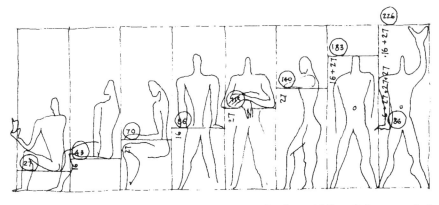

Reference for The Modulor:
Le Corbusier (translated by de Francia and Bostock) – *The Modulor*, 1961.

In the middle of the twentieth century Le Corbusier contrived a more complex system of proportions relating the human frame to those of other natural creations. He used a special proportion called the Golden Section. His system, called *The Modulor*,

Earlier in the twentieth century, however, the German artist and dramatist, Oskar Schlemmer, had recognised that the human frame also measures the world in its movement and projects its measure into the space around it.

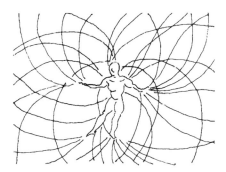

A large doorway exaggerates the status of the occupant, and diminishes the status of the visitor.

A small doorway diminishes the status of the occupant, and enhances the status of the visitor.

A human-scale doorway puts the occupant and visitor at equal status.

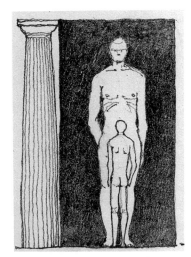

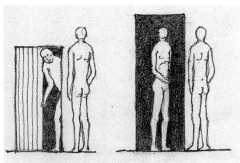

Six-directions-plus-centre

A human being has a front, a back, and two sides; generally speaking, the ground is below, and above is the sky. Each stands (or sits, or lies) at the centre of its own set of these six directions.

with its four walls, ceiling and floor, conforms to this. In such places each of us can compare the orientation of our own six directions, and the position of our own centre, with those of the room, finding places where our six directions are in either formal accord

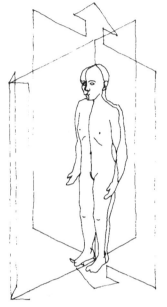
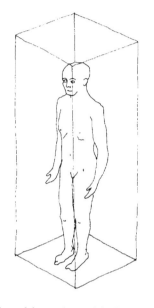
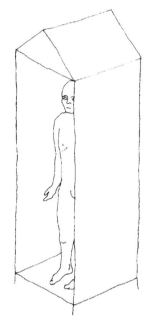

These observations seem almost too obvious to bother stating, but they are simple truths that have fundamental ramifications for architecture. Six directions condition our relationship with the world, in which each of us is our own mobile centre. They condition our perception of architecture – how we find and occupy places, how we relate ourselves to other places – and play into the conception of architecture, presenting a matrix for design.

One way in which architecture can relate to the six-directions-plus-centre is by the evocation of resonance between an enclosure and its occupant, by making it a place which responds to (or deals with in some way) each of the six directions. An ordinary cell,

or relaxed interplay with those of the room. By its six sides a place (a room, a building, a garden) can set out a two- or three-dimensional orthogonal framework, the power of which lies in its provocation in us of a sense of relationship.

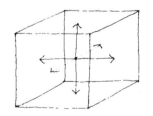

In relating to a place that has a front (an in front), a back (a behind), two sides (a left and a right), a top (the above), and sits on the ground (the below), we feel that in some way we are relating to something which is like ourselves, and which, to this extent, is created in our own image, and to which we can respond through comparison with our own six-directions-plus-centre.

The suggestion of accord between sets of six-directions-plus-centre can be a powerful identifier of place, especially when architecture sets up a centre which a person, or the representation of a god in human form, or a significant object, can occupy.

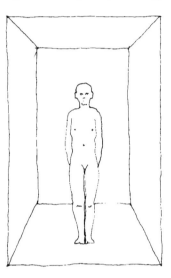

Often in such cases one of the six directions is dominant, usually the forward: as in the case of a soldier's sentry box which allows vision to the front while protecting his back and sides from attack, his top from rain or sun, and his feet from mud or the cold of the ground; or as in the case of a throne room, where the position of the throne against one of the four walls, rather than at the geometric centre of the room, allows the monarch's forward direction to dominate the space. Such a manifestation of direction might be reinforced in other ways, maybe by

positioning the throne opposite the entrance, or by setting out a path – a red carpet perhaps – which identifies the monarch's route to and from the throne as well as emphasizing the forward direction from the throne.

The six directions are evident in human bodies, and these can be responded to in the architecture of spaces and rooms. The six directions are also

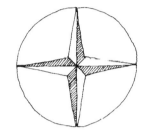

manifest in the conditions within which creatures live on the surface of the earth. The sky is above and the earth below; but each of the four horizontal directions has its own character. Each of the four cardinal points of the

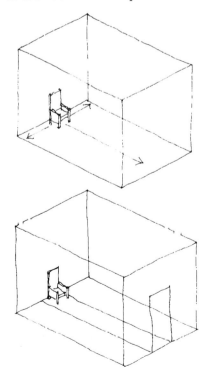

The tank in Damien Hirst's Away from the Flock *forms a three-dimensional orthogonal frame around the sheep. Each face of the tank implies an elevational view of the animal.*

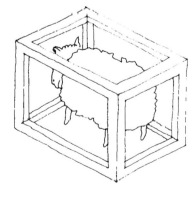

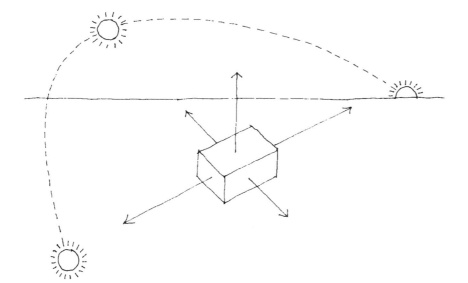

compass relates to the movement of the sun. In the northern hemisphere the sun rises in the east and sets in the west, it is at its highest in the south, and never enters the northern quarter.

Works of architecture can be oriented to these terrestrial directions as well as to those of anthropomorphic form. In this way buildings mediate geometrically between human beings and their conditions on earth. Any four-sided building on the surface of the earth relates in some way, roughly or exactly, to these four cardinal points of the compass. Any four-sided building is likely to have a side which receives morning sun, a side which receives midday sun, and a side to the setting sun; it will also have a side to the north which receives little or no sun. These four horizontal directions have consequences in the environmental design of buildings, but they also tie architecture into the matrix of directions which cover the surface of the earth (and which are formally recognised in the grids of longitude and

latitude by which any position on the surface of the earth is defined).

The four-sided building is directly related to the directions on the surface of the earth as it spins through time; and each side has a different character at different times of day. But such a building can be significant in another way too; for if its six directions are considered to be in congruence with those of the earth – its four sides face each of the four terrestrial directions implied by the movement of the sun, and its verticality accords with the axis of gravity which runs to the centre of the earth – then the building itself can be considered to identify a centre – a significant place that seems to gather the six directions of the earth into its own, and provide a centre which the surface of the earth does not.

In these ways the geometry of the six-directions-plus-centre can be seen to be inherent at three levels of being: in ourselves as human beings; in the original nature of the world on which we live; and in the places that we make through architecture, which mediate between us and the world.

The six-directions-plus-centre are a condition of architecture, and as such are susceptible to the attitudes of acceptance and control mentioned in the chapter on *Temples and Cottages*: one can accept their pertinence and influence; or attempt to transcend them by exploring abstract and more complex geometries, or by tackling difficult concepts such as non-Euclidean, or more-than-three-dimensional space. Some might also argue that the submission of the world's surface to the rule of four directions, or three dimensions, is simplistic; that the movement of the sun through the sky is more complex than the cardinal directions suggest; and therefore that architecture either should not necessarily pay heed exactly to the matrix that the six-directions imply, or should look for more subtle indicators for the positioning and orientation of buildings.

Nevertheless, the notion of six-directions-plus-centre is useful in analysing examples of architecture of many kinds and characters. Its power is found in examples that range from the ways in which directions, axes and grids can be introduced into landscapes to make it easier to know where one is, and how one might get from one place to another...

Reference for the Vitra Fire Station: 'Vitra Fire Station', in *Lotus 85*, 1995, p.94.

Even a fairly rough stone can, like a person, introduce the six-directions-plus-centre into the landscape.

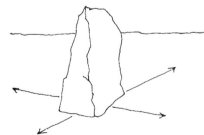

... through the vast stock of orthogonal works of architecture, to attempts to escape or test the boundaries of rectilinear architecture, as in the works of Hans Scharoun, or of Zaha Hadid. Even though distorted, as if by the force of some warp in the gravitational field, the four horizontal directions retain their power in the plan of Hadid's Vitra Fire Station.

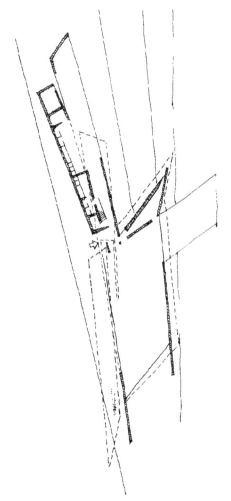

Many works of architecture relate to the four horizontal directions, to the above and the below, and to the concept of centre, in simple and direct ways. The Greek temple is a particularly clear example. The six-directions-

plus-centre operate at various conceptual levels, even in a building whose form is as apparently simple as this.

First, as an object in the landscape, the building has six faces: one to the ground; one (the roof) to the sky; and four sides, each facing one of the four horizontal directions. In this regard the temple establishes itself as a centre.

Second, as an internal place, the cella of the temple has a floor and a ceiling, and four walls that relate directly to the four horizontal directions implied by the image of the god or goddess who was its essential reason for being.

Third, in the relationship between the inside space and the outside world, the doorway (the prime link between the two) allows one of the four horizontal directions (that of the face of the deity, which is reinforced by the longitudinal axis of the temple) to strike out from the inside and relate to an external altar, and maybe also (as a line of sight) to some remote object of significance – the rising sun, or the sacred peak of a distant mountain.

These three ways in which the six-directions-plus-centre are inherent to the architecture of the temple collaborate to reinforce the role of the temple as an identifier of place. The temple itself is a cell and a marker, but its orthogonal form channels the ways in which it identifies the place of the sacred image, making it also a centre.

But there is also a fourth way in which this essentially simple building type relates to the six-directions-plus-centre, one that is of special importance in thinking of architecture as identification of place. This is to do with the way that the directions of the building relate to those of a visitor or worshipper.

The geometry of an ancient Greek temple responds to the six-directions-plus-centre...

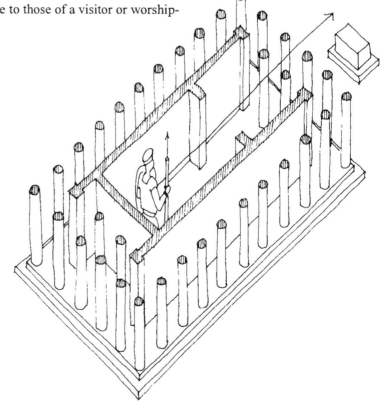

Regarding its external form as a body, we are aware (if we know the building, and are in its presence) when we are at the back, at the front, or at either of its sides. Relative to the building, we know where we are. But in addition to that relationship, we are also aware that there are significant places created by the power of the orthogonal geometry of the building; places that maybe draw us to them. The most important of these is that prominent direction which emerges from the god's statue through the door and strikes out into the landscape; we know when we are standing on this axis and perceive it as special; it excites in us a thrill of connection between our own directions and those of the god.

This powerful axis is established by the architecture of the temple. We are not left as detached spectators, but brought into involvement with the architecture of the building, made part of it. It is exactly the same power, that of the dominant axis, which prompts

the practice of nodding reverently as one crosses the axis of the altar in a Christian church or a Buddhist shrine. It is the same power that draws us to stand at the exact centre of a circular space (the Pantheon in Rome, or under the dome in St Paul's Cathedral in London, or the amphitheatre at Epidavros in Greece).

These simple uses of the six-directions-plus-centre are basic, rudimentary, and seemingly universally recognised as constituting a power of architecture.

Social geometry

The geometry of social interaction between people is perhaps a function of the six-directions-plus-centre that each possesses.

When people congregate they identify their own places, in particular ways. In doing so they overlay a social geometry where they come together. As a process of identification of place, this is architecture in its own right, but while it consists only of people its existence is transient. Works of architecture can respond to social geometries, order them, and make their physical realisation more permanent.

When schoolboys spectate at a playground brawl between two of their number, they form a circle. When there is a formalised bout between two boxers, the area of their battle is defined by a rectangular platform with rope barriers around the edge. Though square it is called a ring, and the boxers' confrontation is represented by their possession of opposite corners.

... as does the geometry of a traditional church.

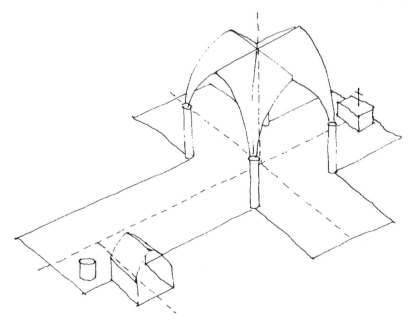

113

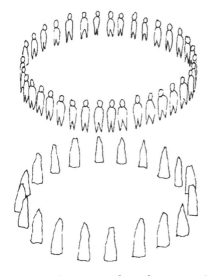

A stone circle makes a people pattern permanent.

People may sit in a rough circle around a fire in the landscape. In the ingle-nook of an Arts and Crafts house that social geometry is transformed into a rectangle, accommodated within the structure of the fabric of the house.

It may not be an example of social geometry, but the grid layout of graves in a cemetery is a function of the geometry of the human frame and the way in which the rectangular shape of the space it needs can be

An ingle-nook formalises the geometry of social interaction around a fire. This imaginary example was drawn by Barry Parker, and is illustrated in the book he produced with his partner in architecture, Raymond Unwin – The Art of Building a Home, *1901.*

There is a social geometry to the space of togetherness...

The radial arrangement of spectators on the slopes of a valley, watching sports or dramatic performances, was architecturally translated by the ancient Greeks into the amphitheatre, with its (more than semi-) circular plan, consisting of many tiers of concentric sitting steps.

tessellated across the land.

People arguing stand opposite each other; when they are friends, they sit next to each other. Both can have architectural manifestations.

In British politics, the confrontation of the Government and the Opposition is physically represented in the benches of the House of Commons, which face each other across the chamber, with the Speaker (or chairman of the debate) sitting on the axis between them.

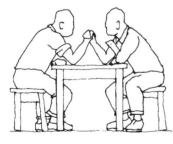

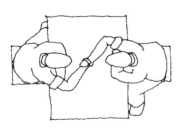

The social geometry of the British House of Commons is a manifestation of the procedural relationship between the Government and the Opposition.

... and to the space of confrontation.

Some chambers for discussion are designed not for argument and opposition but for collective debate. This is sometimes manifested in their architecture. Chapter houses are meeting rooms attached to cathedrals and monasteries. Often they have a circular, or perhaps polygonal, plan which, architecturally at least, is non-confrontational and non-hierarchical. Even the

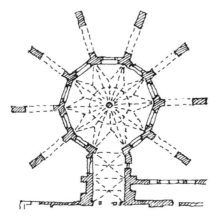

central column, which supports the vaulted ceiling, seems to block direct,

diametrical, opposition across the chamber.

It is a moot point whether such architectural arrangements affect the behaviour of members of parliament or of chapters. Some countries, nevertheless, have chosen to accommodate their parliamentary debates in circular rather than confrontational debating chambers, if only for symbolic reasons. This, as one example, is the debating chamber of the Finnish parliament in Helsinki, which was designed by J.S. Siren and built in 1931.

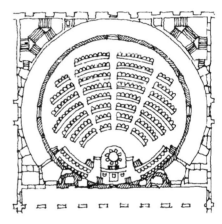

The circle is one of the most powerful symbols of human community; architecturally it seems to speak of people being equal and together in a shared experience of the world. It is the pattern made, loosely, by the people around their campfire; it is the pattern made by people sitting around a picnic; it is a pattern associated with conversation; and it is a pattern associated with spectating at some dramatic or ceremonial event.

Though he avoided many other types of geometry in his designs, even the German architect Hans Scharoun accepted the aptness of the circle as a frame for the social event of a meal. In the Mohrmann House, built in 1939, the dining area is the only place in the plan which has a regular geometric shape: a circular table is accommodated

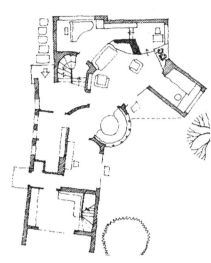

centrally in a semi-circular bay window between the kitchen and living room.

Geometry of making

Many everyday objects have a geometry that is derived from the way they are made. A clay vase is circular

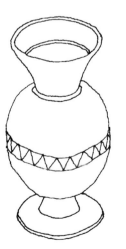

because it is thrown on a potter's wheel; a wooden bowl is circular because it is

turned on a woodturner's lathe; a table is rectangular because it is made of regular-shaped pieces of timber.

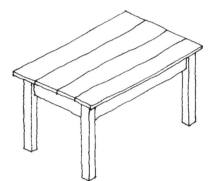

The same is true of building. Often the materials and the way in which they are put together impose or suggest geometry.

When put together into walls, bricks, as rectangular objects themselves, tend to produce rectangular walls, and rectangular openings and enclosures. When using such materials it requires a definite decision to deviate from the rectangular.

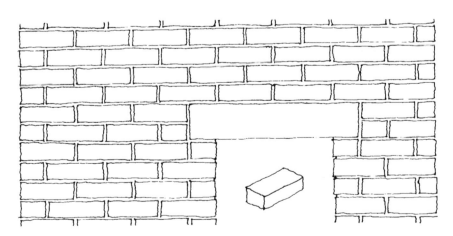

There is geometry to laying slates on a roof...

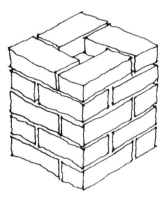

The geometry of bricks conditions the geometry of things that are made from them.

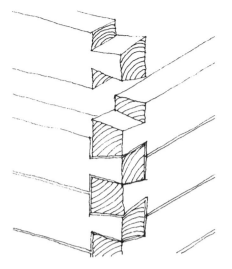

... and to the ways in which pieces of timber can be joined together.

This drawing is based on one in:
Drange, Aanensen & Brænne – *Gamle Trehus,* (Oslo) 1980.

The geometry of making is essential to the construction of buildings. In this traditional Norwegian timber house, as in many traditional houses from around the world, there is an interplay of social geometry and the geometry of making. Social geometry conditions the sizes and the layout of the spaces. But the shapes of those spaces are also conditioned by the materials available and their intrinsic qualities, and by current building practice.

The building is infused with the geometry of making, even though that geometry is not always exact and regular. The fabric of the walls and the structure of the roof is influenced by the sizes of timbers available, and their innate strength. The sizes of roofing tiles influence the design of the roof. The small panes of the window are conditioned by the sizes of pieces of glass. Even the small portions of masonry are conditioned by the shape of the bricks and the subtle and complex geometries of the stones available. And the bracket which holds the cooking pot has its own structural geometry, and describes a locus which is part of a circle as it is swung across the fire.

The geometry of making is not so much a power of architecture as a force which conditions building. The force is not active, but lies latent in materials that are available for building, and in plausible strategies for bringing materials together into building under the influence of gravity. As such the geometry of making is subject, in architecture, to the range of attitudes mentioned in the chapter on *Temples and Cottages*. In producing an archetypal 'cottage', it may be said, the geometry of making is accepted, whereas in an archetypal 'temple' it is transcended. Within this dimension architects can adopt any of a range of attitudes to the geometry of making.

The Scottish architect Charles Rennie Mackintosh designed many pieces of furniture; in some of them he exploited the geometry of making, refining it according to his aesthetic sensibility. This, for example, is a

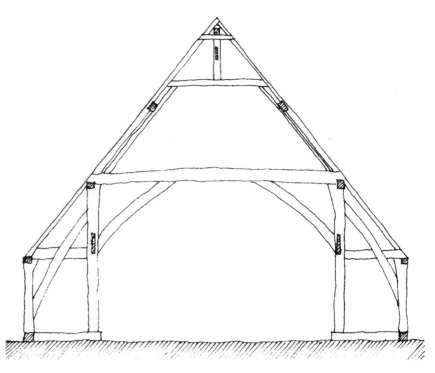

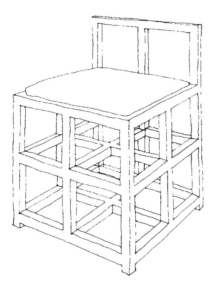

waitress's stool he designed in 1911; it follows the geometry of making, but this has been refined into a matrix of perfect cubes.

There is a constructional geometry too in the shingle and timber buildings designed by the American architect Herb Greene; but it is stretched almost to its limit, and distorted into animal-like forms. This drawing (right) shows part of his Prairie House, built in 1962, on which the shingles are like the feathers of a hen.

The geometry of making includes the geometry of structure, whether it is the timber structure of a medieval tithe barn, or the steel structure of a micro-electronics factory. The geometry of structure is said to be susceptible to mathematical calculation, though there seems to be an infinite variety of ways of arranging a structure to span a particular space. Some are said to be

Reference for Mackintosh furniture:
Charles Rennie Mackintosh and Glasgow School of Art: 2, Furniture in the School Collection, 1978.

Reference for the architecture of Herb Greene:
Herb Greene – *Mind and Image*, 1976.

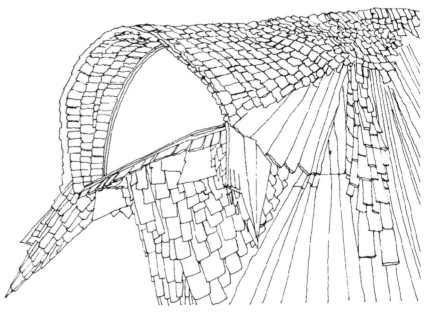

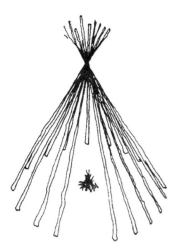

The structure of a native American teepee has an innate conical geometry, which produces a circular plan.

The three-dimensional geometry of some medieval carpentry is quite complex. This is part of the scaffold of the spire of Salisbury Cathedral. The drawing is based on one by Cecil Hewett in his book English Cathedral and Monastic Carpentry, *1985.*

efficient if they use material economically and without redundant members; some have an added quality called elegance. Whether there is a direct correlation between efficiency and elegance is a point of debate.

The geometry of making does not only apply to traditional materials such as brick, stone and timber; it applies just as much to buildings with steel or concrete structures, and to buildings with large areas of glass walls.

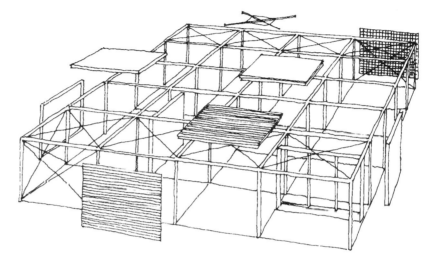

It is also the discipline which controls industrialised building systems. Systems consist of standard components that can be put together as a kit of parts. These parts include structural components, and various types of non-structural cladding panels which form the envelope of the building. The dimensional co-ordination that allows standard components to be manufactured in a factory, transported to a site, and then put together to make a building depends on careful and disciplined appreciation of the geometry of making.

Ideal geometry

The circle and the square may emerge out of social geometry or from the geometry of making, but they are also pure, abstract, figures. As such, they are sometimes thought to have an aesthetic or symbolic power (or both) in their own right. Some architects use them to instil their work with a discipline that is independent of (but perhaps also related to) the various geometries of being.

Ideal geometry does not only include the circle and the square and their three-dimensional forms – the cube and the sphere. It also includes special proportions, such as the simple ratios of 1:2, 1:3, 2:3 or more complex ratios such as 1:√2, and that known as the Golden Section which is about 1:1.618.

In his book, *Architectural Principles in the Age of Humanism* (1952), Rudolf Wittkower explored the ways in which Renaissance architects used ideal geometric figures and ratios in their designs. He also discussed why they believed that such figures and ratios were powerful.

One argument was that natural creations, such as the proportions of the human frame, or the relationships between the planets, or the intervals of musical harmony, seemed to follow geometric ratios, and that if the products of architecture were to possess the same conceptual integrity they too should be designed using perfect figures and harmonic mathematical proportions. Another argument was that through architecture a geometrical perfection could be achieved that was only hinted at in natural creations.

The application of geometry was seen as one way in which human beings could improve the imperfect world in which they found themselves. Geometric purity was thus seen as a touchstone of the human ability, or perhaps duty, to make the world better. It is in this sense that ideal geometry, as a way of imposing order on the world, is a characteristic of the 'temple'.

The result was that architects produced designs for buildings which were composed using perfect figures and geometric ratios.

This, for example, is a copy of Wittkower's diagrams of the geometric composition of the façade of the church of S. Maria Novella in Florence, designed by Leon Battista Alberti and built in the fifteenth century. They

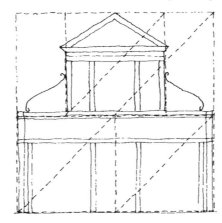 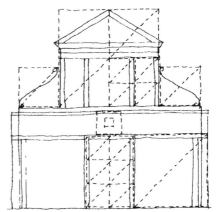

show that the façade of the building may be analysed as a composition of squares. These have a role in the design which is independent of the building's geometry of making; the geometry is displayed on the front wall of the church, as on a screen.

Many architects have designed buildings in which the accommodation is enclosed within a square plan. This is different from composing the design of a façade as a two-dimensional pattern of squares, because it involves the third dimension, and perhaps also the fourth – time.

A square plan is not usually a result of accepting the geometry of making; a square space is not the easiest to frame with a structure; it requires purposeful intent, derived from something other than mere practicality, to make a plan square.

Architects may design a square plan for various reasons: maybe for the philosophical reasons outlined above; maybe because a square can seem to identify a still centre which relates to the six directions mentioned above; maybe as a kind of game – a challenge to fit accommodation within this rigid shape.

Architects are always looking for ideas which will give form to their work and direction to their design. Geometric ideas are some of the most seductive. To design within a square plan is an easy idea to grasp (and a way to break through the problem of getting started). But although it may seem a limitation, the square plan is also open to infinite variation.

There are many examples of square plans. They are rare in ancient and medieval architecture, but became more part of the repertoire of design ideas in the Renaissance.

One very ancient example is of course the Egyptian pyramid. These tombs were generally built on land to the west of the Nile, between the river and the desert, and carefully oriented to what we know as the cardinal points of the compass. They are clear examples of architecture responding to the six-directions-plus-centre.

Below is the plan of the pyramid complex of Pepi II, at Saqqara in Egypt. The pharaoh's pyramid has been cut through to show the burial chamber at its centre. There are three smaller pyramids for his wives. The building to the right of the drawing is the valley temple, which was the ceremonial entrance to the complex and linked to the pyramid temple by a causeway which is too long to be included in the drawing in its full length.

Each side of the pyramid faces a direction with a different character. The temple buildings and the ceremo-

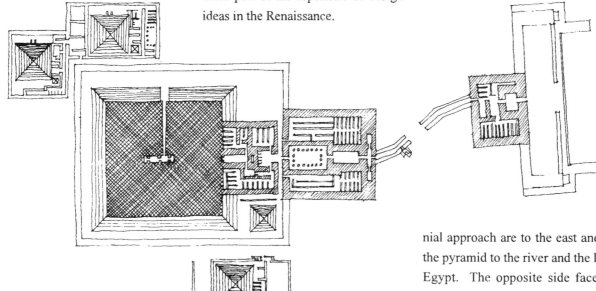

nial approach are to the east and link the pyramid to the river and the life of Egypt. The opposite side faces the desert. The south faces the sun when it is at its highest. The north side seems to have less symbolic significance, and was used for the physical access to the burial chamber, which was perhaps less important than the ceremonial entrance from the east. The pyramid is a centre where these directions meet, and the burial chamber lies at the centre of its geometric form. It is in this way that the ancient Egyptian pyramid was a powerful identifier of place.

Below are the plans of the principal floors of two square plan houses built in England in the 1720s. On the left is Mereworth Castle in Kent designed by Colen Campbell; on the right Chiswick Villa by Lord Burlington. Both architects were influenced in the choice of a square plan by the design on the right, which is of the Villa Rotonda designed by the Italian architect Andrea Palladio, and built some one-hundred-and-fifty or so years before the two English examples.

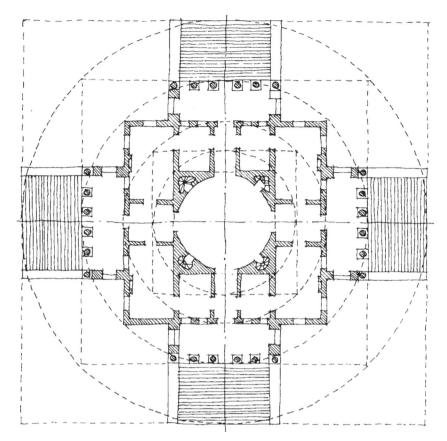

Palladio's plan is the most consistent of the three. As in the ancient pyramid, it gathers the four horizontal directions into a centre – the focus of the circular hall at the heart of the plan, from which the villa gets its name.

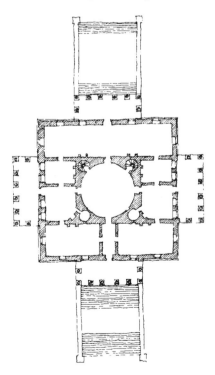

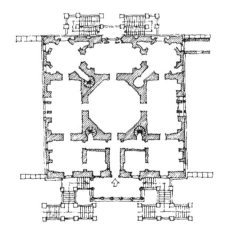

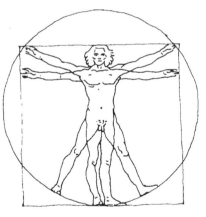

(Unlike the pyramid, the sides of the Villa Rotonda do not face north, south,

Reference for the Villa Rotonda:
Camillo Semenzato – *The Rotonda of Andrea Palladio*, 1968.

east, and west, but northeast, southeast, southwest, and northwest.) The plan is not just one square, but a concentric series of five; the size of each successive one is determined by the radius of a circle circumscribed about the next smallest. The smallest circle is the rotonda itself; and each square (except for the second smallest) determines the position of some substantial part of the building. The largest square gives the extent of the steps which lead up to the porticoes on each side; their depth is determined by the second largest square; and the main walls of the villa are determined by the middle-sized square.

The cross-section through the Villa Rotonda is also a composition of circles and squares, though not such a simple one as in the plan.

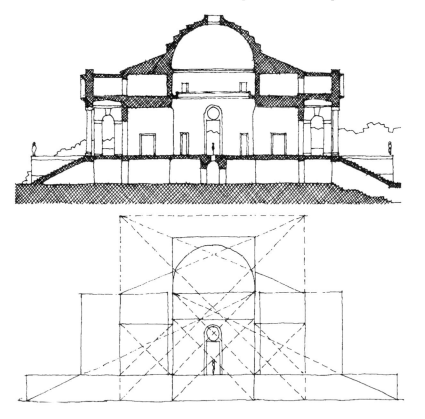

Square plans have been used by architects designing in the twentieth century.

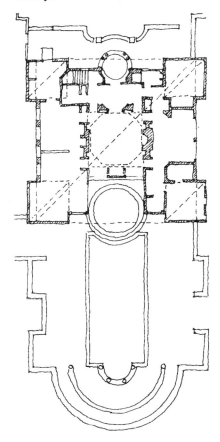

Charles Moore used the square as the basis of his plan for the Rudolf House II. As in the Renaissance examples Moore created a central place, which is here the living room, surrounded by subsidiary places: kitchen, dining room, bedroom, and so on. Perhaps for practical reasons, the plan is not so neatly arranged as that by Palladio.

The Swiss architect Mario Botta bases many of his designs on geometric figures. He has designed a number of private houses in Switzerland; these are often composed of squares and circles, cubes and cylinders.

Botta's design for a family house at Origlio, which was built in 1981, is a composition of rectangles and circles fitted into a notional square. On each

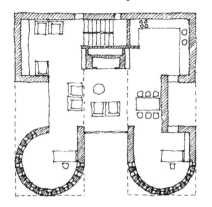

floor he uses the square in a different way. On this floor, the middle of three, the plan is nearly symmetrical, with the living room and fireplace at its heart.

The plan of this house at Riva San Vitale is also based on a square. The house is a tower of five floors built

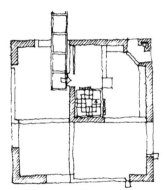

on the sloping bank of Lake Lugano. It is entered across a bridge to the top floor (which is the one shown in the drawing).

In both these houses Botta also appears to have used another geometric figure – the Golden Rectangle – to help him in deciding the layout of the plans. The Golden Rectangle is one which has a particular proportional re-

lationship between its two dimensions: the ratio of the short dimension to the long is equal to that between the long dimension and the sum of the two dimensions. This means that if one subtracts a square from a Golden Rectangle, one is left with another, smaller, Golden Rectangle. This ratio, known as the Golden Mean, is not a whole number, but approximately 1.618:1.

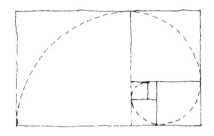

In the house at Origlio it appears that Botta used the Golden Mean to give the proportion between the central section and the side sections of the house. In the Riva San Vitale house

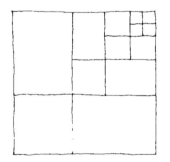

he seems to have used Golden Rectangles in a way similar to that in which Palladio used circles and squares in the Villa Rotonda, that is like Russian Dolls. The square near the middle of the plan accommodates the stair which connects the floors.

Le Corbusier also used the Golden Mean to give geometric integrity to his work. In his book *Vers Une*

Reference for Botta houses:
Pierluigi Nicolin – *Mario Botta: Buildings and Projects 1961-1982,* 1984.

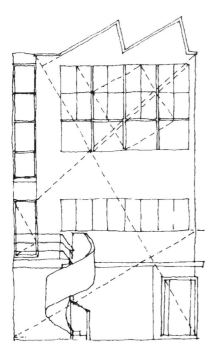

Le Corbusier ordered the elevation of this studio house with 'regulating lines'.

Architecture (1923), translated as *Towards a New Architecture* (1927), he illustrated his geometric analyses of some well-known buildings and the geometric framework on which he had built some of his own designs. He did not only use the Golden Mean, and sometimes his 'regulating lines' (he called them '*traces regulateurs*'), make a complex web of lines. This is a copy of his diagram of the geometric composition of one of the elevations of the studio house which he designed for his friend Amedee Ozenfant; it was built in a southern suburb of Paris in 1923. Rather like in Alberti's S. Maria Novella (shown above), the geometry is displayed on the elevation of the house, as on a screen.

Complex and overlaid geometries

Many twentieth-century architects have used ideal geometry to lend rationality or integrity to their plans, sections and elevations. Some, seemingly bored with simple relationships, have experimented with complex arrangements in which one geometry is overlaid on another.

In some of the house designs by the American architect Richard Meier, the places of dwelling are identified by the spaces which result from a complex interplay of orthogonal geometries.

This, for example, is Meier's design for the Hoffman House, built in East Hampton, New York State, in 1967. The idea for the plan seems to have been generated from the shape of the site, which is an almost perfect square. The diagonal across the square determines the angle of one of the elevations of one of the two main rectangles on which the plan of the house is based.

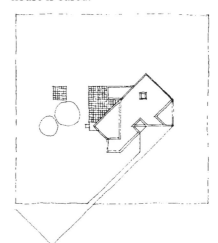

Each of these two rectangles is a double-square. One is set on the diagonal of the site; the other is parallel to the sides of the site. They share one

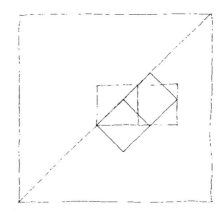

corner. Their geometric interrelationship determines the position of almost everything in the plan.

Places – living room, kitchen, dining area, and so on – are allocated zones which are defined by the interaction of the overlaid geometries. The positions of basic elements – walls, glass walls, defined areas, columns –

are determined in accord with the complex armature of lines which the geometries of the rectangles create. To help in this game the squares are sometimes subdivided to make the geometry even more complex, and thus identify a greater range of different places within the armature.

One interpretation of the geometry which provides the armature of the ground floor of this house is shown in the drawing on the right. The actual plan is below.

In this version one of the squares is divided into thirds in both directions, giving nine smaller squares. The intersections of the third-lines give the positions of the columns set in the glass wall which lights the living room and dining area. The fireplace is positioned on the one corner which the two rectangles share. The entrance – itself a square – seems to be generated by an interaction of the centre line of one of the double-squares with the side of the other, and sits in an axial relationship with the fireplace and the seating in the living room. An alcove in the living room is created by a projection of the middle third of the divided square to meet the corner of the other double-square. And so on.

This may seem complicated, and is certainly difficult to follow when explained verbally. If this is the way that Meier progressed his design for this house, which seems plausible, then he was using geometry as the framework for design decision, a hybrid of that used by Alberti and Palladio. Geometry is used in this way to suggest

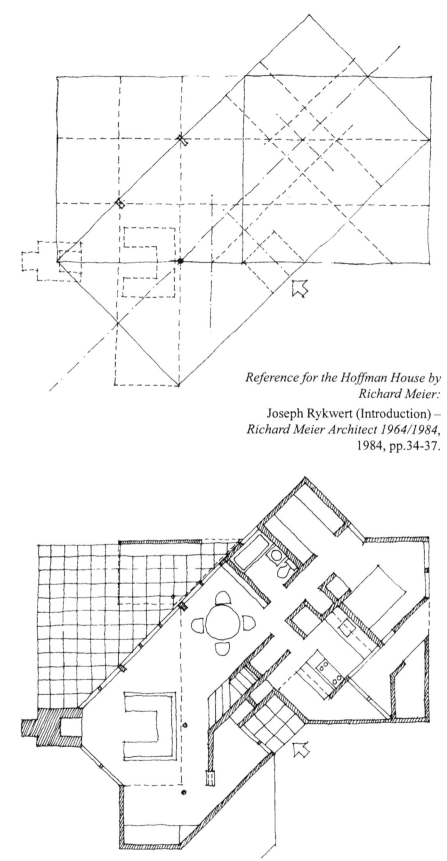

Reference for the Hoffman House by Richard Meier:
Joseph Rykwert (Introduction) – *Richard Meier Architect 1964/1984*, 1984, pp.34-37.

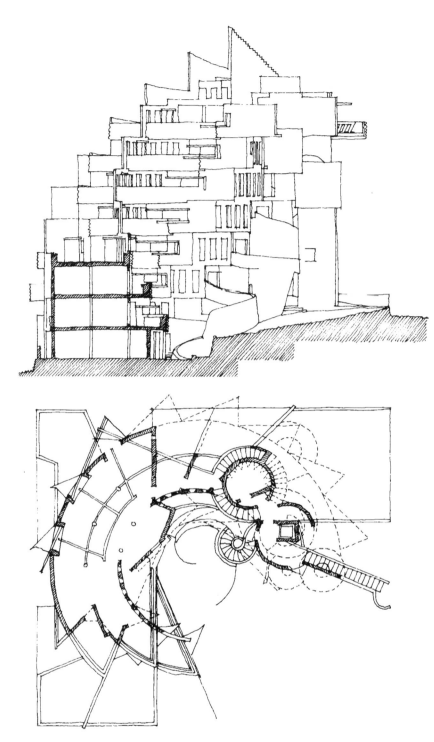

formal and perhaps also aesthetic integrity. In the overlaying of geometries Meier adds a further dimension – intricacy in the quality of the spaces which are created.

Meier's geometric overlays may seem complex, but some other architects have used geometric frameworks more complex than that in the Hoffman House.

On the left and below, as one example, are the section and plan of an apartment building in the Tel Aviv suburb of Ramat Gan in Israel. The architect of this complicated building was Zvi Hecker, and it was built in 1991. It is formed of a spiral of fragmented circles and rectangles, with dwelling places disposed in the spaces which result from the geometric overlays.

This apartment building in a suburb of Tel Aviv is a complicated spiral composition of fragmented circles and rectangles. The places of dwelling are dispersed amongst the spaces which result from the overlaid geometries.

Reference for Tel Aviv apartments by Zvi Hecker:

L'Architecture d'Aujourd'hui, June 1991, p.12.

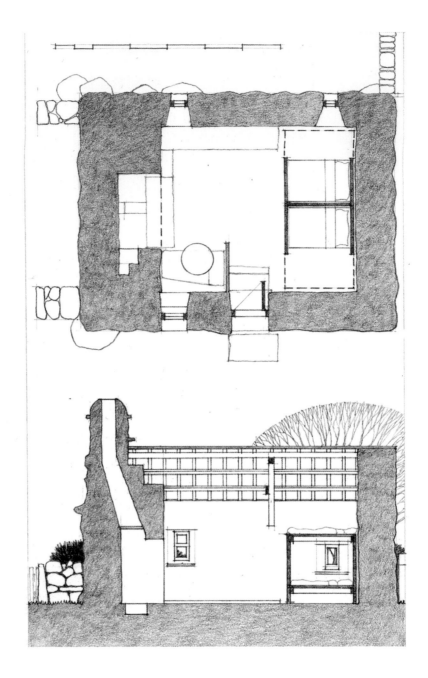

SPACE
AND STRUCTURE

SPACE AND STRUCTURE

Both structure and space are media of architecture. It is by reason of its structure that a building stands. Structure also plays a part in organising space into places. The relationship between space and structure is not always simple and straightforward; it is subject to different approaches.

In terms of attitudes, one can either choose and allow a structural strategy to define the places one wishes to create, or one can decide on the places and, in a way, force structure to cope with them.

There are thus three broad categories of the relationship between space and structure: the dominant structural order; the dominant spatial order; and the harmonic relationship between the two, in which spatial and structural order seem in agreement. In the history of architecture, there have been champions of all three relationships, as evident in the examples below.

There have also been protagonists for a fourth category of relationship, in which spatial organisation is said to be separated from structural, so that they may coexist, each obeying its own logic free of the constraints associated with the other.

As we have seen in the chapter on *Geometry in Architecture*, regarding 'the geometry of making', structure tends to its own geometries. In the sections of that chapter regarding 'the geometry of being' and 'social geometry' we have seen that objects and people, individually and in groups, can evoke their own geometries. In architecture there are vital relationships between these geometries: sometimes they are in tension; sometimes they can be resolved into harmony; sometimes they can be overlaid but remain conceptually separate.

An extra complication is that once a structural strategy is established it can influence (not merely respond to) spatial organisation.

An important aspect of the art of architecture is to choose a structural strategy that will be in some sort of accord with the intended spatial organisation.

The way in which ancient Greek architects evolved indoor theatric places is a good illustration of how spatial organisation can conflict with structural, and how this can be resolved by compromises of different types, in both.

The classic Greek amphitheatre was a geometric formalisation of the social geometry of people sitting on the slopes of a hill watching a performance. Its three-dimensional form was a fusion of social geometry, ideal geometry, and the lie of the land. With no roof it did not have to take account of the geometry of structure.

In some cases however Greeks wished to create an inside place where lots of people could watch something. This meant having to take account of the geometry of the structure which would hold up the roof.

The structures which the Greeks used tended to create spaces which were rectangular in plan; and they could not achieve large spans. Both these characteristics conflicted with the shape of an amphitheatre, which was circular, and needed an uninterrupted large space.

In some instances the Greeks' solution was merely to put the 'round peg' into the 'square hole'; this is the council chamber at Miletus.

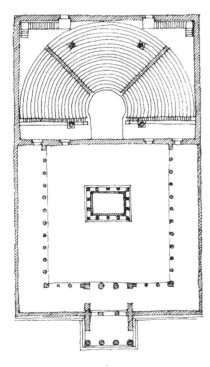

The amphitheatre is enclosed in a quadrilateral cell, leaving corner spaces unused except for stairs back down to ground level. The columns needed as intermediate supports for the

roof have been kept to a minimum; the two at the front are to some extent used to help frame the focal space of the chamber, but the other two are awkwardly intrusive. A minor concession to the geometry of the seating is made in the way the column bases take their alignment from the seats rather than from the orthogonal geometry of the structure.

Almost exactly the same relationship between spatial and structural organisation, but on a smaller scale, is found in the 'new' (late fifth-century BC) council chamber built in Athens (right). Presumably the two pairs of columns, together with the external walls, supported principal structural beams along the lines shown in the plan, which then divided the long dimension of the roof into three smaller, manageable, spans.

In other examples the shape of the seating is made to fit the rectangular geometry determined by the structure. This is the *ecclesiasterion* at Priene.

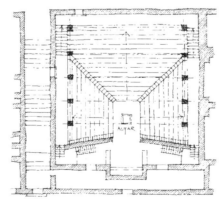

Here the seating has been mutated to the closest rectangular equivalent of the segmental amphitheatre. There is compromise in the structure too, in that the intermediate supports –

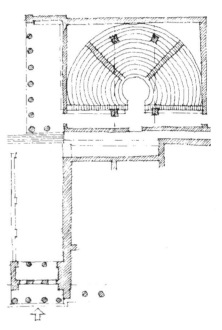

In the council chamber at Athens an amphitheatre of seating was enclosed within a rectangular cell. The columns needed to support the roof were kept to a minimum and carefully positioned to create the least obstruction to view.

the columns introduced into the space to reduce the spans of the roof timbers – are not positioned at the 'third points' where they would divide the width of the hall into three equal spans, but have been placed much nearer to the outside walls so that they do not obstruct views from the seats.

In early buildings that tried to create large roofed spaces columns were indispensable. This is an ancient Egyptian 'hypostyle' hall, from the temple of Ammon at Karnak dating

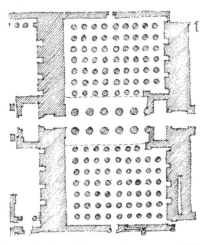

from the late fourteenth century BC. Whatever the space was used for, it would have had to contend with the forest of huge columns, the smaller of which had a diameter of more than three metres.

The ancient Egyptians may have just been impressed by a space filled with huge columns, but the same arrangement would be a problem in spaces for performance.

This is the case in the *telesterion* at Eleusis, built in the sixth century BC as a place for the performance of the secret 'Mysteries'. It has seats for spectators around the periphery of a square

space. Over the performance area is a regular grid of columns to support the

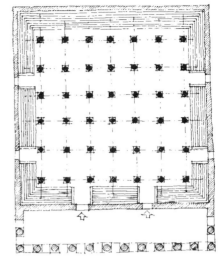

roof. These obstructed everyone's view of what was happening on the floor.

The next plan – of the *thersilion* at Megalopolis (fourth century BC) – appears to have a similar profusion of obstructive columns, except that at first sight they seem to be scattered irregularly across the floor.

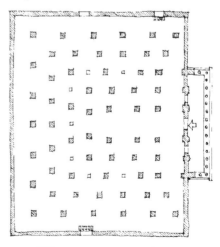

If however one superimposes an interpretation of the grid of the roof structure, one can see that the columns were arranged with a particular spatial

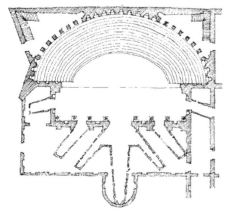

The Renaissance architect Andrea Palladio, wishing to evoke the spirit of the ancient theatres, had to use ingenuity to contrive this oval amphitheatre inside the Teatro Olimpico (AD 1584). In the auditorium the mismatch between the curved seating and the outside walls is masked by an arcade of non-structural columns. The stage setting includes a sophisticated scene incorporating false perspectives.

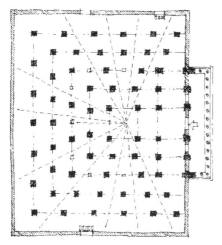

within the building are identified by the structure; the sacred place itself is identified from the outside by the structure of the dome.

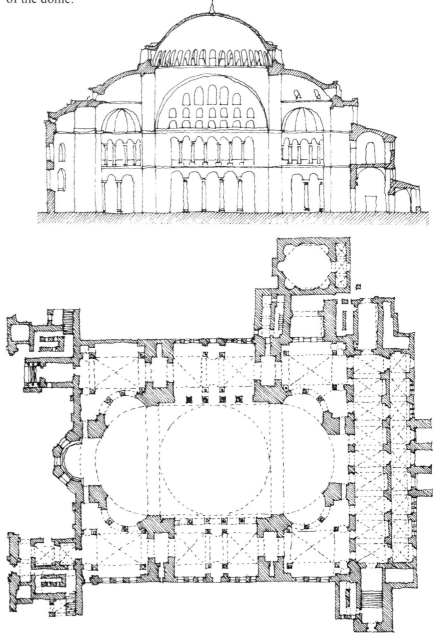

intent, one that responds to the lines of sight which radiate from a point of focus under the four columns which do make a square on plan. This appears to have identified the place where a speaker would stand; and the distortion of the grid of columns was a compromise in favour of a spatial arrangement that would allow him to be seen as well as heard.

Through history, many works of architecture have been created under the power of a conviction that structure is the fundamental form-giving force in architecture, and that the geometric order inherent in resolved structure is the most appropriate order for space too. This conviction is perhaps most apparent in the religious architecture of the Romanesque and Gothic periods, but it has been the impetus behind many nineteenth- and twentieth-century buildings too, both religious and secular.

In the Hagia Sophia in Istanbul, built as S. Sophia in the sixth century AD, the structure *is* the architecture: the spaces it contains are ordered by the pattern of the structure; the places

This intimate relationship between space and structure is illustrated in medieval churches and cathedrals too. Their places – the sanctuary, chapels, nave, etc., are all identified structurally, by resolved stone vaults.

The Hagia Sophia and the medieval cathedrals were built in stone, but the intimate relationship between structure and spatial organisation that they exhibit occurs in structures of other materials too.

The French architect and pioneer in the use of reinforced concrete, Auguste Perret, translated the structural and spatial clarity of the medieval churches into concrete structure. This

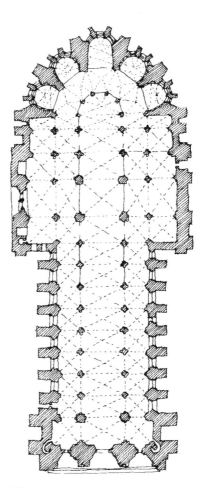

In Rheims cathedral space is ordered by structure.

Reference for the work of Auguste Perret:

Peter Collins – *Concrete*, 1959.

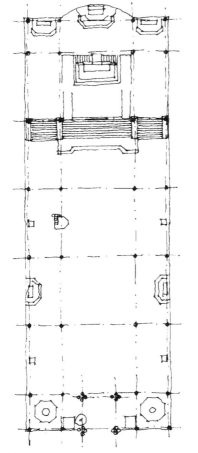

is his church of Notre Dame at Le Raincy just outside Paris, which was built in 1922. It is a smaller building than Rheims cathedral, but even so the proportion of the floor area taken up by the structural supports is much less, because reinforced concrete is much

stronger, structurally, than stone. The relative distance between the columns in Le Raincy is much greater than in Rheims for the same reason. The structural and spatial clarity in both churches is however the same. In Perret's church all the places are identified by the structure: the position of the main altar, the positions of the secondary altars, the pulpit, the font, and so on, are all determined by the spaces defined by the structure.

The space planning requirements of religious buildings are usually fairly simple: the places to be identified can be easily accommodated in the geometric order of structure which also seems to reinforce the spiritual order offered by religion. But in domestic architecture the relationship between structural order and spatial organisation can be more fraught.

The relationship between space and structure in a simple single cell house is straightforward: all the places to be accommodated happen under the

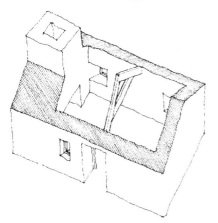

shelter of the roof and within the enclosure of the walls. There may be some principal roof timbers, like the simple truss in the example above, but this is unlikely to influence spatial organisation in the room below. This room is defined by walls which clearly and inseparably perform the dual functions of enclosure and structural support simultaneously.

At the other end of the scale of complexity, large houses built of loadbearing wall structures tend to have their spaces organised into many cellular rooms. Probably the heyday for this type of house was during the Victorian age when many people with newly acquired wealth had large houses built for them.

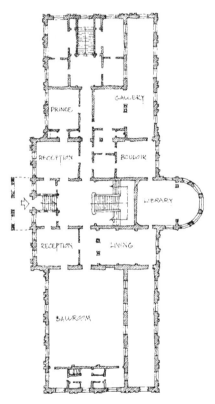

There are many types of traditional house in which the two functions of enclosure and structural support of the roof are distinguished from each other. In these the roof is supported on a frame of timber, and the spaces are enclosed by non-loadbearing screen walls. These framed buildings may be simple single cell houses, or they may consist of a number of rooms. In traditional examples the rooms or places within the houses tend to be organised according to the geometric order suggested by the structural frame.

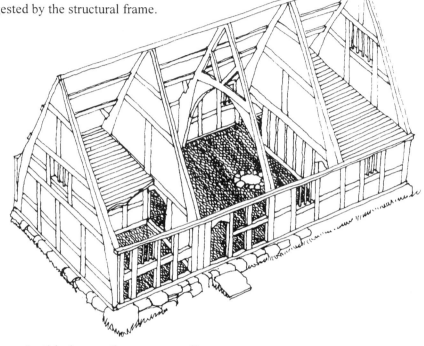

In this house there are small rooms on two storeys set in the two end structural bays, and a larger hall occupying the central two structural bays. The walls are filled in with light wattle and daub panels.

The plan of this house is a rectangle, but timber-frame structures can also have more complex plans.

Traditional Malay houses are built using a simple timber-frame structure. By processes of addition, they can become quite extensive, and composed of many spaces. The places they accommodate tend to be defined by the structural bays, which are sometimes accompanied by changes in levels.

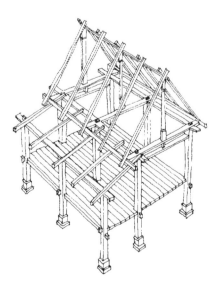

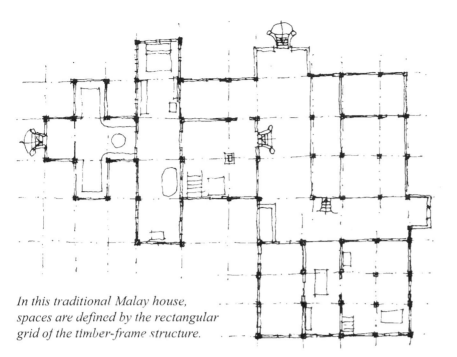

In this traditional Malay house, spaces are defined by the rectangular grid of the timber-frame structure.

Reference for Malay houses:
Lim Jee Yuan – *The Malay House,* (Malaysia) 1987.

in a southern suburb of Berlin. There are places: for sitting by the fire look-

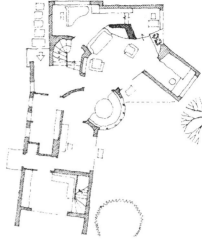

ing out through a glazed wall into the garden; for playing the piano; for eating; for growing decorative plants.... The disposition of these takes priority over the structural organisation of the house.

This house too has a complex plan. It is the Casa Romanelli, designed by the Italian architect Angelo

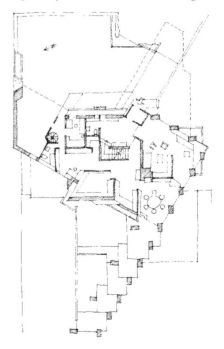

In the examples given so far, the geometry of structure has suggested that space be organised into rectangles. As we have seen in the section on 'the geometry of making', structure can tend to make circles as well as rectangles. Some houses of all ages have their space organised according to the circular order of a conical roof structure.

Some architects, particularly in the twentieth century, have argued, through their designs for houses, that the spaces associated with life are not necessarily rectangular or circular, and that dwelling places should not be forced into the geometric plan forms suggested by resolved structures.

During the 1930s in Germany, Hans Scharoun designed a number of private houses in which the disposition of places took precedence over the geometric order of structure. Here again is the Mohrmann house, which stands

Reference for Casa Romanelli:
Architectural Review,
August 1983, p.64.

Masieri and executed by Carlo Scarpa in the north Italian town of Udine in 1955. Though, as in the Scharoun plan, the geometry of this house is complex, its spatial organisation is more a result of the overlay of different geometries to create complexity. The disposition of places does not direct the design, but rather accommodation is found for them amongst the walls and columns. Though the structural pattern is complex, it leads and spatial organisation follows.

Some architects have tried to separate structural order from spatial organisation and place making.

There is a small house on Long Island, New York, designed by the architects Kocher and Frey and built in 1935. All its accommodation is on the first floor, which stands some two-and-a-half metres above the ground on six columns, and is reached by a spiral stair; on top is a roof terrace. This is a plan of the structural layout of the main living floor. Although the living place

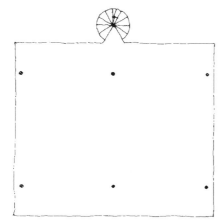

is defined by the extent of the platform, the structure of six columns positioned regularly across the plan makes no suggestion of how the floor should be laid

out to make places. The drawing alongside shows how it was laid out; the walls are not load bearing. The movable screens which give the bed space some privacy are wrapped around, not another column, but the water downpipe.

This Kocher and Frey house is an example which follows the principle set by Le Corbusier some twenty years earlier in the 'Dom-Ino' idea. He

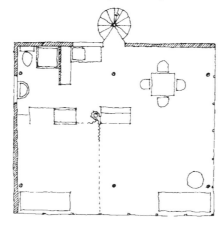

suggested that the planning of buildings could be freed of the restrictions of structural geometry by the use of columns supporting horizontal platforms.

Le Corbusier designed a number of houses using the Dom-Ino idea. Mies van der Rohe also experimented with detaching spatial organisation from structural order. Both however tended to allow structure a part in place identification. Both experimented with space between horizontal planes.

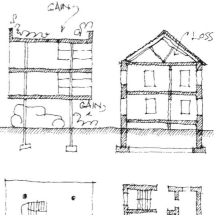

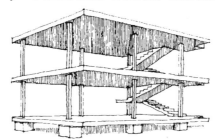

This is one of Le Corbusier's diagrams arguing the benefits of the Dom-Ino idea in the architecture of house design.

Reference for house on Long Island:
F.R.S. Yorke – The Modern House, (6th edition) 1948, p.218.

This is the structural diagram of the Villa Savoye at Poissy, near Paris, built in 1929. Clearly, as in the

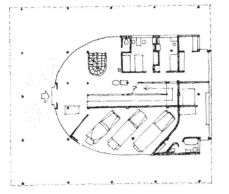

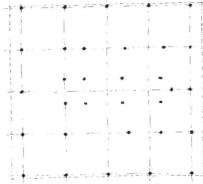

thersilion at Megalopolis, the structural grid has been distorted. Although the structure does not determine places within the plan, Le Corbusier does use it to help in the identification of places, as one can see, for example, in the drawing alongside: where the columns define the space occupied by the central ramp; where a column picks up the corner of the stair; and where two columns frame the main entrance.

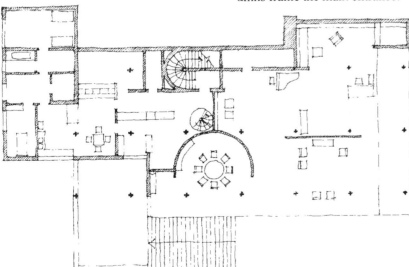

In the Tugendhat House at Brno, (1931), Mies van der Rohe preserved the geometric order of the structural

grid of cruciform columns, but he too used the columns to help identify places: two of the columns, together with the curved screen wall, frame the dining area; two others help define the living area; and another column suggests the boundary of the study area, at the top right on the plan.

In the Barcelona Pavilion (1929), however, in which Mies van der Rohe was almost totally free of the need to identify places for particular purposes, he managed to create a building in which space is liberated, almost completely, from the discipline of structure, and channelled only by solid, translucent and transparent walls.

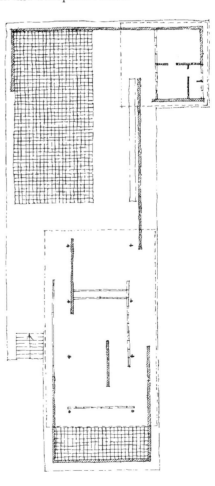

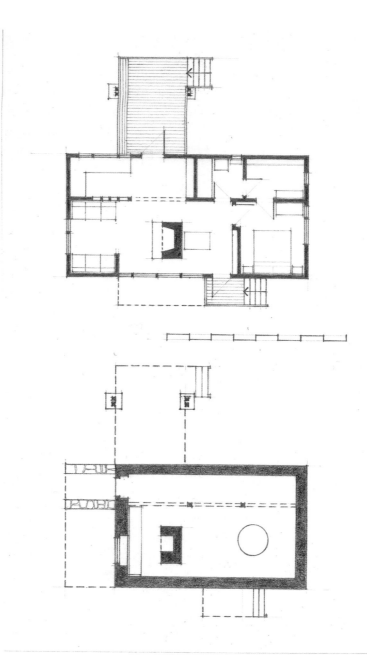

PARALLEL WALLS

PARALLEL WALLS

One of the simplest, oldest, and yet most enduring of architectural strategies is based on two straight parallel walls.

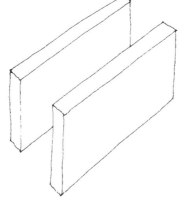

This strategy is found in prehistoric architecture, and it continues to be useful. Architects have explored its possibilities right into the twentieth century, developing variants and hybrids. It is unlikely that its potential has yet been exhausted.

The obvious attraction of this most uncomplicated arrangement is its structural simplicity – it is easier to span a roof between two parallel walls than any other form.

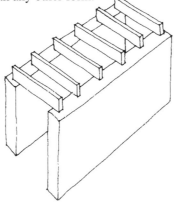

But although it is simple, the parallel wall strategy is not without its subtleties. As with many ancient forms of

architecture these subtleties may have caused a sense of wonder in the minds of those who first used them; a wonder that we have only lost through familiarity. The causes of that wonder are still available for rediscovery and use in design.

In the chapter on *Geometry in Architecture*, and in particular the section on the 'six-directions-plus-centre', it was said that terrestrial architecture relates, in some way or another, to the earth, the sky, the four horizontal directions, and the idea of centre. The strategy of parallel walls relates particularly to the four horizontal directions. Its power lies in its control over these directions, in definite ways which can be used to create a sense of security, direction, and focus.

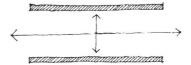

Protection is provided by the roof which shelters the 'inside' from the rain or the sun, but also by the side walls which limit the directions of approach to two – 'front' and 'back' – or, with the addition of a non-structural rear wall, to one – 'front' – making this simple building like a cave.

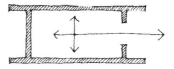

The sense of direction, or dynamic, is created by the long shape of the space between the walls. The line

Opposite page:
In many buildings, space is organised using parallel walls.

of direction can run either way, straight through between the walls

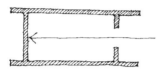

... or culminate within the building, terminated by a back wall.

These characteristics of the parallel wall strategy are to be found in some of the most ancient buildings on earth.

In the nineteenth century the archaeologist Heinrich Schliemann discovered a city thought to be the ancient city of Troy, made famous by the stories of Homer. Some of the houses he found there were based on the simple form of two parallel walls.

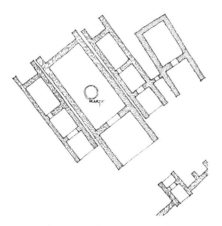

The gateway, or propylon, was formed of two parallel walls too, extending the experience of transition from outside the city wall to inside.

Although the houses of Troy would have had focuses in their hearths, they do not appear to have

taken advantage of the focusing power of parallel walls. This comes about by combination of the line of direction, the convergence of perspective lines, and the frame created by the walls with the roof above and the ground below.

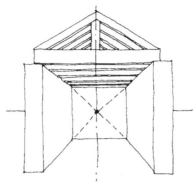

Vincent Scully, in his book *The Earth, the Temple, and the Gods*, suggested that the ancient Greeks used the sense of direction and focus (or framing) created by parallel walls to relate their buildings to sacred sites on the peaks of distant mountains.

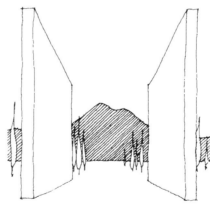

The evolution of ancient dolmens (right) shows the discovery of parallel walls as a structural and a spatial strategy. It seems a particularly human development from the amorphous cave; born of structural order, and producing 'magical' architectural effects that

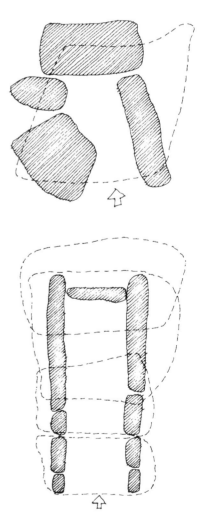

add to the ways in which places can be identified.

This strategy also underlies the architecture of: the Greek temple, from

on an altar; and the Gothic church, which identifies the place of the altar in a similar way but with a more sophisticated vaulted roof structure.

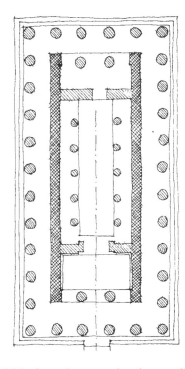

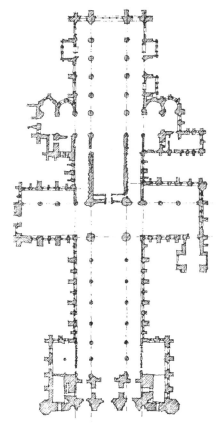

which the axis set up by the parallel walls strikes out into the landscape; the Romanesque basilica, in which the perspective of the walls focuses the axis

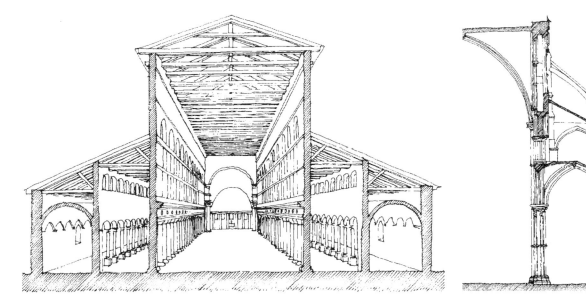

In the twentieth century some architects have experimented with parallel walls as a basis for spatial organisation.

When Michael Scott designed a new church at Knockanure in Ireland in the 1960s he reduced the parallel wall strategy to its most basic form.

woods is identified by the two flank walls, and the implied movement through the building is from right to left on the plan and section. Progress through the church is controlled by cross walls. The plan defines five zones along this route.

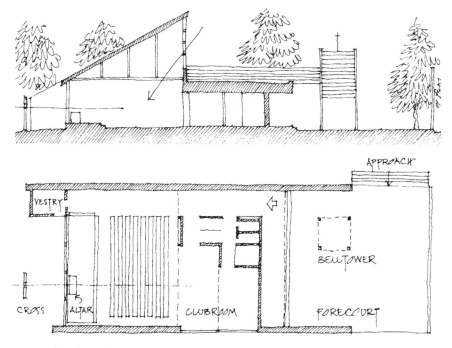

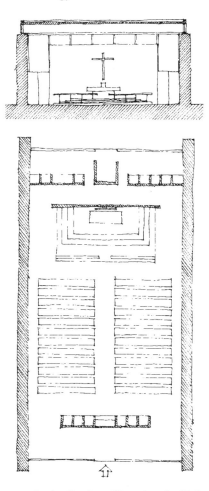

In the Student Chapel at the University of Otaniemi near Helsinki in Finland, two parallel walls are used to channel a progression from a secular to a spiritual view of nature. The chapel was designed by Kaija and Hiekki Siren and built in 1956-7 on a low hill amongst pine and birch trees. The special place of the church in the

The first of these is the world through which one approaches the church. The second is the courtyard, entered from the side and partially enclosed by walls and screens like basket work woven from twigs. Inside the courtyard there is a bell tower which acts like a marker. From the courtyard one passes through to the chapel itself, which is the fourth zone, past the third which is a clubroom and overspill space for the chapel. The fifth zone, into which one cannot progress, is the transformed nature which one sees through the totally glazed end wall of the chapel. The focal cross stands outside the building amongst the trees.

Reference for Knockanure church: World Architecture 2, 1965, p.74.

Reference for Finnish churches:
Egon Tempel – *Finnish Architecture Today*, 1968.

The 'nib' which houses the vestry helps to separate the nature through which one approached the chapel from the nature one sees from one's pew, the setting of the cross.

A number of Scandinavian architects in the late 1950s seem to have experimented with the parallel wall strategy. The next example is a cemetery chapel at Kemi (also in Finland) designed by Osmo Sipari and built in 1960. Here the two parallel walls are triangular in section, and the ceremonial axis of the cross and catafalque has been turned through 90 degrees to run across rather than with the longitudinal grain of the parallel walls. The entrance too, which relates to the cross, is in one of the walls rather than through one of the open ends of the parallel wall plan. There are two other significant walls in the plan: a third parallel wall which runs from within the chapel out into the garden; and one at right angles to the parallel walls, which connects the gate into the cemetery to the main door of the chapel.

The parallel wall strategy has been used in house design too. Because it allows extended repetition it is the basis of the terrace house, in which the place of each family is identified between two party walls.

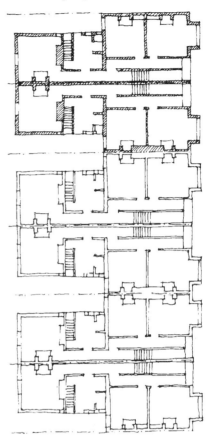

The American architect Craig Ellwood put two dwellings between each pair of party walls in this group of four courtyard apartments in Hollywood (1952).

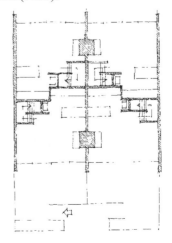

Reference for terraced houses:
Stefan Muthesius – *The English Terraced House*, 1982.

This low-cost house (right) was designed by Charles Correa for a hot climate. The use of parallel walls means that it can be almost endlessly repeated. The irregular section allows some more private upstairs sleeping accommodation, but with the openings in the roof, it also allows ventilation through the house.

In these examples of houses using parallel walls each dwelling unit has been accommodated between its own pair of walls. In the next two examples a single house occupies a number of intramural spaces.

The diagrams and drawings along the bottom of this and the opposite page illustrate a house in Switzerland designed by Dolf Schnebli, built in the early 1960s. The section through the house shows that its structure is composed of five barrel vaults supported on six walls. These walls form the structural order and the basis of the spatial organisation of the house.

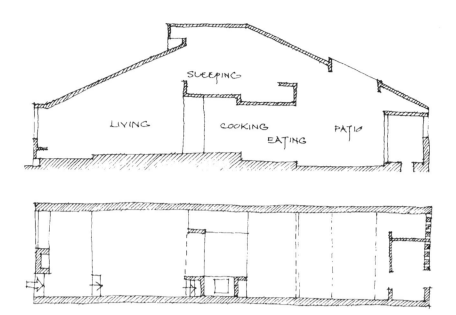

In the ancient tradition, each of the spaces between the walls is given a single directional emphasis by one end being closed with a cross wall. The other end is visually open, but sealed against the weather by a glass wall.

The places of the house are disposed within this armature of parallel walls. Some are accommodated between walls (the bedrooms for example); some stretch across more than one bay of space, necessitating the removal of some portions of the walls from the structural diagram. The hearth is positioned as an additional place identifier, across the structural grain. There is a terrace, also defined by the walls.

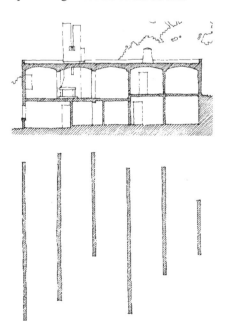

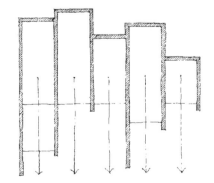

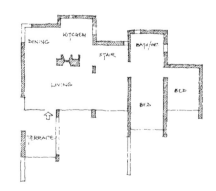

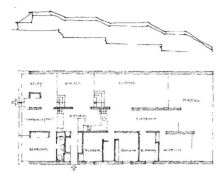

This parallel wall house was designed by Norman and Wendy Foster with Richard Rogers. In it the sense of movement from entrance to terrace is with the grain of the walls, which run down a sloping site. Here there are three zones created by the four walls: the zone for meeting people, which includes the study, dining room and living room; an intermediate zone for the conservatory, kitchen and playroom; and a private zone for the bedrooms.

Reference for Greek summer house: World Architecture 2, 1965, p.128.

Reference for Lichtenhan house by Dolf Schnebli: World Architecture 3, 1966, p.112.

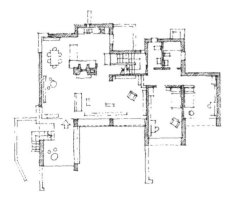

This house too uses more than one bay of space in a parallel wall plan. It is a summer house on a Greek island, designed by Aris Konstantinidis.

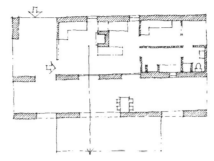

In this plan the implied direction runs across the grain of the parallel walls, that is from top to bottom on the drawing. The three walls are used to create four zones. The house stands on the coast. First there is the approach zone; then the living zone which accommodates the living room, dining room, kitchen, bedroom, and also the car port; then a shaded terrace; and finally the fourth zone which is open to the sea. In this house a reinforced concrete roof is supported on rough stone piers. The hearth divides the living from the dining places; and the pier by the entrance has been turned through 90 degrees to allow access for the car.

Some architects have experimented with parallel walls that are not straight, or with layouts in which a parallel wall strategy has been distorted.

The drawing to the right shows the plan of the ground floor of a student residential building in the City University which lies in the southern suburbs of Paris. It was designed for Swiss students by Le Corbusier, and built in 1931. It is called the Pavillon Suisse.

The rectangle of dotted lines indicates the block of accommodation which is lifted off the ground on massive columns. This block thus also forms a large 'porch' which protects the entrance into the building.

As one goes in there is a reception desk in front and to the right. Behind that there are the private quarters of the director, and an office. Past the reception desk is the common room. And to the left there is a lift, and the stair which leads up to the student rooms.

The plan of this part of the building is not rectangular. Its furthest extent is defined by a convex curved wall; and the stair seems to wriggle its way upwards rather than having a straight flight. At first the plan does not appear to conform to the parallel wall strategy.

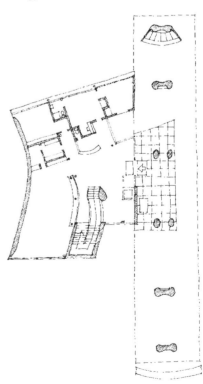

One can however reinterpret the plan as an orthogonal layout; this shows that the subtleties of Le Corbusier's plan seem to have derived from a distortion of a parallel wall layout. The drawing below shows the ground floor of the Pavillon Suisse 'straightened out'. In this version the block of student accommodation forms one of the parallel walls, and the wall at the left of the plan the other. Between them are other walls, framing the stair and the entrance, and dividing the rooms of the director's flat and office.

By comparing this straightened version with Le Corbusier's own plan, one can see what he gained by deviating from the parallel grain. This is an example of a subtlety of layout doing more than one thing at once. One effect is that there is more space for the private accommodation. Also the curve of the wall tends to turn the lines of sight of the private accommodation, and of the common room, away from the block of student rooms. In addition the reception desk is turned more towards the entrance, and the stair is given a more sculptural curved form in which lines of passage interact with lines of sight. Finally, Le Corbusier takes advantage of the curve to make a bench seat, along the glass wall of the entrance of the common room, more sociable.

Le Corbusier experimented with concave as well as convex deviations from the parallel. Earlier than the Pavillon Suisse, in the early 1920s, he designed a house for a Monsieur La Roche. It stands at the end of a *cul de sac* in northwest Paris. On its first

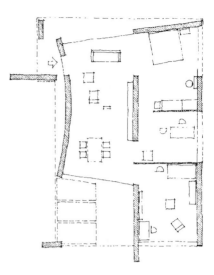

In this plan for a small house at the Bristol building exhibition in 1936, the architects Marcel Breuer and F.R.S. Yorke curved one of a set of parallel walls, in a way similar to Le Corbusier in the Pavillon Suisse (but maybe without the subtlety).

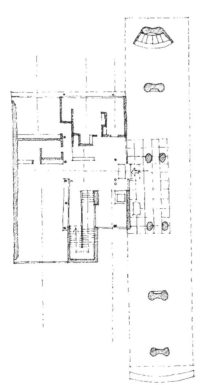

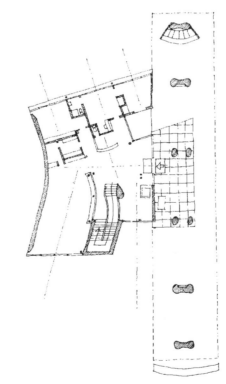

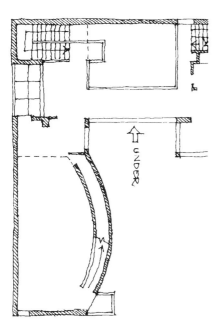

floor, supported above the ground on a short wall and three columns, he designed a gallery (left), in which Monsieur La Roche could display his collection of paintings. This room has one straight wall and one which is, from the inside, concave. Along the curved wall there is a ramp which leads up to the next floor. The curve of the wall and the ramp make the room more of a place to stop; it lies on a route – an 'architectural promenade' – which begins outside the house and finishes on a roof terrace, passing through the triple height hallway, up the stairs, into the gallery, up the ramp, to the library on the second floor, 'and out onto the roof terrace. The curved wall also plays a part on the outside, tacitly guiding visitors to the front door.

Richard MacCormac, in his design for a new library building at Lancaster University, dedicated to John Ruskin, has adapted the parallel wall strategy by curving the walls together at the ends to exaggerate their effect of enclosure and protection. Inside, more parallel walls channel movement through the building.

In a temporary sculpture pavilion in Sonsbeek Park near Arnhem in the Netherlands, built in 1966, Aldo van Eyck distorted the parallel wall strategy in another way.

Conceptually, he began with six simple parallel walls on a defined area of ground. Built of simple blockwork they were about 3.5 metres high and 2 metres apart, supporting a flat translucent roof. These walls set up a pattern of movement through the pavilion.

He disrupted this plan with openings and semi-circular niches, to create places for the exhibits, to allow more routes through the pavilion, and to open up lines of sight across the grain of parallel walls. The result is a complex frame for sculpture and people.

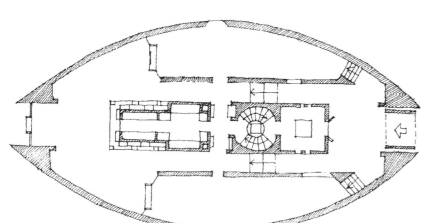

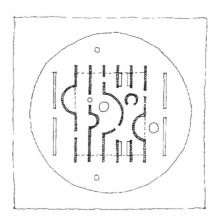

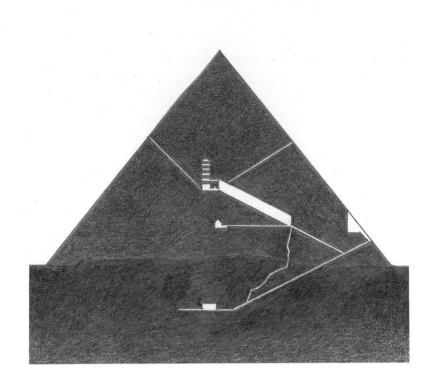

STRATIFICATION

STRATIFICATION

Human architecture would no doubt be different if we could fly freely in three dimensions. Because we walk and are held down by gravity, our lives mainly take place on flat surfaces, and architecture is concerned with the planning of floors. With this limitation in movement, human life and architecture have a particular emphasis in the two horizontal dimensions.

Some architects have accepted, or even celebrated, this emphasis by designing buildings in which movement and places are organised between strictly horizontal planes of platform and roof.

The German architect Mies van der Rohe celebrated the horizontal emphasis of human life in many of his projects. This is the plan of a 'Fifty-by-fifty' (foot) house which he designed in 1951, but which has not been built. The house consists of a square flat roof over a paved area.

The roof is supported in the most minimal way possible, on four columns, one in the middle of each side of the square. The walls are completely of glass.

All the spaces of the house are contained between these two horizontal planes; and the glass walls do not obstruct lines of sight in the horizontal dimensions.

It may be said that the Fifty-by-fifty house is a building of one stratum. It controls and organises a particular portion of the land's surface at ground level; it has no changes of level – no pits or platforms; there are no upper floors, or cellars excavated out of the earth.

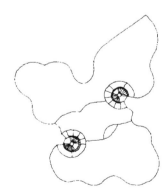

In 1922 Mies van der Rohe designed a skyscraper which, though the plan was irregular, was composed of many horizontal slices of space.

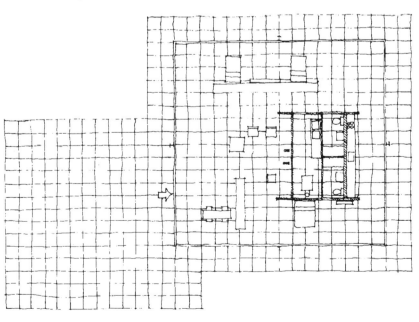

This is the section through a part of a small house designed by the Italian architect Marco Zanuso, and built near Lake Como in 1981.

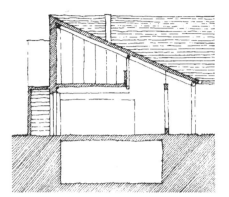

It has three strata, each with its own character. There is the ground level stratum, which has easy access to the outside; it has a stratum under – a cellar which is excavated from the earth and which probably has particular characteristics of darkness and coolness; and it has a stratum above – a sleeping gallery, which is secluded away from the ground floor, and has a sloping ceiling because it is directly under the pitched roof.

Stratification plays a part in the identification of place.

Below is a much grander house, in Kent; it too has three strata. This is a section through Mereworth Castle, designed by Colen Campbell, and built in 1725. (The plan of its main floor is on page 122.)

It has a lowest level of rooms which are partly above ground level, but this has some of the characteristics of a cellar – its ceilings are vaulted to carry the weight of the floors and walls above, and it is cool and not well lit.

The most important level is the one above, with the grandest rooms. This is known as a *piano nobile* – a 'noble floor' – which suggests that some sense of nobility was attached to its being above the level of the ground.

There is a strata of rooms above the noble floor, but you can see that this layer is penetrated to allow a dome over the space at the centre of the house.

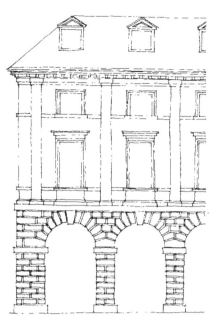

The strata of a building can often be seen in its elevation, but their different characters can also be experienced inside the building. The ground floor is accessible from outside; the upper floors are separate from the ground, perhaps more aloof; the character of the top-most floor is affected by the geometry of the roof, and perhaps by the availability of light from the sky.

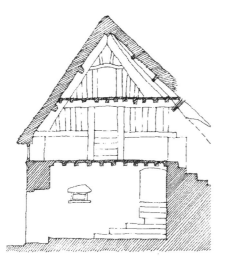

In Ernest Gimson's Stoneywell Cottage, there are almost two storeys within the structure of the roof. He wanted to reduce the scale of the house from the outside, and emphasize the importance of the sheltering roof.

In this part of the library of Uppsala University, there is a lecture theatre on the topmost level. In masonry structures it is easier to support large spaces over small ones than vice versa; the walls or columns of the smaller spaces can support the floor of the large.

Many buildings are stratified in similar ways. This is an agricultural laboratory designed by a Swedish architect – Fredrik Blom – in 1837.

It has a ground floor with its entrance, (and which at the far side becomes a first floor because of a change in ground level); it has a cellar, which seems excavated from the ground, and which has a structure appropriate to carrying the weight of the building above; it has a middle floor which has its own particular character – separated from the ground but not in the roof; and it has an attic where the shape of the space is affected by the geometry of the roof structure – in this case the triangular section of the roof has been translated into a curved ceiling.

There is similar stratification in this Italian farmhouse (right) designed by Giovanni Simonis. Each level has its own character: the vaulted lowest level; two middle levels, the upper with a jettied window seat under the eaves of the roof; and an attic within the roof. The levels are linked by the series of stairs, the angle of which seems to relate to the pitch of the roof, allowing the close relationship between the roof and the stair to the attic.

In the 1920s Le Corbusier radically re-evaluated the stratification of buildings. In his 'Five points towards a new architecture' (1926) he said that

buildings could have gardens on their roofs, and open ground floors.

Le Corbusier used these ideas in some of his house designs, and in other building types. In place of a garret would be a terrace open to the sky for sunbathing; in place of a cellar, or ground floor, a space open for free movement under the house.

Le Corbusier also experimented with the interrelationships between the

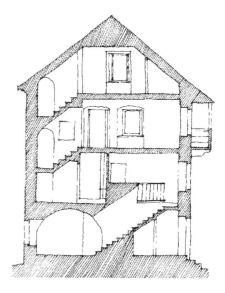

levels in buildings. In this small house for a site in Carthage, Greece, designed in the 1930s, he made the layers interlink. The roof terrace is shaded against the strong Greek sun.

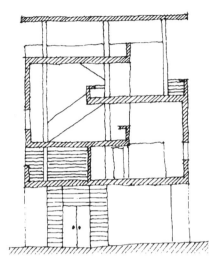

And in the *Unités d'Habitation*, some large apartment blocks he designed after World War II, the dwellings interlock with each other across the section of the building, and around a central access corridor. This drawing is through only a small portion of a block, which was designed to accommodate some 1600 people, together with community services.

Le Corbusier also recognised the greater freedom in the manipulation of space that an architect has on the top floor of a building. A lower level is restricted in that its 'roof' is often also the floor of the level above, and in that the possibilities of allowing light in directly from above are severely limited. On the top floor these restrictions do not exist (the 'above' is no longer hampered by the 'below' of a floor above); there is more opportunity for moulding space in the vertical dimension and using light from above.

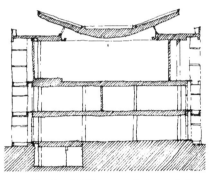

In the Millowners' Association Building for Ahmedabad (1954) Le Corbusier follows the structurally sensible convention that a large space is supported on smaller spaces below. This also allows the large space – the

By using rooflights and openings in floors, John Soane created spaces where light from the sky could penetrate into the lowest stratum. In some parts heavy glass floors allow light to filter down through the levels. This is a section through part of his own house; a place where kept his large collection of sculpture and architectural fragments.

Reference for John Soane:
John Summerson and others – *John Soane* (Architectural Monographs), 1983.

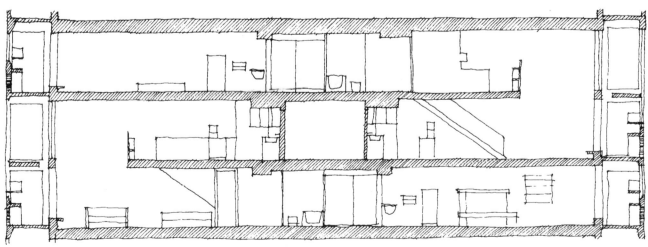

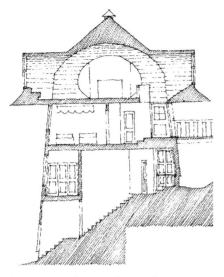

Sometimes the usual stratification can be inverted. In this house by Robert Venturi the attic is vaulted, as if it is supporting weight above, and the lowest floor follows the irregular geometry of the ground. The main entrance is at mid-level, over a bridge.

Reference for Venturi:

Papadakis and others, *Venturi, Scott Brown and Associates, on houses and housing*, 1992.

Reference for Schinkel:

Karl Friedrich Schinkel, *Collection of Architectural Designs*, (in facsimile, 1989).

discussion chamber) to be lit from above, through a convex roof (with the same freedom from the restrictions of floor above as the dome over the central hall of Mereworth Castle).

Associated with the 'temple' attitude to the identification of place (discussed in the chapter *Temples and Cottages*), is the idea of creating levels above the ground – worlds above the mundane. The stage for performance is an example of this; so is the *piano nobile*.

At the Schloss Charlottenhof, a villa built in 1827 in the extensive grounds of the Sanssouci Palace at Potsdam (near Berlin), Schinkel designed a terraced garden raised approximately three metres above the flat landscape around.

The garden is at the same level as the *piano nobile* of the house. The lower levels of the house were for the servants. The ascent from the mundane to the noble level is by a pair of staircases in the entrance hall.

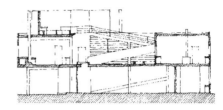

In the Villa Savoye, Le Corbusier created three main strata: a ground floor accommodating the entrance hall, the servants quarters and the garage; the first floor with the living and sleeping rooms, and with an open terrace enclosed within the almost square enclosure of walls; and a level above with a solarium for sunbathing. All three levels are linked by the ramp at the core of the house.

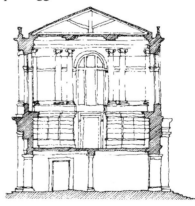

The library is a building type which in many instances has a particular stratification. Traditionally, for various reasons, libraries were built on a floor above ground level: to avoid damp (in days before damp proofing of walls); to increase security for the valuable books; and possibly also because their large spaces could be built over cellular rooms.

The library of Trinity College in Cambridge was designed by Christopher Wren and built by 1684. Wren followed the precedent of earlier college libraries by putting the library on the first floor, in this case over an open loggia.

The Bibliotheque Ste Genevieve in Paris, designed by Henri Labrouste, and built by 1850, is also on the first floor. The library has a steel vaulted ceiling, and is supported on columns and cellular rooms beneath. The library hall itself is reached by passing through the columned ground floor hall, under the books, to a pair of staircases at the rear of the building where one turns to face the opposite direction and then enter.

There is a sense, in approaching both these libraries (and the many other examples), that physically rising to a level above the ground is equivalent also to rising to a higher intellectual level. The sense seems to have been consciously intended by Gunnar Asplund, the Swedish architect, when he designed the Stockholm City Library, which was built in 1927.

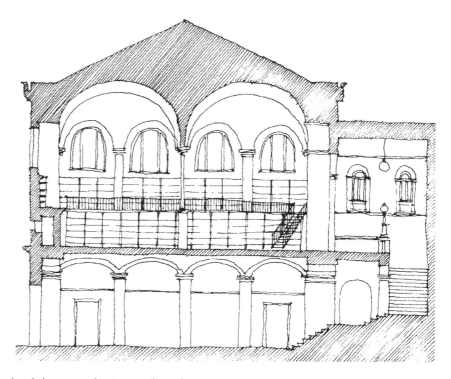

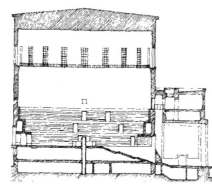

Here one enters up a staircase that emerges almost in the centre of the circular, and very high, library hall. The hall is lit by a ring of high windows which create rectangles of sunlight which slowly track across the white walls. The bookstacks are on three tiers around the circumference, each with its own walkway. The administration of

book issues and returns takes place at the centre of the floor.

In the Viipuri Library, Finland, designed by Alvar Aalto, and built in 1935, one rises through various levels of bookstacks. The children's library

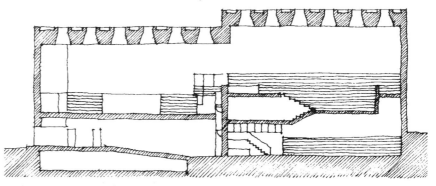

is on the ground floor, and the main bookstacks on three higher levels that gradually ascend under the high ceilings.

The upper floors are lit by an even pattern of circular roof-lights, with deep conical sides that reflect the light evenly through the spaces.

The Cranfield Institute Library was designed by Norman Foster and built in 1992. It too has the bookstacks on the upper floors, with the smaller spaces – a lecture theatre and some seminar rooms – on the ground floor.

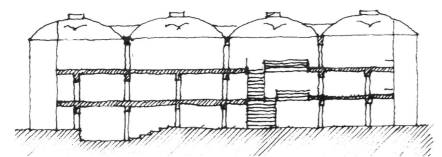

Like Labrouste's library, this is a metal-framed building with vaulted ceilings. Like Asplund's it has a staircase which rises through each floor. Like Aalto's it has a means of diffusing daylight through roof-lights to illuminate the spaces evenly. The number of columns is doubled on each of the lower floors to take the extra weight of the books.

The new National Archive in Paris was built in the early 1990s, designed by Stanislaus Fiszer. Its section shows a number of aspects of stratification. It has three principal strata, each of which has two levels. The entrance level has a central atrium, with a ramped stair which takes library users up to the higher levels. The offices and administration are also in this stratum. The lowest stratum, below ground, contains storage rooms. The upper floors are large, and take advantage of the possibility of being lit through the roof. On various levels Fiszer has used changes in ceiling height to help to identify different places, especially to suggest a separation between peripheral and central zones (this is done by suspended ceilings which conceal services), but it is only in the top stratum that he has the freedom to vary the sizes of the volumes of space significantly. The central reading room, lit by the sloping roof-light, is flanked by two levels which accommodate bookstacks, computer facilities, and so on.

The National Archives building in Paris has three strata, each of two floors. The lowest is below ground, and houses the stores. The middle stratum accommodates the entrance concourse and offices. The reading rooms, book stacks, and computer facilities are in the top stratum, where ceilings are free from the constraints of a floor above, and light can be admitted from the sky.

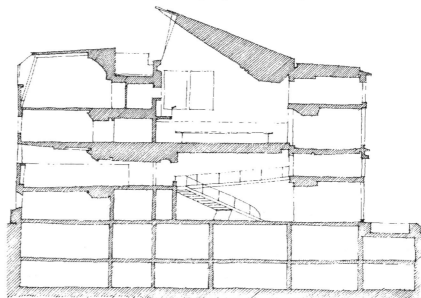

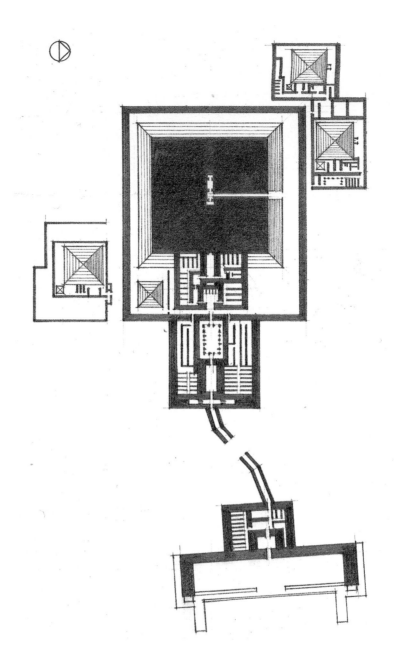

TRANSITION,
HIERARCHY,
HEART

A porch not only marks an entrance, it also identifies a place of transition between outside and inside.

The propylon is a building through which one must pass to reach the temenos of a Greek temple. This is the propylon on the acropolis in Athens; it marks the transition from the everyday world into the sacred area of the temples.

Opposite page:
An ancient Egyptian pyramid complex can be interpreted as a transition from life into death. There is a hierarchy of places from the river to the desert. The heart of the complex is the tomb of the pharaoh. The point of symbolic transition is the place where the mortuary temple meets the base of the pyramid.

TRANSITION, HIERARCHY, HEART

Experiencing products of architecture involves movement. One passes from outside to inside, or through the serial stages of a route. Even in a simple enclosed space it is not possible to look in all directions simultaneously, so one moves around.

One might tend to think of a place as somewhere one stops – a market square, a living room, an operating table. These may be called static places, or perhaps nodes. But the pathway one takes to get from one static place to another is a place too. One might call this a dynamic place. Dynamic places play an essential part in the conceptual organisation of space.

Dynamic and static places have characters that derive from the basic and modifying elements by which they are identified. The character of a static place might be affected by that of the dynamic places that lead to it; and the character of a dynamic place might be affected by that of the static place to which it leads. The experience of a corridor that leads to a cell in which there is an electric chair is affected by one's awareness of the place to which it leads. The experience of the burial chamber at the heart of one of the ancient Egyptian pyramids is affected by the nature of the route by which you reach it – penetrating the mass of the pyramid.

Even in quite mundane examples, transitions form part of the experience of works of architecture. The door of a house is a significant interface between the public and the private realm. Many religious sites have some form of gateway which marks the entrance: the lych gate of an English churchyard; the propylon through which one enters the temenos of a Greek temple; the gates and forecourt of a Chinese temple. All contribute to the effect that a static place – the hearth of a house, the altar of a temple – is set apart from the rest of the world.

Transition places are important in the ways that static places relate to each

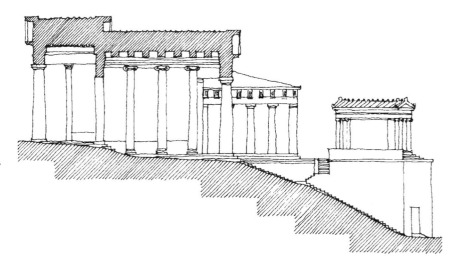

other. They play a part in the relationship between a place and its context. Often there is a sequence, or hierarchy of stages between one static place and another. When entering dwellings, for example, one usually has to pass through a number of different zones of increasing privacy. Sometimes this hierarchy or serial experience of places culminates in a place which is conceptually at the core of the work of architecture – its heart.

This is the plan of the palace of Tiryns in Greece. It was a hilltop citadel built more than 3000 years ago. If one begins at the top of the drawing one can trace a path through a hierarchy of places leading up to the most important, the king's throne room – the megaron.

From the entrance court, itself surrounded with thick walls, one would have passed into a long and narrow passage, through a couple of gateways, and then to a smaller court where there was the first of two formal propylons. Passing through this, one would have entered another courtyard, and then through the second propylon into the innermost courtyard, which seems to have been cloistered. Off this courtyard was the megaron itself; but to reach its hearth and the throne one still had to pass through a porch or portico, and then an anteroom.

This was not the shortest possible route from the entrance to the throne – one changes direction twice during the course of it. Perhaps it was made tortuous like this to lessen the slope of the climb up the hill; but it also

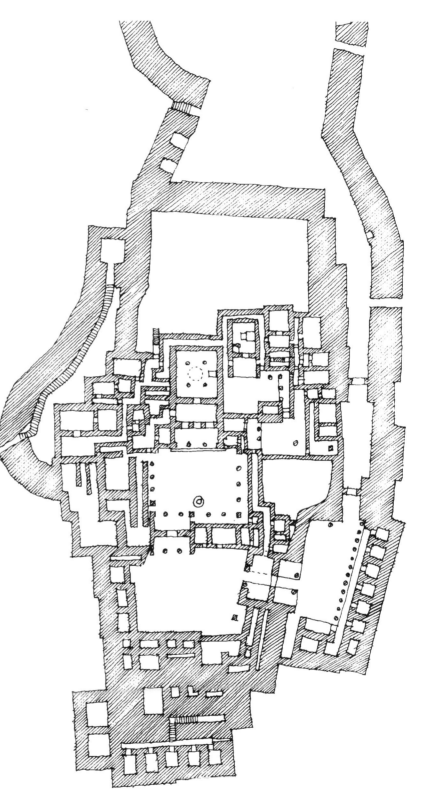

Reference for Greek architecture:
A.W. Lawrence – *Greek Architecture*, 1967.

158

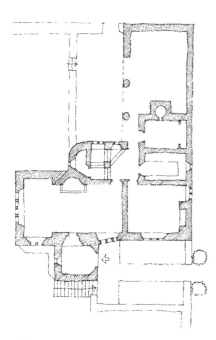

Reference for Gimson's house:
Lawrence Weaver – *Small Country Houses of To-day*, 1912, p.54.

made the heart of the palace seem much more deeply embedded in its body, and allowed the creation of a number of transitions, each of which could successively be defended in the event of enemy intrusion.

Transitions, hierarchies, and hearts can be found in less dramatic works of architecture too. The drawing on the left is the ground floor plan of a house that Ernest Gimson designed for himself at the end of the nineteenth century. It was built in the Cotswold village of Sapperton.

The main entrance into the house is from the right hand side of the drawing, from a village lane. The heart of the house may be said to be the hearth in the hall (living room), which is the largest room in the plan. To reach the hearth from the lane one passes first between two bushes (like sentinels), through a gate which is set in a waist-height wall, into a small entrance court, along a stone path which is flanked by flower beds, through an arch into the stone porch (there are some steps down

into the garden alongside it), through the front door which is set in a very thick wall (that actually supports a fireplace on the floor above), and into the living room. If the lane is 'public', then the entrance court is 'semi-public'; the porch is 'semi-private', and the living room is 'private'. This sequence of places and transitions creates a hierarchy from the public realm to the privacy of the interior. Each stage in this hierarchy is accounted for in the architecture that Gimson gave his house.

[One passes through a sequence of places when entering by the back door too: through a wall into a back courtyard where there is an open-sided shed whose roof is supported by two columns; the back door is tucked under this shed roof.]

At around the same time, Frank Lloyd Wright was designing the Ward Willits House, built in Highland Park, Illinois in 1902. As in the Gimson house, the heart is the hearth that in Wright's design lies right at the core of the plan. In this example the hierarchy of places between the public realm and the private includes the motor car. The route begins in the bottom right-hand corner of the plan. The car drives up to and under the *porte corchère* which projects out from the house over the driveway. Emerging from the car, under the shelter of the roof, one climbs three steps onto a small platform which leads to the front door; passing diagonally across the small hallway one climbs some more steps, and then turns sharp left into the main living room. The hearth, in a sort of ingle-nook, is

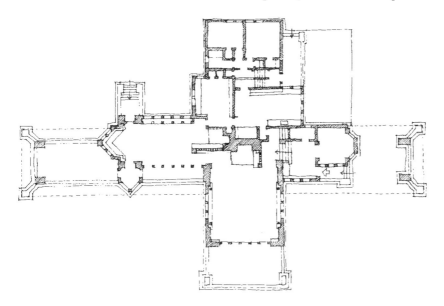

behind a screen which hides it from the entrance.

Transitions, and the hierarchy of places, draw out the passage from the public realm to the private. Often, as in the case of the Ward Willits house, the architect avoids the most direct route, so that the person approaching and entering the house can be 'led' through a progressive sequence of experiences.

Transitions also provide a buffer between one place and another, particularly between 'an inside' and 'the outside'. This may have practical benefits, such as when a draught lobby helps to insulate the inside of a building from a cold outside; but they may also have a psychological effect too, such as that between a busy street and the quiet interior of a church.

In 1953 Alvar Aalto built a summer house on the island of Muuratsalo.

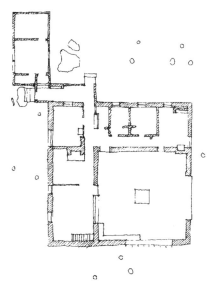

Its plan is a square enclosed by high walls. The living accommodation is ranged along two sides of the square, leaving a square courtyard. This court-

yard creates a transition between the interior of the human dwelling and the nature that surrounds it. The opening in the courtyard sets up a line of sight along the shore of the lake in which the island sits.

The ideas of transition, hierarchy, and heart do not only apply in the architecture of dwellings. They are used in works of architecture with different purposes. They may be very simple, or grand and complex.

This is the chapel of the President's Palace in Brasilia, Brazil, designed by Oscar Niemeyer, and built in 1958.

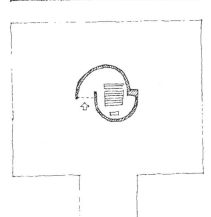

Its plan is very simple, but also subtle. The first basic element of the architecture of the chapel is a flat platform supported on stilts; this defines the circle of place of the chapel. On this simple platform, which is approached across a flat bridge, stands the altar. The altar is hidden from view and protected by a simple white wall that curves around it and rises to a pin-

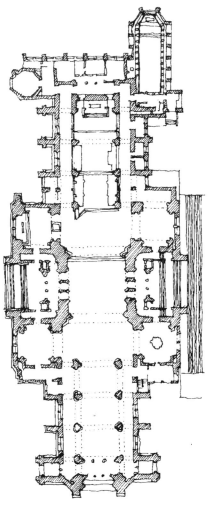

In his plan for Liverpool Cathedral, Sir Giles Gilbert Scott created a hierarchy of spaces between the outside and the sanctuary, designed to set the altar well apart from the everyday world. Like all medieval cathedrals, this building is a manifestation of transition from the secular world to the sacred.

Reference for President's Chapel, Brasilia:
Albert Christ-Janer and Mary Mix Foley – *Modern Church Architecture*, 1962, p.77.

Reference for Aalto summer house:
Richard Weston – *Alvar Aalto*, 1995.

Reference for Paris Opéra:
Nikolaus Pevsner – *A History of Building Types*, 1976, p.85.

nacle surmounted by a cross. This defines a more intimate circle of presence of the altar. The transition from the 'outside' to the 'inside' of the chapel is simple, but it includes various stages: crossing the bridge onto the platform; approaching the chapel; and going in, which must be like entering a shell – entry is progressive rather than immediate, and the modifying element of light, which enters through the door too, washes progressively more dimly on the curving wall.

The *Opéra* in Paris is a grander example. It was designed by Charles Garnier, and built in 1875. The section has been simplified to show only the major internal spaces. The heart of the *Opéra* is of course the auditorium – the tiers of seating, and the stage. The transition is from the everyday world of the city outside to a place where one is in the presence of the magic, or make-believe, of opera or ballet.

The first stage in this transition is the flight of steps at the entrance which immediately raises one onto a plane above the mundane. The second is the entrance through the thick walls into the first lobby. From here one can see through to the second lobby where there is the grand staircase. This space is richly ornamented and brightly lit. It is like a stage itself, on which the audience can display themselves before going into the auditorium for the performance. The proscenium arch is the ultimate transition.

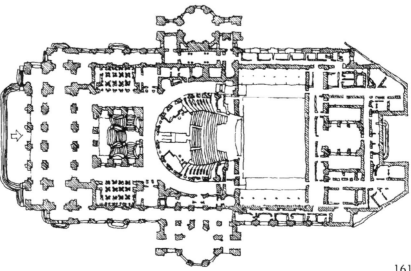

In the Paris Opéra there is a sequence of transitions from the street to the make-believe world of the stage.

POSTSCRIPT

POSTSCRIPT

The framework of themes in this book is not complete. There are many still to be identified; and probably an unlimited amount to be invented.

I am aware of some that I have not had space to include: the theme of 'datum place' – a place by reference to which one knows where one is; the theme of 'places made by excavation', rather than by building; the theme (related to transition, hierarchy, heart) of 'places between' – places within walls – zones between inside and outside which are not quite either; the theme of 'implied place' – that place is not always clearly defined by basic and modifying elements of architecture, but can be implied in minimal and subtle ways; and then there is the theme of 'non-orthogonal architecture' (which has only be touched upon here) – where orthogonality and the six-directions-plus-centre are denied or subverted.

There is more work that could be done on those themes that have been included in this book; each of them could be the subject of its own full-length study. There is more to do on the ways in which geometry contributes to identification of place; the subtleties of the parallel wall strategy have not been exhausted here; the philosophical and poetic ramifications of the 'temple–cottage' dimension need to be more fully explored.

One intention of this book has been to help to open this field of research, rather than to provide a comprehensive survey of it. The latter would be impossible anyway, because the boundaries of architecture are not known and there may not be any.

The key that let me into this field was the realisation that architecture is, before all else, identification of place. This is discussed in detail in the first chapter but, although it is not always mentioned, it can be seen to underpin all the others too: the purpose of basic elements is not just to be themselves, but to identify place; the effect of the different attitudes associated with the 'temple' and the 'cottage' is to identify place in different ways; the power of the six-directions-plus-centre is that they identify place; the purpose of organising space – by structure, by parallel walls, into stratified layers, or into hierarchies with transitions and hearts – is to identify place.

This is a key into architectural design as well as analysis. If one thinks of architecture as designing 'buildings', one designs in one way; if one thinks of it as identifying places, then one designs in another. The focus of attention shifts from tangible form to include inhabited space. In the latter, a 'building' is seen not as an end in itself, but as a means to an end.

This is not a new thought, but it remains a significant one. It can be found, in varying degrees of clarity, in most of the texts included in the list of supplementary reading given at the end of this book.

It is a thought that seems to require restatement from time to time, because it can be elusive, and also because it can be easily lost beneath a mound of seemingly more pressing concerns. The practise of architecture is so beset by constructional, contractual and commercial pressures that this silent and seemingly undemanding core of its 'reason for being' can easily be ignored.

Through history, other factors have helped push 'architecture as identification of place' down the list of priorities for concern. (These are in addition to the common tendency that people find it easier to think in terms of the tangible – i.e. buildings – rather than the intangible – e.g. places.)

First is the suggestion, implicit in a lot of architectural writing, that the word architecture can be reserved for a special class of building. This is contained in Nikolaus Pevsner's famous assertion, 'A bicycle shed is a building; Lincoln Cathedral is a piece of architecture'. To think like this might be satisfactory for an architectural historian, because it relates to a quality of buildings as perceived, but it throws definition of the activity of architecture into turmoil.

In thinking of architecture as identification of place one is on firmer ground: both the bicycle shed and the cathedral are architecture, though of different character and quality; the shed identifies a place for storing bicycles, the cathedral a place for worship. The people responsible for both are architects, though one of them may be better at it in some ways than the other.

Thinking of architecture as iden-tification of place, everyone is to some degree an architect. Setting out the furniture in a living room is architecture; so too is laying out a city. The difference is only a matter of degree, and at different scales there are different levels of responsibility.

The legislative bodies in some countries rule that the responsibilities of building – in that they involve contractual problems and spending large sums of money – should only be handled by people with particular qualifications which make them professionals. In some cases, the United Kingdom included, the title 'architect' is protected by law. But there is another justification for architecture being a profession, which can be understood by thinking of it as identification of place. It is architects who, by definition (whether or not they are legally entitled to the name), organise the world into places for life and work. This is a responsibility which is on a par with medicine, law, religion. There is a level where everyone deals with their own concerns (as in health, dispute, and spiritual belief), but there are also levels where matters can be complex and require the education, experience and commitment of people who accept professional responsibility.

A second factor which has pushed 'architecture as identification of place' down, has been a conscious fascination, in some strands of architectural theory, with its contrary – the idea of 'placeless' architecture. There is not space here to follow this strand in detail, but it was recognised and described by Oswald Spengler in his book *The Decline of the West* (1918), as a preoccupation with 'the infinite'; it was evident too in Mies van der Rohe's interest in 'universal space'; and it has been brought to realisation in many 'anti-street' urban developments. In 1931, the Swedish architect Erik Gunnar Asplund gave a lecture in which he illustrated one such development, declaring triumphantly that 'PLACE GIVES WAY TO SPACE!'

The third factor which has worked against 'architecture as identification of place' has been technology, partly because people tend to focus more on how buildings are built rather than on what they do in identifying places, but also because many primitive place types have been made redundant.

The 'hearth' is no longer an essential place in a home; heating is provided by a boiler perhaps kept in a cupboard and heat distributed through pipes and radiators. From its heyday in the time of the pharaohs, the 'tomb' has plummeted to almost total irrelevance in the repertoire of architecture. The 'market-place' was superseded by the shop, but even that is under threat from telemarketing and the Internet. Most significantly perhaps, the pulpit, the look-out and the stage have been overtaken by television, which allows politicians to preach into people's living rooms, viewers to see great distances (even to the moon and outer planets of the solar system), and performances to be watched from almost anywhere.

Related to this is the enormous increase in the prevalence of the framed image. As has been said in the chapter *Architecture as Making Frames* the two-dimensional image of a work of architecture, set as it usually is within the four sides of a frame, does not allow one to experience it as a place or series of places. This is true of a painting, or a photograph, a film, or a television image. Even if the picture presents the illusion of three dimensions, even if it includes movement, it diminishes the experience of place. Even so, these images are perhaps the most common ways in which the products of architecture are viewed; there are only a limited number of buildings that each of us can actually experience; the vast majority – especially those which architects are urged to emulate, by critics in the press – are seen as framed images. This has the effect of reinforcing the perceived importance of visual appearance in works of architecture (and even pictorial composition), further undermining the importance of place identification.

It is probably true to say too, that architects involved with large projects worry more about whether the roof will leak (or similar matters to do with the performance of the fabric of a building), or whether they will lead their client into some expensive legal battle (against themselves perhaps), than about whether they are making good places; at the least such worries must seem more immediate, and have more potential to give architects personal problems or spoil their lives. Concerns about construction, about performance, about legal and contractual matters, can easily occupy all of an architect's time, leaving none for issues, which can easily (but wrongly) be disregarded as worthless, of identification of place.

Hearths, tombs, shops, schools, libraries, museums, art galleries, meeting rooms, places of work, offices... all are challenged by developments in technology which complicate and confuse issues of place. But this is not to say that the idea of place is no longer relevant.

Architecture, like language, is always changing; new types of place emerge while others become redundant. Architecture now has to take account of: places for televisions, for computers, for skate-boarding; airports, cash-dispensing machines, motorways; none of which existed in ancient times. And there are still many primitive place types that are still relevant: places to sleep, to cook, to eat, to walk, to grow plants, to meet people, and so on.

*   *   *

These are all points which indicate something of the nature of the theoretical ground on which the present book stands. But its main purpose has been to show that architecture, its products and its strategies, can be subject to analysis within a consistent conceptual framework.

This is not to say that the whole framework is understood, nor even that the framework is finite in its extent. Nor is it to say that all the themes that have been described and discussed in this book are relevant to every work of architecture that has been achieved, or applicable to every new work of architecture that will be proposed.

Indeed it is apparent that different movements in architecture through history, and different individual architects, have had different preoccupations in their works. Within the creative field of architecture different themes may be given different weights, independently and relatively. One architect or movement may concentrate on the relationship between space and structure; another might stress the ways in which social geometry influences the organisation of buildings, and give the ordering power of structure a lower priority; one might exploit the powers of the six-directions-plus-centre, where another might see them as best subverted; one might seek to concentrate on the modifying elements of architecture – light, sound, touch, where another might be more interested in the formal powers of the basic elements – wall, column, roof. The variety of permutations is endless.

Architecture is not a matter of system, but of judgement. Architecture, like play-writing, composing music, law-making, or even scientific investigation, is subject to drive, vision, and interest. It is a creative discipline that accommodates varying views on the interactive relationship between people and the world around.

Architecture is, because of this, a political and a commercial field too. It is political in that there are no 'right' answers and 'wrong', but answers which find favour, and those which do not; 'favour' lies with those who have the most powerful voice. It is commercial in that the products of architecture have to survive in a consumer market – a new building is like a newly launched product; whether it succeeds or not depends on whether or not its 'customers' 'like it'. And this leads into the debate about who architecture's 'customers' are.

Despite the unnerving complexity and uncertainty of the conditions within which it is done, architecture as a creative discipline is susceptible to reasoned understanding.

If one considers architecture not in terms of material *things* (objects, buildings) – not as a catalogue of formal types, or a classification of styles or technologies of construction – but

in terms of frames of reference for *doing*, (which is another term for the themes or 'filters' in this book), then it is possible to build a framework for analysis which is consistent yet not restricting; one that allows the creative mind to learn from the works of architecture of the past, and to generate ideas for the future.

Architecture should not be limited by classifications that deal only with what *is* or *has been*; there will always be potential for new ways of identifying places. Architecture's vitality depends upon invention and adventure, but any field of human endeavour – music, law, science – needs a base in knowledge that can be presented to students of the subject as a foundation upon which they can build and develop. Architecture is no different.

CASE STUDIES

References

Peter Blundell Jones – 'Holy Vessel',
in *Architects' Journal, 1 July 1992,*
p.25.
'Dreams in Light',
in *Architectural Review, April 1992,*
p.26.

CASE STUDY ONE - FITZWILLIAM COLLEGE CHAPEL

The small chapel at Fitzwilliam College in Cambridge, UK, was designed by the British practice MacCormac Jamieson Prichard, and built in 1991. It is a clear and understandable building which illustrates a number of the themes discussed in this book.

Identification of place

The chapel has been attached to the end of a wing of the existing college accommodation (designed by Denys Lasdun in the 1960s). It faces a large tree (which was already there) almost in the centre of the rectangular college grounds. The circle which outlines the plan of the chapel identifies a place which enjoys a particular relationship with this tree.

The fundamental purpose of the building was to establish this place as a place of worship. It has done this 'first' by cupping the place between two brick walls curved around like protecting hands; these form a cylinder which contains the chapel.

Basic and combined elements

The principal architectural elements of the chapel are *wall, platform, aedicule, focus, cell, column* and *glass wall.*

The platform is the main floor of the chapel (see the Section, on the next page). Being raised it makes the chapel interior feel apart but, because of the glass wall that faces the tree, not separate from the land outside.

On this platform is the aedicule – apparently composed of four pairs of columns arranged at the corners of a square. The columns in each pair are structurally separate: the inner four columns support a central square flat roof; the outer four support a secondary pitched roof which spans between the outer walls and the roof of the aedicule.

The focus of the aedicule is the altar, a simple table covered with a red cloth.

Below the platform there is the cell – a crypt-like meeting room totally secluded from the outside world. Its

Plan of main floor

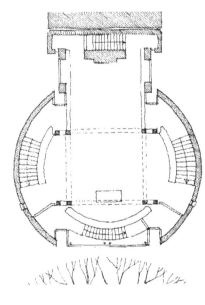

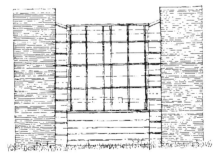

Elevation

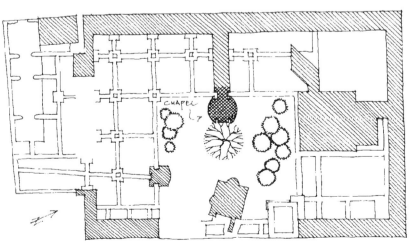

Site plan

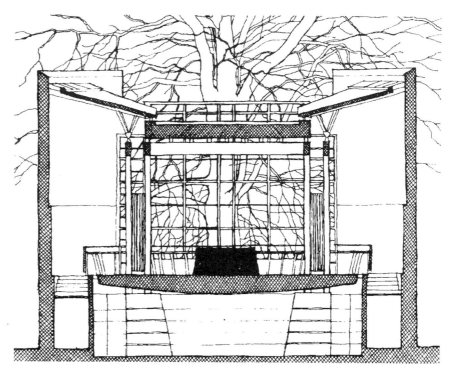

floor level is slightly lower than that outside. Within this meeting room, and enhancing its crypt-like quality, the structural supports of its ceiling, which align with the columns of the aedicule in the chapel above, appear as heavy masonry piers – battered as if to suggest they need to spread a heavy load – providing a strong and visible foundation.

The platform, the aedicule above with its altar, and the cell beneath, are all enclosed and protected by the two curved side walls, arcs of the circular plan. The open end, between these two walls, is the large clear glass wall through which the tree can be seen.

Though there are many subtleties, the building makes simple and direct use of these elements. Each seems to fulfil its timeless purpose: the *walls* enclose and protect; the *platform* raises a special place above ground level; the *aedicule* frames a specific place – that of the altar which is the *focus* and heart of the building; the *cell* separates a place from everywhere else; the *columns* act structurally bearing the loads of floor and roof, but also help to define space; and the *glass wall* allows in light and is certainly for looking through.

Modifying elements
• light

In the morning sunlight streams into the chapel from the east through the branches of the tree and the large window.

In both the chapel and the 'crypt' there are narrow perimeter rooflights

that allow light to wash down the walls: softly on overcast days, and with a pattern of sharp shadows when the sun shines. With the changing light and slowly moving sun patterns the interior is never quite the same twice. At night the lights inside turn the chapel into a lantern or lighthouse.
• colour

By contrast with the harsh purple brick on the outside, the inside colours are soft and warm. This image of a warm interior is further reinforced at night when the inside light and colour contrasts with the darkness. The altar cloth has the warmest colour.

Elements doing more than one thing

The platform is a floor and a roof; and the glass wall allows both a view out and makes a lantern at night.

The aedicule defines the main chapel space and the place of the altar, but it also helps to create four subsidi-

This section is drawn facing the tree. You can see the platform (which has a curved under surface) supporting the aedicule in the chapel above, and supported by the piers in the meeting room below. The altar stands on the platform in front of the large east-facing glass wall. You can also see the gaps at the perimeter of the roof and around the edge of the platform floor, which allow light to wash down the walls of the chapel and the meeting room.

170

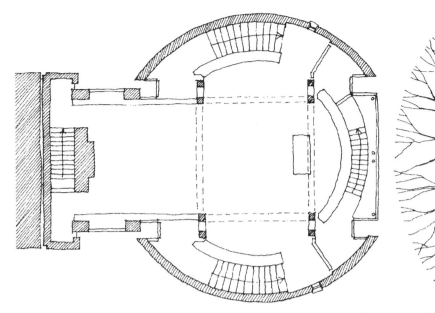

Plan at chapel level, showing the square aedicule and the four subsidiary spaces it helps to make: the place of the two stairs from the entrance; the place of the priest's stair rising under the glass wall from the meeting room beneath; and the place of the organ at the rear of the chapel.

Plan at 'crypt' level, showing the entrance, and the four piers which support the floor of the chapel.

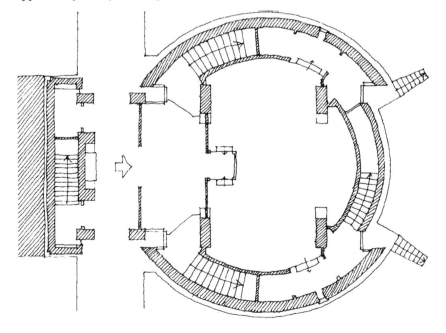

ary spaces: the place of the organ (at the rear of the chapel); the places of the two stairs which curve up from the entrance below; and the place of the priest's stair up from the 'crypt'.

The inner walls which are the boundaries of the crypt, and which define all three stairs, also form the bases of circumferential seating in the chapel.

As in any building there are many other things doing more than one thing at once: the spaces between each pair of columns accommodate the vertical radiators; the organ is housed in a wall which also contributes to the enclosure of the chapel, and defines the place of another stair.

Using things that are there

The chapel uses the end of the existing wing as an anchor; it uses the tree as a companion. But it also uses, and exploits, the place between the two which previously lay dormant.

Primitive place types

The chapel identifies a place of an altar together with its associated place for worshippers. There are many precedents for such 'primitive' places being bounded by a circle or aedicule; here it is both.

Architecture as making frames
• 'outside-in' framing

The chapel sits in the frame made by the other college buildings and their gardens. The circle of the building itself is a frame for worship. Within, the seating on the circumference is a frame within that frame; the aedicule is a frame within a frame within a frame; the altar is a frame within a frame within a frame within a frame... like 'Russian Dolls'.
• 'inside-out' framing

The glass wall frames a particular view of the tree, as an abstract picture, but also making a link between the internal space and nature outside, (rather like the *Student Chapel* at Otaniemi, where the cross is an external focus).

171

Temples and cottages

Architecturally as well as in purpose the chapel is a 'temple'. The aedicule stands on a platform above the natural ground level. The form of the chapel is geometrically disciplined; its materials are carefully finished. And although it is attached to an existing building and relates to the tree, it does not submit to either. The building's one submissive characteristic is perhaps its use of bricks which match those of the older building.

Circles of presence

The chapel creates its own circle of presence, which houses the altar with its circle of presence, and which responds to, and exists within, the circle of presence of the tree. Through these overlapping circles one may carry one's own.

Six-directions-plus-centre

Inside the chapel the six directions are defined by the six sides of the cubic geometry of the aedicule.

The *lateral* directions are blocked by the side walls. The direction to the *rear* loses itself in the area of the organ; the *down* direction is the floor and the 'crypt' beneath (see the Villa Rotonda by Palladio), the presence of which one is reminded of by the stairwells.

The two directions which hold greatest importance in this chapel, as in most traditional religious buildings, are the *up* and the *forward*: the forward passes through the altar and the glass wall to the tree and the rising sun be-

yond; the vertical – the *axis mundi* – though not strongly emphasised by the architecture of the building (there is no spire, or vault, or cupola), is simply implied by the coincidental axes of the cylinder of the outer walls and the cube of the aedicule; this centre, together with the four horizontal directions, is recognised, but undemonstratively indicated, by a faint cross of pairs of parallel lines inscribed across the ceiling of the aedicule.

Social geometry

Like the *Woodland Chapel* by Asplund in Stockholm (*Case Study Five*) the internal shapes of both the chapel and the meeting room recognise and establish the social circle.

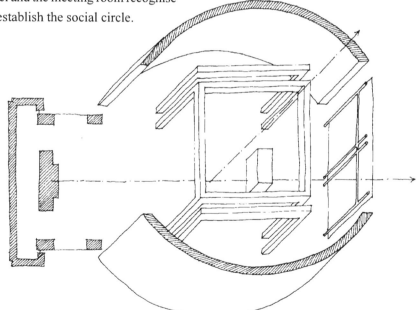

This is a simplified three-dimensional drawing of the chapel space; it does not show the staircases up from below. It does show the position of the aedicule between the two curved side walls, and the two main directions: the up and the forward.

Space and structure

The principle structural elements of the chapel – the frame of the aedicule and the flank walls – are also the principle space defining elements.

In the 'crypt' the space is defined by the four structural piers. The space is also defined by the curved walls of

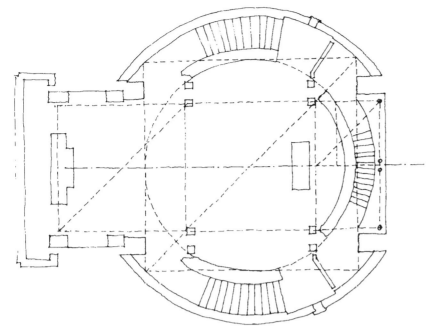

The form of the chapel seems to hang on an armature of geometric shapes and volumes. In the plan you can see a pattern of squares and circles.

The geometric arrangement of the section is not so simple, but you can still extract lines which appear to regulate the shapes and positions of elements.

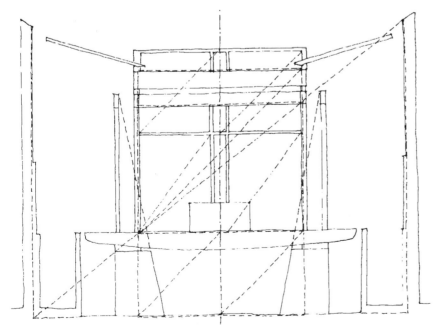

the three sets of stairs, which are not roof supporting.

Ideal geometry

Although it is sometimes difficult to establish exactly which ideal geometric shapes and volumes an architect used in determining the form and disposition of a building, it is clear that the Fitzwilliam Chapel is organised on a conceptual armature of circles and squares, cylinders and cubes.

The aedicule is a central cube, which is extended by half a cube towards the tree, and a full cube to the rear, making the organ place. On plan, the central square of the aedicule (which laterally is measured to the centre-lines of the columns, and longitudinally to their outer faces) sits within another square, one-third larger, which determines the radius of the curved walls; and a circle subscribed within it seems to determine the positions of the four outer columns of the aedicule and the radius of the circumferential seating and rail behind the altar.

(As in the Villa Rotonda), the geometry of the section is not as clear and simple as that of the plan. The central cube of the aedicule is there, but it is not a purely spatial cube – its height is measured from the platform floor to the top of the upstands around the flat roof.

The square of the aedicule in section is extended downwards as half a square to determine the height of the 'crypt', though again this includes the depth of its roof – the platform.

There appear to be some other alignments: the angles of the batters on the piers in the crypt seem to align with the tops of the outer columns in the chapel above; and the angle of the slope of the capstones on the side walls seems to derive from a long diagonal line through the section, from the notional bottom corner, through the base of the inner aedicule columns on one side, and through the top of the aedicule columns on the other.

Transition, hierarchy, heart

For such a small building the transition from outside to inside is elaborate. This accords with the idea that holy spaces should be reached through 'layers of access' (as suggested by Christopher Alexander in 'Pattern 66' of *A Pattern Language*).

The route follows an *architectural promenade* through a hierarchical arrangement of spaces, and culminates in the chapel itself, where there is a view of the outside from which one has come; (comparable with the 'window' on the upper roof terrace which is the terminus of the architectural promenade through the Villa Savoye).

To get into the chapel one first goes under the link between it and the existing wing of college accommodation. Thus the way in is provided with an integral protective 'porch'. (This was intended to have been part of a covered walkway, following the line of the innermost pathway on the site plan, creating an inner courtyard garden for the college. The walkway has not been built.) Through the entrance there is a vestibule with the door to the meeting room opposite. One rises into the chapel up either of the two stairways which run just inside the curved walls. In this way one emerges into the chapel, not on its main axis, but at either side.

Parallel walls

Notwithstanding the circular plan and the related arcs of the side walls,

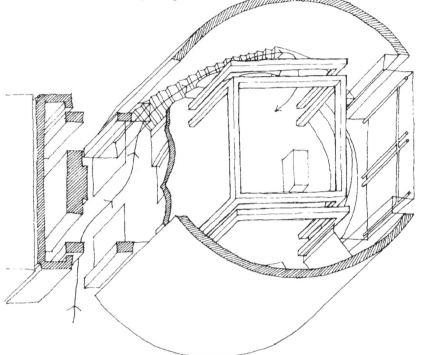

the chapel has some of the characteristics of the architecture of parallel walls.

A comparison has already been made with the Student Chapel by Siren and Siren at Otaniemi. In both it is the side walls that identify and protect the place of the chapel; in both, these act like blinkers blocking the lateral directions and framing a particular view; in both, one's passage through and into the chapel transforms one's view of the outside world. But whereas in the Otaniemi chapel (where the chapel is not lifted on a platform) the drift of movement runs longitudinally along one of the walls, here the dynamic is an upward spiral – or rather a pair of spirals running in counter directions, up each of the staircases onto the raised platform.

CASE STUDY TWO - THE SCHMINKE HOUSE

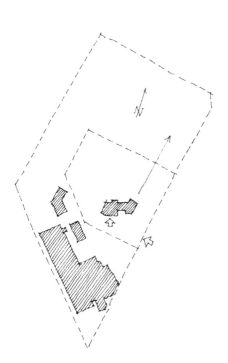

Reference

Peter Blundell Jones – *Hans Scharoun*, 1995, pp.74-81.

The Schminke House was designed by Hans Scharoun, and built for the German industrialist Fritz Schminke in 1933. Schminke owned a noodle factory in Löbau, close to the border with Czechoslovakia. The house was built on land to the north of his factory.

Conditions

The site available for the house was generous in size. The adjacent factory lay to the south, and the best views were to the north and northeast. (This of course set up a conflict between sun and views.) The land had a slope, though not a dramatic one, from the southwest down to the northeast.

Scharoun was designing at a time when the new architecture promoted by Le Corbusier and others in the aftermath of the First World War was an exciting prospect. In 1923 Le Corbusier had published *Vers Une Architecture*, in which he celebrated (amongst other things) the beauty and adventure associated with ocean-going liners.

Scharoun had been a contributor to the *Weissenhof* housing exhibition in Stuttgart in 1927, alongside Le Corbusier, Mies van der Rohe, Walter Gropius, and others.

The use of large areas of glass and of steel as a structural material were well-established, and some architects – Le Corbusier in particular – had been experimenting with the free-planning that framed structures made possible (for example in the 'Dom-Ino' idea of

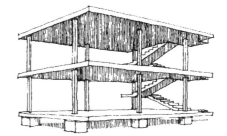

1914 and in the Villa Savoye of 1929), and the reduced division between inside and outside which large areas of glass allowed. The development of central heating had also made planning less centred on the hearth; and electric lighting had been available for some years

Scharoun had an adventurous and wealthy client who seemingly wanted a house which manifested his forward-looking, 'modern' mentality. Mr Schminke would have had one or two resident servants.

Identification of place

Scharoun's task was to identify places for all the mixed activities of dwelling: eating, sleeping, sitting being sociable, bathing, cooking, playing, growing plants, and so on.

Basic elements

The basic elements which Scharoun employed were, primarily: the platform, the roof, the wall, the glass wall, and the column. Most important of these are the two horizontal platforms and the roof, between which all the internal spaces of the house are contained, and which also form the terraces at the eastern end.

Other basic elements used include: the path, only clearly defined when in the form of staircases and in the landing on the upper floor; the pit, which identifies the area of the conservatory; and the canopy which identifies the place of the main entrance. There is a hearth which is a focus, though not a particularly imposing one, in the living area. Also, the chimney stack to the central heating boiler, at the western end of the house, acts as something of a marker, though possibly Scharoun wanted to play this vertical element down, against the prevailing horizontality of the platforms and roof.

Although these basic elements combine to form the house in its setting, Scharoun seems to have tried, for the most part, to avoid the traditional combined elements of enclosure and cell. These are found only where unavoidable: in the maid's bedroom, the sanitary provisions, and in the children's bedrooms. Elsewhere, in the main living spaces, and in the master bedroom at the eastern end of the house, the cell is not used; such enclosure being negated by the use of glass walls.

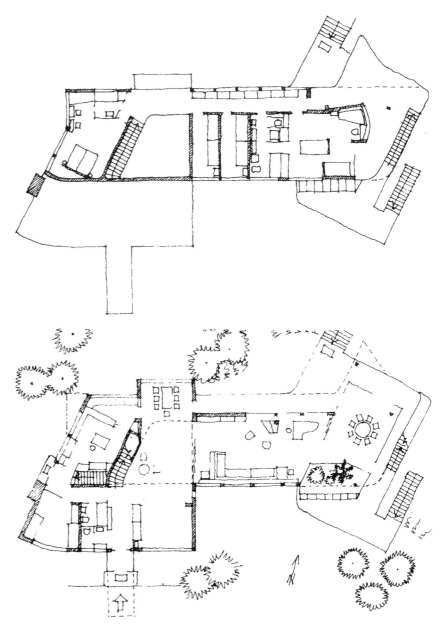

Modifying elements

The most important modifying element in the Schminke House is light. It has been carefully planned with sunlight and views uppermost in the mind of the designer. Also, the provision of electric light has been very carefully thought about, and used precisely to identify different places in the house.

The views and the sunlight exert opposing forces on the house. To the south of the site, in the direction from which the sun shines, is the less attractive prospect – the factory. The better views are to the north and northeast. Scharoun tackled this dilemma by allowing the sun's light into the building through the south-facing walls, part of which is formed into a conservatory, but also orienting the living spaces towards the views, through glass walls on the northern face of the house. On both of the main living levels of the house he projected decks out to the north (the pointed deck on the upper level is particularly distinctive), seemingly designed to catch the summer evening sun from the west.

The lighting plan shows the care with which Scharoun used different kinds of electric light to help identify

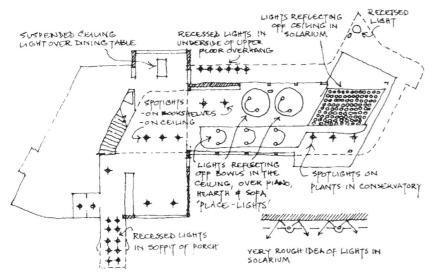

different places within the house. He designed light fittings especially to achieve a variety of effects; some of them he actually called *Platzleuchte* – place-lights. (Two photographs, reproduced in the book on Scharoun by Peter Blundell Jones, show the great difference in the character of the living spaces in sunlight and at night, and the dramatic effect of the different kinds of electric light used by Scharoun.)

Elements doing more than one thing

The house contains the living places, but it also acts to divide the site. Its angle creates an entrance area off the access road; and its mass separates the factory from the garden.

Inside, the main internal stair and the hearth in the living space are two distinctive examples of elements used by Scharoun to do more than one thing at once.

The stair between the entrance level and the upper level of the house is situated just opposite the main entrance. It has a slight change of direc-

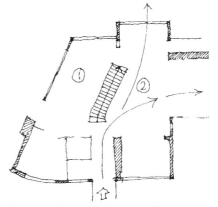

tion, curving on the bottom three steps. The primary purpose of the stair is obviously to make a pathway, a link for moving between the two levels. It is also used as the main part of the physical separation between the service end of the house (1) and the living parts of the house (2). The stair also does a third, more subtle, thing: its precise position and its angle on plan work to 'nudge' people entering the house to the right – i.e. towards the living places.

The hearth in the living space performs its timeless purpose as a focus, but it also acts as a divider between the piano place (2) and the living area (1).

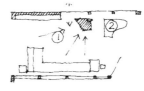

Using things that are there

Scharoun used the views to the north and northeast to help in the organisation of his plan. But probably the most effective thing he used that was already there was the slope of the land. The effect of this is most appar-

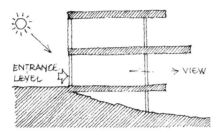

ent at the important east end, which accommodates the principal living spaces. The slope allowed entrance into the house not at the lowest level (the traditional ground floor), but at the intermediate level, rather like boarding a boat. It also meant that, although one enters at ground level, without rising up steps or a ramp one finds oneself, once one has reached the eastern end of the house, a storey above ground. This effect is further exaggerated on the upper level – on the 'prow' outside the master bedroom, where one may survey the rolling land from a commanding height. The most frequently encountered photographs of this house show it like a small modern pleasure boat at its moorings.

Primitive place types

The house contains, but does not seem to celebrate in traditional fashion, the usual primitive place types one finds in any dwelling.

There is a hearth in the living area (which plays the various roles men-

tioned above) but it does not seem to be the *raison d'etre* of the living spaces; there are other, more interesting architectural things going on.

Architecture as making frames

Like any house, the Schminke House frames the lives of its inhabitants. It does this in particular ways.

It emphasizes the horizontality of those lives, with its division into three pronounced horizontal levels which relate to the landscape around.

It doesn't enclose those lives in a protective carapace; its platforms and roof protect them from the sky, but the transparent sides make them open to the horizon.

And its allusion to ships and sailing seems to suggest that the house is a vessel rather than a cell; accommodating adventure and change through time and space, rather than security in enclosure and stasis.

Temples and cottages

Three particular characteristics of the Schminke House belong to the 'temple': its separation of the living spaces from the ground level at the eastern end of the house; its use of highly finished materials; and its apparent arrogance in the face of climatic forces (Scharoun was no doubt depending on the central heating to make up for the heat lost through the large areas of glass, and on modern materials to prevent the flat roof from leaking).

Otherwise the house exhibits some 'cottage' characteristics: its responsiveness to site – sun and ground;

In the lower of these two drawings you can see (reading from left to right) the distorted circles of presence of the dining table, the hearth, the piano, and the table in the solarium. It also shows the lines of passage which thread between and through them.
The upper drawing shows the principal lines of sight in the plan. Notice that they follow three principal directions: one set up by the main entrance; another by the living area; and a third, at an angle, by the main stair and the solarium.

and its thorough relation of planning to purposes.

Although in this house there is an underlying armature of orthogonal geometry (a 'temple' characteristic) it is Scharoun's responsive attitude – to sun, to site, to views, to function – that twists this geometry into an irregular plan form. Though this results in a sculpturally interesting form, particularly at the picturesque east end of the house, Scharoun was not motivated solely by a desire to make form or paint pictures with his architecture.

Thus Scharoun's plans exhibit subtle conflicts between different kinds of geometry.

Geometry

First, there appear to be no instances where Scharoun has allowed the shapes of his spaces to be determined by ideal geometric figures, no circles, no squares, no rectangles with particular harmonic proportions.

Dismissing ideal geometry as a way of making decisions about the positions of things, his conflicts seem to have been between the geometries of being and of making. To these were added his perception that the site had within it two different grains.

One of the most obvious characteristics of the house is that it is not a simple, orthogonal form. The geometry of making is not given the highest priority, but is allowed to be distorted by other pressures.

These other pressures begin with the circles of presence, distorted as they are in most instances into rectangles of presence, and with the social geometries which constitute the various places in the house: the dining place, the place around the hearth, the place around the table in the solarium (at the extreme east end of the main living floor).

Next there are the lines of sight, within the building, and also from the inside to the outside. Scharoun seems to have seen the latter – the views – as being at an angle to the lie of the land which set the datum for the general grain of the house.

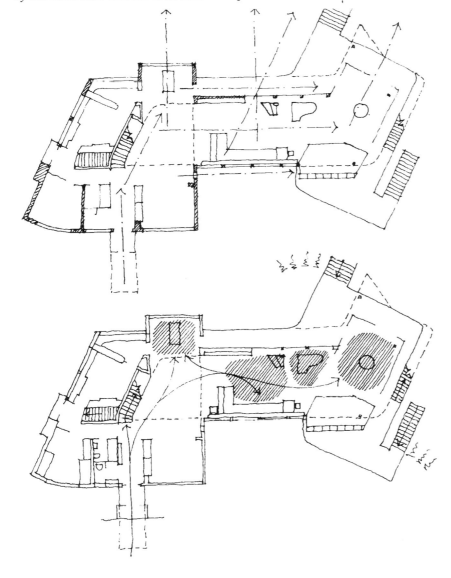

This overlaying of the different geometries, with a refusal to submit to the geometry of making, produced a distinctive response to the six-directions-plus-centre. The plans of the house have two overlapping grains. The 'up' and the 'down' direction are, at most positions, contained by the horizontal platforms and the roof. But with the four horizontal directions, the situation is more complex.

Taking the entrance as the starting point one is aware of the 'forward' and of the 'rearward'; one is also, as one enters, very much aware of the 'right', but the 'left' is diminished, being replaced by the deflection of the stair, (in the way already mentioned,) to reinforce the 'right' direction.

At the other end of the house, at the solarium, something different happens with the four horizontal directions. Here it is the 'forward' (roughly to the north) which is deflected, to focus the space more on the better views.

The house has no one centre, but a number: the hearth, the dining table, the table in the solarium, ... It seems that for Scharoun the most important centre was the mobile person.

Space and structure

The structure of the house is a skeleton of steel frame. Its columns are not laid out on a regular grid, but respond to the complex attitude to the six-directions mentioned above.

At the east end of the house the vertical structure – the columns – are reduced to a minimum to increase the openness of the spaces. Even so they

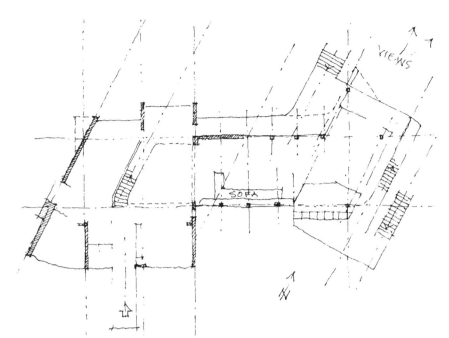

still contribute to the identification of places.

There is a column in the solarium which seems to help to identify its extreme corner; there is another on the deck outside which supports the prow above, and which also makes a 'doorway' between the deck at the top of the steps down to the garden and the narrower deck outside the solarium; and there is a third column in the conservatory, about which Scharoun seems perhaps to have been less happy – it looks as if he tried to camouflage its structural identity by painting it with small

In this drawing you can see the complementary grains of the house. They distort the simple geometry of making to take account of the alternative grains suggested by the lie of the land, the views, and the direction of the sun.

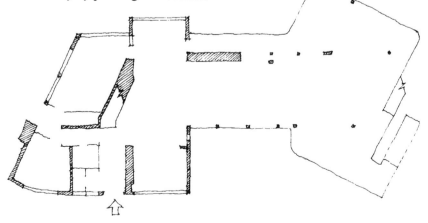

squares of different colours, making it into an elemental sculpture (as distinct from a place identifier) amongst the cacti.

At the other end of the plan the spaces are more definitely enclosed by walls and windows. The boiler chimney stack, at the extreme west end of the house is built of brick – a weighty contrast to the apparent levitation of the decks at the other end of the house.

The static places in the plan tend to be at the extremities: the dining area; the solarium; the conservatory; the bedroom and the prow of the deck on the

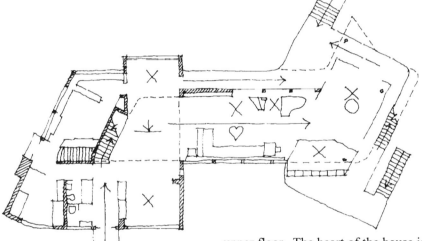

upper floor. The heart of the house is probably the living area, with its static focus the hearth. In some circumstances however, this heart also works as a dynamic space, a route from the hallway, which is the datum place of the house, to the solarium. Other, clearer dynamic spaces are the stairs, the deck outside the piano place, and the corridor landing on the upper floor.

The canopy over the main entrance begins a process of transition from outside to inside the building. This process of fairly abrupt enclosure

is reversed by the progressive openness of the rest of the house.

Scharoun was adept at making zones between the inside and outside. There are the various decks on both levels, which create an intermediate zone which is neither inside nor wholly outside. There is the conservatory too, an inside space which also, unlike the majority of spaces in the house, has contact with the sky. And there is the solarium itself, which is a space more open than the living room but less so than the decks – a zone between the two.

The dining area, not quite a zone between, is defined by the overhang of the landing above. It is at one end of what looks to be the remnants of a parallel wall space, which sets up an axis into the countryside through the broad window over the dining table.

On the upper floor the layout is more cellular, until one comes to the master bedroom which insinuates itself amongst a composition of planar walls, mostly arranged orthogonally, but with one wall slightly skewed to broaden the view to the northeast. This one piece of wall obeys neither of the two grains

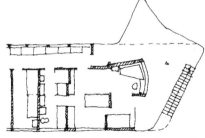

set up on the main living floor beneath; its 'freedom' is due to the independence of the two floors allowed by the 'Dom-Ino' idea.

The house is clearly stratified. There is an undercroft dedicated to the services of the house – the boiler room etc. The entrance floor, in the middle, is at one end a *piano nobile*. The upper living floor, further from the ground, is the sleeping floor, its contact with the sky manifest in the deck prow outside the master bedroom which, in the summer, basks in evening sun.

Postscript

The Schminke House was the last house that Scharoun designed before the Nazis in Germany imposed restrictions on the styles in which architects could work. Unlike some of his Modern contemporaries Scharoun chose not to leave Germany. He designed a number of houses during the Nazi years, each with the outward appearance of traditional cottages. Scharoun expressed his rebellion against Nazi constraints covertly, by continuing to explore the potential of the non-orthogonal organisation of space into places. These are the plans of his Baensch House, which dates from 1935, two years after the Schminke.

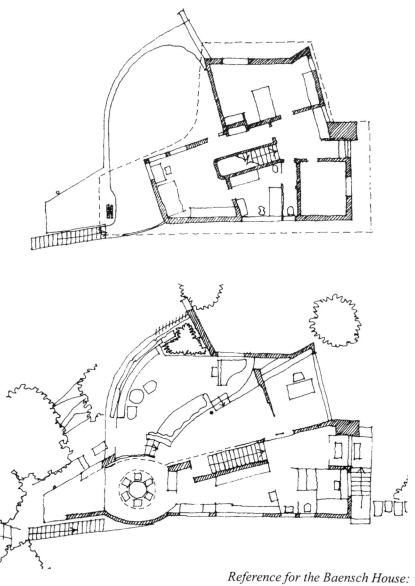

Reference for the Baensch House:
Peter Blundell Jones – *Hans Scharoun*, 1995, p.13.

Reference for Merrist Wood:
Andrew Saint – *Richard Norman Shaw*, 1976, pp.112-113.

CASE STUDY THREE - MERRIST WOOD

Merrist Wood is an English Victorian house, designed by Richard Norman Shaw, and built at Worplesdon in Surrey, in the mid-1870s.

I shall not look at every aspect of this house, nor even at the house as it was built, but at an early version of the floor plan of the house, for a comparison can be made between this and the floor plan of the Schminke House (*Case Study Two*) which illustrates some crucial differences between nineteenth-century and twentieth-century 'Modern' organisation of space.

Merrist Wood was built in the Old English style for Charles Peyto Shrubb, who would have had a body of servants.

In designing it Shaw thought primarily in terms of load-bearing walls; as distinct from the 'Dom-Ino' idea which was available to Scharoun fifty years later. Shaw did not have central heating available as an option.

The plan of the house as built clearly shows the consequences of these conditions. The rooms are mostly cellular. The hall, which is at an angle to the rest of the plan, is a double-height space, with a tall bay window looking down a slope into the garden and across the landscape. All internal space is compartmentalised into these cells, and apart from at the porch to the main entrance there is, on this ground floor, very little exploration of the zone between inside and outside.

A small courtyard allows light into the centre of what would otherwise be a deep and dark plan.

Windows are generally mullioned holes-in-walls. The nearest Shaw comes to creating a glass wall is the large bay window in the hall.

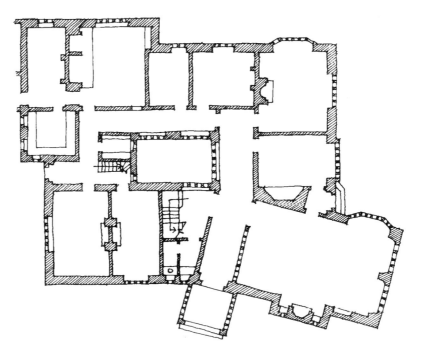

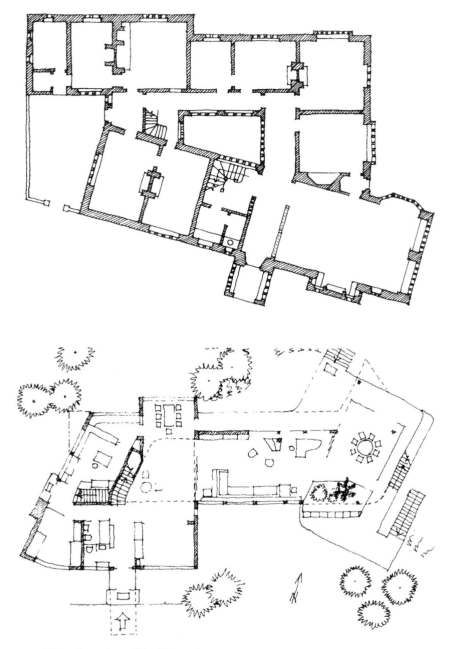

The plan of a previous version of this house is additionally interesting because it shows the whole of the front portion of the house set at an angle. It is this version that can be compared with the plan of Scharoun's Schminke House. (This is not to suggest that there is a direct historical connection between the two designs; though Merrist Wood was mentioned in Hermann Mutthesius's book *Das Englische Haus,* 1904, which publicised in Germany the virtues of late nineteenth-century English house design, of which Scharoun would have been aware.)

In both plans the servants' accommodation is set to the left, with its own entrance, and separated from the living spaces by the main stair to the upper floors and the ablutions. In Merrist Wood the servants' accommodation is larger, occupying at least fifty per cent of the ground floor area.

The most notable comparison between the two plans however is the juxtaposition of two grains set at an angle to each other. In the Scharoun plan the angle between the two main sections of the house is about 26 degrees; in the Shaw plan about 29 degrees. Rather like the Schindler plan (The Falk Apartments, 1943) discussed in the chapter on *Elements Doing More Than One Thing*, Shaw manages to condense all the difficulties which might arise from using two orthogonal grids at an angle to each other, into an odd-shaped servants' stairwell, the non-rectangular light courtyard, and a small link between the hall and the drawing room.

The orientation of the Shaw plan, with the sun and the view in the same direction, is approximately the opposite of that of the Scharoun plan.

Though both used two orthogonal grains or grids as the bases of their plans, the distinct difference between the ways in which these were used is that whereas Scharoun overlaid

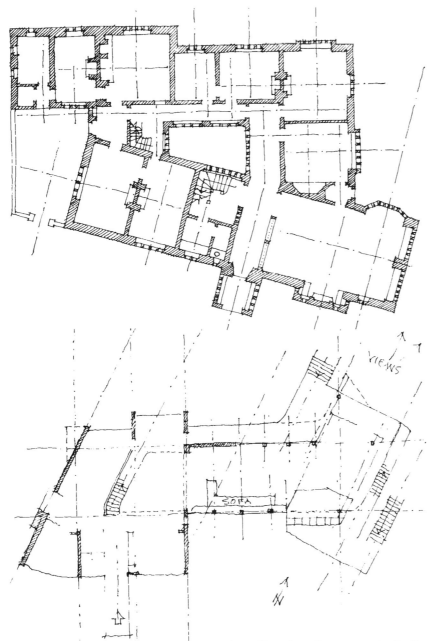

The comparison between these two plans illustrates a great deal about the difference between Modern and Victorian space planning. Both houses had similar though not identical briefs. Their site conditions were similar, even though the orientation was opposite. The places that the two architects had to identify were more or less the same: servant accommodation; living space; morning space; eating space. Both architects were concerned about light and views.

The differences between the ways in which they planned their houses were influenced by differences in the technologies available – frame structure versus load-bearing masonry; central heating versus hearth; glass wall versus hole-in-wall window – and by a more adventurous attitude (on the part of Scharoun) to the use of the various kinds of geometry.

This is not to suggest that Shaw was always content to accept the constraints of load bearing masonry structure on his organisation of space. Here

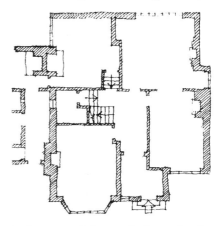

them, Shaw kept them separate. Partly, if not mainly, this difference is a consequence of the greater planning freedom allowed to Scharoun by the frame structure, and of the greater flexibility in lines of sight allowed by the glass wall. Shaw, by contrast, working fifty or so years earlier, was restricted to using the cell, window, and load-bearing wall.

is the ground floor of a house he designed for Kate Greenaway, the Victorian children's author. On this floor,

185

and the floor above, the house is fairly conventional in its structural layout.

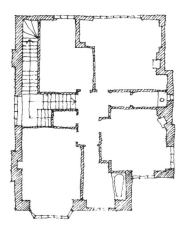

But on the top floor, where he wanted to provide his client with a studio lit from the northeast, Shaw allowed his space planning to contradict the structural geometry of the lower floors.

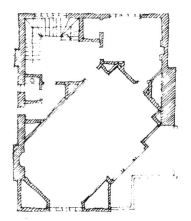

Even though diagonally set against the orthogonal grain established on the floors below, this studio remained largely a cell, closely bounded by its own four walls.

In other houses, however, Shaw explored how the structural authority of the load-bearing wall might be breached to allow a more flexible moulding of space.

On the right is part of the ground floor plan of an unbuilt house designed for F.W. Fison. Linking the main entrance with the grand hall of the house there is a structural wall (double-hatched in the drawing) which along its length changes its character a number of times. It starts as a barrier between the entrance passage and the butler's room – an interface between the staff quarters and the hallway; then it crosses the stair hall, adding to the sculptured quality of that space; after becoming an orthodox wall with two mullioned windows, and then an archway to a rectangular bay window, it terminates as an external buttress.

And at Dawpool (1882, below) Shaw repeatedly allowed 'bubbles' of space to penetrate the structural walls of the rooms, breaking their rectangles, and inhabiting the zone between inside and out.

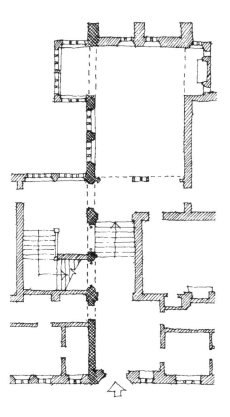

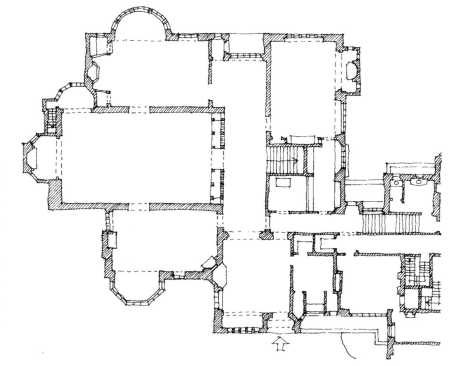

Reference for Vanna Venturi House:
(Venturi) – *Venturi Scott Brown & Associates, on houses and housing* (Architectural Monographs No. 21), 1992, pp.24-29.

CASE STUDY FOUR - VANNA VENTURI HOUSE

Robert Venturi designed this house for his mother. It was built at the prevailing orthodoxies of the Modern Movement, questioned them, and

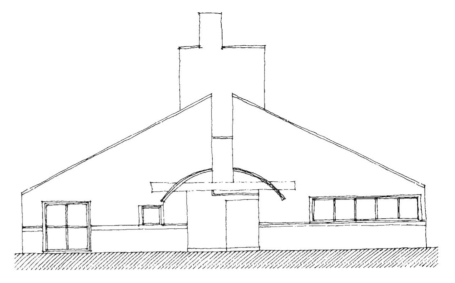

Chestnut Hill, Pennsylvania, in 1962. At about the same time, he was writing a book called *Complexity and Contradiction in Architecture*, which was published in 1966. The design of the house is related to the argument of the book.

rebelled against them. His arguments are set out in detail in his book. In general he rejected the quest for simplicity and resolution associated with Modernism (arguments for which are found particularly in the writings and works of Frank Lloyd Wright, Mies van der

The site of the Vanna Venturi House is flat. Around its boundaries it is enclosed by trees and fences. It is entered through a neck of land, and the house is positioned to present its gable elevation to the approach.

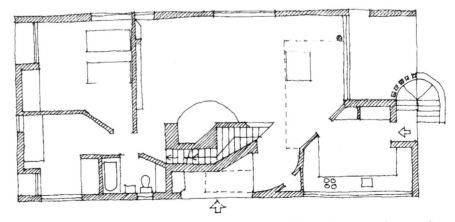

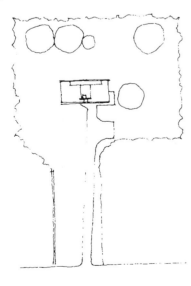

Conditions

At the time of both the house and the book the teaching and practice of architecture were dominated by Modernism. Venturi, rather than accepting

Rohe and of Louis Kahn), in favour of complexity and contradiction, which he argued made products of architecture more witty and less boring; more appropriate (poetic) reflections of the complexities and contradictions of life, and more stimulating, intellectually and aesthetically.

Venturi used the design of his mother's house to express through architecture his reaction against the orthodoxies and seriousness of Modernism. In it he consciously avoided what might be considered 'right answers', and contrived conflicts in the arrangement of forms and the organisation of space.

Basic elements

Even in his choice of basic elements Venturi expressed his reaction against Modernism.

The distinctive palette of elements used by orthodox Modernist architects included: the flat roof; emphasis (externally) of the horizontal floor; the column (*piloti*), allowing the opening up of the ground level and 'free planning'; and the glass wall, which reduced (visually) the cellular division of space internally and between inside and outside. Modernist architects also tended to play down the formal importance of the hearth, and of its external expression in the chimney stack. (Scharoun used this palette in his design for the Schminke House, *Case Study Two*.)

In his mother's house Venturi directly contravened every one of these 'rules' of Modernism. The roof is pitched; the horizontality of the floors is not expressed externally; there are no columns (except one – an expedient to hold up the roof over the dining area, and which is omitted in some pub-

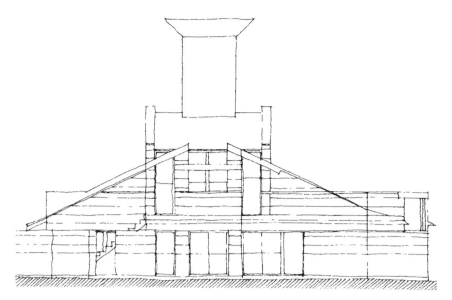

lished plans of the house), and the house is firmly set on the ground; there is a glass wall (between the dining area and a covered terrace) but in the main elevations Venturi prefers to make windows (almost caricatures of traditional windows) in the walls; he also gives significant emphasis internally to the central hearth, and externally to its chimney.

Space organisation and geometry

There are quirks in Venturi's design which are well-discussed elsewhere in critiques of this house: his 'mannerist' touches (the broken pediment of the front elevation for example); his (counter-Modern) use of ornament (the appliqué 'arch' superimposed on the clearly structural lintol over the entrance); the 'ingrowing' bay-windows in the downstairs bedrooms, and verandah off the dining area; the stair going up to nowhere from the upstairs bedroom; and so on. But Venturi's attitude of complicating and contradicting orthodox ways of doing things is perhaps most architectural (in the terms set out in this book) in his

In this early version of the Vanna Venturi House, the chimney stack is even more prominent than in the built version. In his architecture Venturi borrowed ideas from historical examples; he took the idea of prominent chimneys from British domestic architecture (of the Arts and Crafts and Edwardian period, and from the eighteenth-century work of John Vanbrugh) and from similar houses in the United States. Venturi was also interested in conflicts of scale: in this version the chimney is 'too big' for the house; in the final version (on the previous page) the chimney appears to be both 'too big' and 'too small'.

188

spatial organisation of the house and in the ways in which he deals with various of the sorts of geometry.

The design of the house 'begins' with two parallel walls, which define the area of ground of the inside of the house.

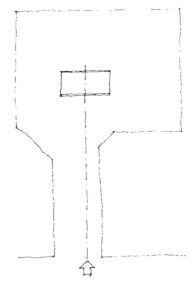

In positioning the house, Venturi lays the parallel walls across the main axis of the site.

As discussed in the *Parallel Walls* chapter, these tend to establish a longitudinal axis which sets up a dominant direction within the plan and also begins to order relationships between 'inside' and 'outside'. But Venturi contradicts the orthodox architecture of parallel walls in a number of ways.

First he positions the walls perpendicular to, rather than parallel with, the principal axis of the site, which is the axis of entrance (left).

Then he contradicts the arrangement of gables found in ancient parallel wall buildings (temples), by placing the gables of his complex roof

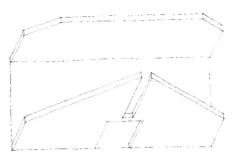

on the long sides of the rectangular plan. In ancient temples it was the geometry of making that influenced the three-dimensional geometry of the roof, resulting in triangular pediments

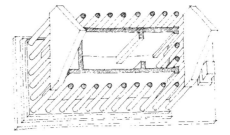

at each end. Venturi's contradictory arrangement, together with his avoidance of columns, results in the 'front' of his mother's house being like a pediment on one of the 'wrong' sides of the rectangular plan, and resting directly on the ground.

As can be seen in the sections (below), the geometry of Venturi's roof

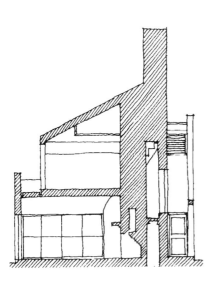

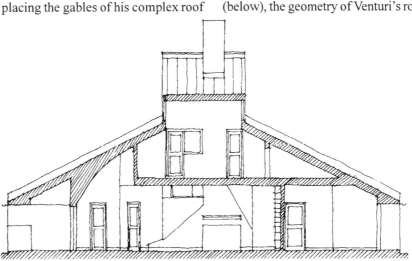

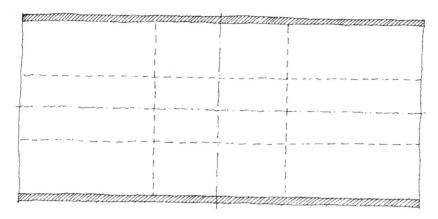

is complex: there are slopes in three different directions; it doesn't always reach the walls that 'should be' its support. (This happens over the entrance, and at the 'ingrown' balcony outside the upstairs bedroom, and reinforces the sense that these very two-dimensional walls are 'masks', screening rather than expressing the inside – another counter to the Modernist suggestion that barriers between inside and outside should be broken down.)

Venturi's contradiction of orthodoxy informs his plan too.

In his own explanation of the house in *Complexity and Contradiction in Architecture*, Venturi describes his plan as deriving from, but a distortion of, 'Palladian rigidity and symmetry'.

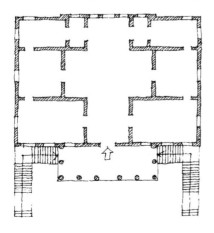

As Rudolf Wittkower has shown in *Architectural Principles in the Age of Humanism*, Palladio's villa plans, whether square or rectangular, were generally arranged according to a division into three in both directions; they were given a dominant central space, surrounded by subsidiary rooms. (Bottom left, for example, is Palladio's Villa Foscari.)

If Venturi's design had followed these Palladian arrangements, it might have turned out something like this:

If he had adhered to Palladian principles, the plan of Venturi's house might have been like this.

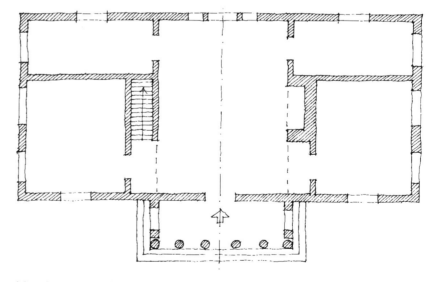

with a large room in the middle, and secondary rooms arranged symmetrically at the sides. There might have been a portico protruding at the front. Windows would, as far as possible, have been arranged symmetrically within rooms. The staircase and fireplace might have occupied equivalent positions in the two halves of the plan.

Venturi broke this Palladian discipline in various ways, establishing and then destroying symmetry; creating then denying axes.

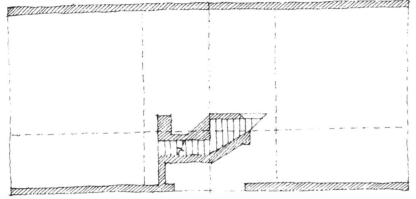

The fireplace and the stair compete for space with the entrance...

... and partition walls distort Palladian geometry to accommodate different-sized spaces.

The contradictory 'move' that he appears to make first (above), is to bring the stair and the fireplace together, and to position them centrally so that they block the axis of entrance. In the Palladian plan that axis would be open, as a line of passage leading into the main central space (and maybe also as a line of sight out into the surroundings). Venturi, having set up the axis, denies it with solid.

This 'move' does other things too. It creates a porch, but one that recedes into the building rather than projecting out from it.

It also gives Venturi another opportunity for complexity by setting up a situation in which entrance, stair and fire all vie to occupy the same part of the plan. The orthodox form of each is changed in some way in response to this (contrived) 'competition' for space: the fireplace is moved off axis to allow room for the stair; the stair is narrowed half-way up conceding to the chimney stack; and Venturi makes the entrance doorway, which itself has been usurped from its axial position, 'push' the adjacent wall to an angle that nudges into the stair.

The angle of this wall seems intended to acknowledge the line of passage into the house, now made diagonal, mitigating slightly the blocking effect of the stair and fireplace. The line of passage is further managed by the quadrant curve of the closet wall, turning an axial Palladian line of entry, into a chicane.

Elsewhere in the plan (left) partition walls are positioned both to accord with and to distort Palladian orthogonality. The wall between the living room and the bedroom (to the left on the plan) is at a right angle to the parallel walls, whereas the walls which run across the plan, which help delineate the small bedroom, the bathroom, entrance, and kitchen, are afflicted by a spatial warp, seemingly caused by the position of the stair and fireplace.

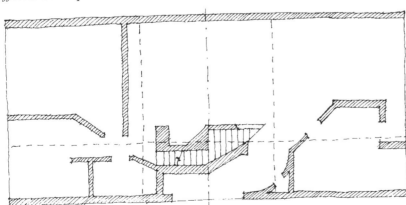

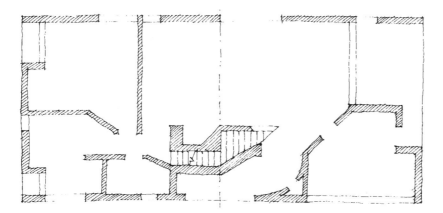

Venturi breaks a classical rule of architecture by positioning a window so that its edge, rather than its centre-line, aligns with the axis of the house. Another window has the end of a partition wall intruding into it.

Finally, the positioning and nature of the window and door openings presents Venturi with more opportunities for architectural contradiction.

A Modernist use of the parallel wall strategy would probably make a clear differentiation between the characters of the 'ends' and the 'sides'. In Craig Ellwood's design for example,

(below) the end of each apartment is fully glazed, and there are no openings in the side walls. In the Maisons Jaoul (bottom) by Le Corbusier openings in the side walls are clearly such, while the end walls are screens.

Venturi refuses such clarity, putting a mix of types of opening in each elevation of the house.

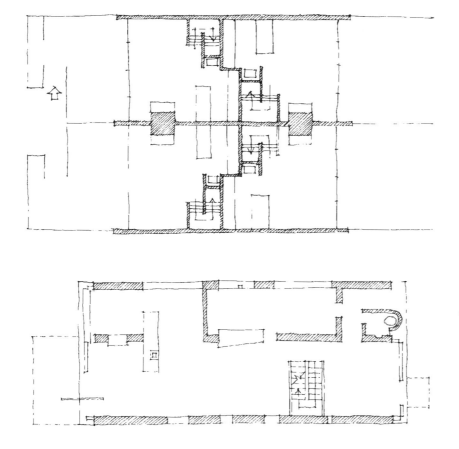

In these apartments designed by Craig Ellwood (above), and in the Maisons Jaoul by Le Corbusier (one of which is shown below), the nature of the interface between inside and outside is very different at the ends of their parallel-wall plans from the sides. The ends tend to be glass walls, and the sides walls with windows in them. Venturi, in contrast, mixes the two types of wall on all four faces of his mother's house.

Reference for The Woodland Chapel:
Caroline Constant – *The Woodland Cemetery: towards a spiritual landscape*, 1994.

CASE STUDY FIVE - THE WOODLAND CHAPEL

The Woodland Chapel stands in the extensive grounds of the Woodland Crematorium, on the outskirts of Stockholm. Designed by Erik Gunnar Asplund, just after the First World War, it was intended for the funerals of children.

interest was in the power of traditional forms and methods of building – a movement which has been called 'National Romanticism'.

The chapel is reached through the grounds of the Woodland Crematorium. Around the main crematorium –

At first sight the chapel appears simple and without pretensions to being anything more than a rudimentary hut in the woods. But Asplund managed to imbue this unassuming, elemental building with a remarkable range of apt poetic ideas. The underlying subject of the 'poem' is, of course, death.

Conditions

Asplund designed the Woodland Chapel at a time before Modernism had become the dominant movement in Swedish architecture. The prevailing

a later building also by Asplund – the landscape is open, undulating, and with a 'big' sky. By contrast, the Woodland Chapel is hidden away, in a dark wood of pine trees.

Identification of place

Asplund's task was to identify a place for funeral services; where family and friends could come together to mourn.

Basic elements

Basic elements are used in clear and straightforward ways. There are defined areas of ground, columns, walls, and a roof. There is a pathway leading to the building, a platform on which the coffin is placed, and another used as the lectern. The floor, walls and roof form a simple cell, in which there is a doorway on the line of the approach, and a small domestic window in one corner. The floor around the perimeter of the inside of the chapel is raised by two steps, suggesting that the main place is a shallow pit.

Modifying elements

The chapel stands in the dappled light of the wood. There is the faint smell of pine. Walking towards the building, one's footsteps are muffled by the carpet of pine needles, except on the stone paving which defines the area of the chapel floor, inside and under the porch.

Inside, the main place is lit by a roof-light at the highest part of its domed ceiling. Sounds are reflected by the hard surfaces.

Elements doing more than one thing

As one approaches, the roof appears as a pyramid, and acts as a marker. The porch columns support the roof, but also channel the route into the building. The returns of the walls alongside the entrance help to create small subsidiary places off the main chapel space, but they also make the cell walls appear much thicker than they are, increasing its cave-like quality. This effect is reinforced by the deep reveals of the small window, and the niche in which the lectern stands. The

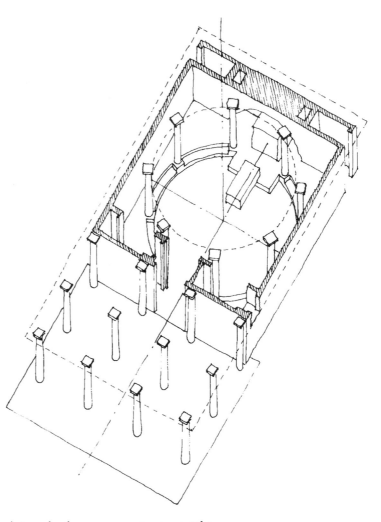

internal columns appear to support the dome above, but also define the main place.

Using things that are there

Asplund uses the woods to give the chapel a particular setting. The pathway to the building, which begins at a gateway some distance from it, strikes a straight line through the irregularly spaced trees. The porch columns are themselves like trees, though regularly positioned, bringing something of the character of the surrounding woods in under the roof.

Primitive place types

The niche in which the lectern stands is not a hearth, but like one.

(Externally there is a chimney stack in the same position, but this leads from the basement.) The lectern itself is like an altar. The catafalque, on which the coffin rests, is both a bed and an altar. It is also the focus of the performance place – like a clearing in the woods – defined by the shallow pit, surrounding columns and domed ceiling.

Architecture as making frames

The building is a temporary frame for the body of a dead child, and for the ceremony associated with its funeral.

In its outer form the chapel is like a house, framed by the surrounding woods. The porch frames the gathering mourners, who mingle with the columns (which have a presence like ancestors come to the funeral).

Under the roof there is also the cell which separates the special place of the ceremony from everywhere else, and inside that there is the pit and the ring of columns like a primitive henge. This circle, lit from the sky above,

frames the catafalque, which frames the coffin, which is itself a frame for the body. The lectern is framed in its own niche. The henge, catafalque, lectern, coffin, and the mourners are all framed, pictorially, by the entrance doorway, but architecturally by the womb-like interior.

Temples and cottages

The chapel is a 'temple' in 'cottage' clothing; the unquestionable authority of death is cloaked in the appearance of domestic simplicity. The building, though not raised on a platform, is formal and symmetrical. It has no pragmatic irregularity, though its materials are simple and natural. Its scale is small; it is a building for human beings.

Geometry

Asplund employs many of the various kinds of architectural geometry.

The circle of columns – again like ancestors standing around the shallow pit – define, literally, the circle of pres-

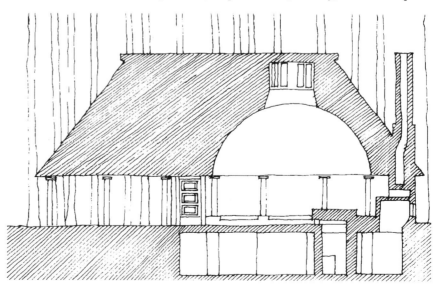

ence of the catafalque and coffin; it is within the social geometry of this circle that the mourners sit.

The line of passage and the line of sight from the entrance gateway coincide. In experience and symbolically the building – the pyramid – terminates this axis. It establishes two of the six directions inherent in the chapel – stretching from the symbolic hearth to the western horizon and the setting sun.

The circle of eight columns set up the cross axis – the other two horizontal directions blocked by the side walls – and thus establish a centre. Below is the basement; and above is light coming through the 'sky' of the dome, (the ideal geometry of which disrupts the geometry of making of the roof). Through the centre is the vertical axis – the *axis mundi* (axis of the earth).

The catafalque is positioned, not at the centre of the circle on the *axis mundi*, but between the symbolic hearth and that vertical axis – suspended for the duration of the ceremony between home and eternity.

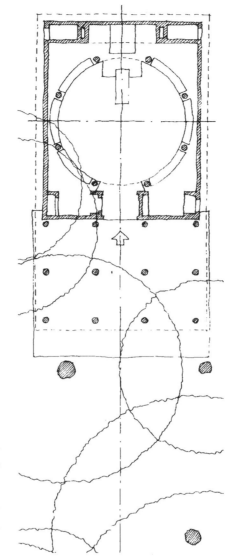

SELECT BIBLIOGRAPHY AND REFERENCES

Select Bibliography

The following may seem at first sight a disparate set of books, but the principles by which they have been selected are consistent. All contain discussion of architecture either as (what I have termed) *identification of place*, or put forward ways of analysing architecture according to conceptual themes, or discuss related theoretical issues. As such they deal with architecture in ways to which architects, concerned with design generation, can relate. No particular one can however be said to be the authority for the present book.

Some of the authors cited have produced other related works; only those most immediately pertinent to the arguments in this book are included here.

Alexander, Christopher and others – *A Pattern Language: Towns, Buildings, Construction*, Oxford UP, New York, 1977.

Alexander, Christopher – *The Timeless Way of Building*, Oxford UP, New York, 1979.

Atkinson, Robert and Bagenal, Hope – *Theory and Elements of Architecture*, Ernest Benn, London, 1926.

Bachelard, Gaston, translated by Maria Jolas – *The Poetics of Space* (1958), Beacon Press, Boston, 1964.

Eliade, Mircea, translated by Sheed – *Patterns in Comparative Religion*, Sheed and Ward, London, 1958.

Frankl, Paul, translated by O'Gorman – *Principles of Architectural History* (1914), MIT Press, Cambridge, Mass., 1968.

Heidegger, Martin, translated by Hofstader – 'Building Dwelling Thinking' and '... poetically man dwells...', in *Poetry Language and Thought* (1971), Harper and Row, London and New York, 1975.

Hertzberger, Herman – *Lessons for Students in Architecture*, Uitgeverij Publishers, Amsterdam, 1991.

Hussey, Christopher – *The Picturesque, studies in a point of view*, G.P. Putnam's Sons, London and New York, 1927.

Lawlor, Anthony – *The Temple in the House*, G.P. Putnam's Sons, London and New York, 1994.

Le Corbusier, translated by de Francia and Bostock – *The Modulor, a harmonious measure to the human scale universally applicable to architecture and mechanics*, Faber and Faber, London, 1961.

Lethaby, William Richard – *Architecture: an introduction to the history and theory of the art of building*, Williams and Norgate, London, 1911.

Lynch, Kevin – *The Image of the City*, MIT Press, Cambridge, Mass., 1960.

Martienssen, R.D. – *The Idea of Space in Greek Architecture*, Witwatersrand UP, Johannesburg, 1968.

Moore, Charles and others – *The Place of Houses*, Holt Rinehart and Winston, New York, 1974.

Norberg-Schulz, Christian – *Existence, Space and Architecture*, Studio Vista, London, 1971.

Parker, Barry and Unwin, Raymond – *The Art of Building a Home*, Longman, London, New York and Bombay, 1901.

Rapoport, Amos – *House Form and Culture*, Prentice Hall, New Jersey, 1969.

Rasmussen, Steen Eiler – *Experiencing Architecture*, MIT Press, Cambridge, Mass., 1959.

Relph, Edward – *Place and Placelessness*, Pion, London, 1976.

Rowe, Colin – 'The Mathematics of the Ideal Villa' (1947), in *The Mathematics of the Ideal Villa and other essays*, MIT Press, Cambridge, Mass., 1976.

Ruskin, John – *The Poetry of Architecture*, George Allen, London, 1893.

Schmarsow, August, translated by Mallgrave and Ikonomou – 'The Essence of Architectural Creation' (1893), in Mallgrave and Ikonomou (editors) - *Empathy, Form, and Space*, The Getty Center for the History of Art and the Humanities, Santa Monica, Calif., 1994.

Scott, Geoffrey – *The Architecture of Humanism*, Constable, London, 1924.

Scully, Vincent – *The Earth, the Temple, and the Gods; Greek Sacred Architecture*, Yale UP, New Haven and London, 1962.

Semper, Gottfried, translated by Mallgrave and Hermann – *The Four Elements of Architecture* (1851), MIT Press, Cambridge, Mass., 1989.

Spengler, Oswald, translated by Atkinson – *The Decline of the West* (1918), Allen and Unwin, London, 1934.

Sucher, David – *City Comforts*, City Comforts Press, Seattle, 1995.

van der Laan, Dom H., translated by Padovan – *Architectonic Space: fifteen lessons on the disposition of the human habitat*, E.J. Brill, Leiden, 1983.

van Eyck, Aldo – 'Labyrinthian Clarity', in Donat (editor) - *World Architecture 3*, Studio Vista, London, 1966.

van Eyck, Aldo – 'Place and Occasion' (1962), in Hertzberger and others - *Aldo van Eyck*, Stichting Wonen, Amsterdam, 1982.

Venturi, Robert – *Complexity and Contradiction in Architecture*, Museum of Modern Art, New York, 1966.

Vitruvius, translated by Hickey Morgan – *The Ten Books on Architecture* (first century BC), Dover, New York, 1960.

Wittkower, Rudolf – *Architectural Principles in the Age of Humanism*, Tiranti, London, 1952.

Zevi, Bruno, translated by Gendel – *Architecture as Space: how to look at architecture*, Horizon, New York, 1957.

Zevi, Bruno – 'History as a Method of Teaching Architecture', in Whiffen (editor) - *The History, Theory and Criticism of Architecture*, MIT Press, Cambridge, Mass., 1965.

Zevi, Bruno – *The Modern Language of Architecture*, University of Washington Press, Seattle and London, 1978.

References in the text

The following is a list of the references given in the main text of this book, and in the margins. Most of these are references to publications where more information can be found on the particular examples used. More general texts cited are included in the *Select Bibliography*.

Ahlin, Janne – *Sigurd Lewerentz, architect 1885-1975*, MIT Press, Cambridge, Mass., 1987.

Blaser, Werner – *The Rock is My Home*, WEMA, Zurich, 1976.

Blundell Jones, Peter – 'Dreams in Light', in *The Architectural Review*, April 1992, p.26.

Blundell Jones, Peter – 'Holy Vessel', in *The Architects' Journal*, 1 July 1992, p.25.

Blundell Jones, Peter – *Hans Scharoun*, Phaidon, London, 1995.

Bosley, Edward – *First Church of Christ, Scientist, Berkeley*, Phaidon, London, 1994.

Brawne, Michael – *Jørgen Bo, Vilhelm Wohlert, Louisiana Museum, Humlebaek*, Wasmuth, Tubingen, 1993.

Christ-Janer, Albert and Mix Foley, Mary – *Modern Church Architecture*, McGraw Hill, New York, 1962.

Collins, Peter – *Concrete, the vision of a new architecture*, Faber and Faber, London, 1959.

Collymore, Peter – *The Architecture of Ralph Erskine*, Architext, London, 1985.

Constant, Caroline – *The Woodland Cemetery: towards a spiritual landscape*, Byggforlaget, Stockholm, 1994.

Crook, John Mordaunt – *William Burges and the High Victorian Dream*, John Murray, London, 1981.

(Dewes and Puente) – 'Maison à Santiago Tepetlapa', in *L'Architecture d'Aujourd'hui*, June 1991, p.86.

Drange, Aanensen and Brænne – *Gamle Trehus*, Universitetsforlaget, Oslo, 1980.

Edwards, I.E.S. – *The Pyramids of Egypt*, Penguin, London, 1971.

(Foster, Norman) – 'Foster Associates, BBC Radio Centre', in *Architectural Design 8*, 1986, pp.20-27.

(Gehry, Frank) – 'The American Center', in *Lotus International 84*, February 1995, pp.74-85.

Greene, Herb – *Mind and Image*, Granada, London, 1976.

Hawkes, Dean – *The Environmental Tradition*, Spon, London, 1996.

(Hecker, Zvi) – (Apartments in Tel Aviv), in *L'Architecture d'Aujourd'hui*, June 1991, p.12.

Hewett, Cecil – *English Cathedral and Monastic Carpentry*, Phillimore, Chichester, 1985.

Johnson, Philip – *Mies van der Rohe*, Secker and Warburg, London, 1978.

(Kocher and Frey) – (House on Long Island), in Yorke, F.R.S. – *The Modern House*, Architectural Press, London, 1948.

(Konstantinidis, Aris) – (Summer House), in Donat, John (editor) - *World Architecture 2*, Studio Vista, London, 1965, p.128.

Lawrence, A.W. – *Greek Architecture*, Penguin Books, London, 1957.

Le Corbusier, translated by Etchells – *Towards a New Architecture* (1923), John Rodker, London, 1927.

Lethaby, W.R. and others – *Ernest Gimson, his life and work*, Ernest Benn Ltd, London, 1924.

Lim Jee Yuan – *The Malay House*, Institut Masyarakat, Malaysia, 1987.

(MacCormac, Richard) – (Ruskin Library), in *Royal Institute of British Architects Journal*, January 1994, pp.24-29.

Macleod, Robert – *Charles Rennie Mackintosh, Architect and Artist*, Collins, London, 1968.

March, Lionel and Scheine, Judith – *R.M. Schindler*, Academy Editions, London, 1993.

(Masieri, Angelo) – (Casa Romanelli), in *The Architectural Review*, August 1983, p.64.

Murphy, Richard – *Carlo Scarpa and the Castelvecchio*, Butterworth Architecture, London, 1990.

Muthesius, Stefan – *The English Terraced House*, Yale UP, New Haven and London, 1982.

Nicolin, Pierluigi – *Mario Botta: Buildings and Projects 1961-1982*, Architectural Press, London, 1984.

Pevsner, Nikolaus – *A History of Building Types*, Thames and Hudson, London, 1976.

Pevsner, Nikolaus – *An Outline of European Architecture*, Penguin, London, 1945.

Robertson, D.S. – *Greek and Roman Architecture*, Cambridge UP, Cambridge, 1971.

Royal Commission on Ancient and Historical Monuments in Wales – *An Inventory of the Ancient Monuments in Glamorgan, Volume IV: Domestic Architecture from the Reformation to the Industrial Revolution, Part II: Farmhouses and Cottages*, H.M.S.O., London, 1988.

Rudofsky, Bernard – *Architecture Without Architects*, Academy Editions, London, 1964.

Rudofsky, Bernard – *The Prodigious Builders*, Secker and Warburg, London, 1977.

Rykwert, Joseph (Introduction) – *Richard Meier Architect 1964/84*, Rizzoli, New York, 1984.

Saint, Andrew – *Richard Norman Shaw*, Yale UP, New Haven and London, 1976.

Schinkel, Karl Friedrich – *Collection of Architectural Designs* (1866), Butterworth, Guildford, 1989.

(Schnebli, Dolf) – (Lichtenhan House), in Donat, John (editor) - *World Architecture 3*, Studio Vista, London, 1966, p.112.

(Scott, Michael) – (Knockanure Church), in Donat, John (editor) - *World Architecture 2*, Studio Vista, London, 1965, p.74.

Semenzato, Camillo – *The Rotonda of Andrea Palladio*, Pennsylvania State UP, University Park, Penn.,1968.

Smith, Peter – *Houses of the Welsh Countryside*, H.M.S.O., London, 1975.

Summerson, John and others – *John Soane* (Architectural Monographs), Academy Editions, London, 1983.

Tempel, Egon – *Finnish Architecture Today*, Otava, Helsinki, 1968.

(Venturi, Robert) – *Venturi, Scott Brown and Associates, on houses and housing*, Academy Editions, London, 1992.

Weaver, Lawrence – *Small Country Houses of To-day*, Country Life, London, 1912.

Weston, Richard – *Alvar Aalto*, Phaidon, London, 1995.

Weston, Richard – *Villa Mairea* (in the Buildings in Detail Series), Phaidon, London, 1992.

Yorke, F.R.S. – *The Modern House*, Architectural Press, London, 1948.

INDEX